C0-AYL-271

LIBRARY OF HEBREW BIBLE/
OLD TESTAMENT STUDIES

430

Formerly Journal for the Study of the Old Testament Supplement Series

THE GOOD, THE BOLD, AND THE BEAUTIFUL

The Story of Susanna and Its Renaissance Interpretations

Dan W. Clanton

t&t clark

NEW YORK • LONDON

T & T Clark International, 80 Maiden Lane, New York, NY 10038

T & T Clark International, The Tower Building, 11 York Road, London SE1 7NX

T & T Clark International is a Continuum imprint.

Library of Congress Cataloging-in-Publication Data
Clanton, Dan W.
The Good, the Bold, and the Beautiful: The Story of Susanna and Its Renaissance Interpretations / Dan W. Clanton.
p. cm. — (Library of Hebrew Bible/Old Testament Studies, 430)
Includes bibliographical references and index.
ISBN 0-567-02991-3 (hardcover : alk. paper)
1. Bible. O.T. Apocrypha. History of Susanna—Criticism, interpretation, etc. I. Title. II. Series.

BS1795.52.C53 2006
229'.6—dc22 2005031447

Printed in the United States of America

06 07 08 09 10 10 9 8 7 6 5 4 3 2 1

CONTENTS

List of Figures

ACKNOWLEDGMENTS

I would like to take this opportunity to thank several people without whom this project would never have come to fruition. A book of this length is never a solitary endeavor, and this work is no exception.

First, I would like to thank Drs David Petersen, Greg Robbins, and M. E. Warlick, the members of my Dissertation Committee, whose encouragement and advice has been invaluable. Special thanks must go to my advisor, Dr Pamela Eisenbaum. Without her guidance and sense of humor, this project would have taken twice as long and only been half the fun.

Henry Carrigan, Andrew Mein, and Amy Wagner at T&T Clark deserve many thanks for their help in leading me by the hand through the complex and sometimes mysterious process of publishing one's first book. This project simply wouldn't have seen the light of day without the expertise and hard work of Duncan Burns at Forthcoming Publications.

I also need to express my appreciation to the staff of the Taylor Library at the Iliff School of Theology (especially Katie Fisher), the Penrose Library at the University of Denver, and the Virginia Village Branch of the Denver Public Library. A book without sources is impossible, and my work would have been unfeasible without the assistance of these libraries and their staff.

There are also numerous people who belong on my personal Honor Roll for offering consistent encouragement and aid during the writing of this project. These include: Dr Andy Tooze, Joe Leader, Richmond West, Sarah Sweetman, Patricia Roux, Marty Michelson, Dr Glenn Pemberton, Kabamba Kiboko, Dr Susan Brayford, and Dr Mark George. I must also extend a heartfelt thanks to my co-conspirators in the realm of religion and popular culture whose work and collegiality has been an inspiration to me: Melinda Campbell, Jeff Scholes, Terry Clark, and Dr Jeffrey Mahan.

I also want to acknowledge my debt to Dr Dana Thomason and Jim Owen, two extraordinary teachers who put me on this path and who have always inspired me by their knowledge, humor, and humanity.

My parents, Dan and Kaye, and siblings, Kristin, Jeff, and Kara, deserve a large *Merci* for their support during this process and for always believing I had something important to say.

I must thank our son Danny and our daughter Hannah for reminding me that the small joys in life are often the most important.

Finally, I would like to dedicate this book to my wife Missy, whose constant support and love gave me the strength and will to complete it. In the words of Robert Earl Keen, *I love her more than roses love the sun…*

Part I

SUSANNA IN BIBLICAL LITERATURE, CULTURE, AND HISTORY

Chapter 1

INTRODUCTION

1.1. *Introduction to Project*

The story of Susanna and the Elders is one of the most interpreted and reproduced tales from the Apocrypha, and for good reason. In its compact narrative, it touches on attempted rape, female sexuality, abuse of power, punishment for the wicked, and voyeurism, to name but a few themes. The basic story is as follows:[1] the Elders see Susanna and each lust after her. They then admit their lust to one another, and go immediately to Susanna and grab her. Susanna refuses to acquiesce to their desire (and her own rape), at which point the Elders simply walk away. However, they later summon her, accuse her of adultery, and the people condemn her to death. At this point, the Lord comes to Daniel in some fashion, and he publicly cross-examines the elders concerning their testimony. Their stories conflict, thus exposing their deception. The people then administer the same punishment that the Elders had previously mandated for Susanna: they kill them.

The story has been richly interpreted by various musicians and artists. For example, in G. F. Handel's 1748 oratorio, the tale is told in much the same way as it appears in the Theodotion version in the Apocrypha.[2] However, in Alessandro Stradella's 1681 oratorio, Susanna is portrayed as a strong, resistant character, teasing the Elders and even calling to a guard to have them arrested after they approach her.[3] In Laurits Tuxen's nineteenth-century painting of Susanna, she is pictured as a young, strong character, looking down on the Elders as she covers her nakedness. However, in George Pencz's etching (*Susanna and the Elders*, 1532),[4] Susanna is seen sitting on the lap of one of the Elders as he is forcing her to kiss him. He, in turn, fondles her breast as the other Elder holds her wrists firm, not allowing her to escape. This is just a sample of the multifarious interpretations of the story of Susanna, but one can already see the intensification of sexual overtones within the interpretive tradition.

1. There are two versions of the story of Susanna preserved in the Apocrypha: the Old Greek (OG) and the Theodotion (Th). The outline of the story provided here represents those elements that the two stories have in common.

2. For a recent recording of this piece, I recommend George Frideric Handel, *Susanna* (Philharmonia Baroque Orchestra; cond. Nicholas McGegan; Harmonia Mundi 907030.32, 1990 [1748]).

3. The only recording I know of this piece is Allessandro Stradella, *La Susanna: Oratorio in due parti di Giovanni Battista Giardini a cinque voci, due violini e basso continuo* (Complesso Vocale Strumentale Camerata Ligure; cond. Esteban Velardi; Bongiovanni GB 2121/22–2, 1991 [1681]).

4. Online: http://www.spaightwoodgalleries.com/Pages/Pencz.html.

The thesis for which I will argue in this study consists of three interrelated claims. First, I will argue in Chapter 2 that the story of Susanna was written in the first century B.C.E., and I will provide a brief description of that century. In Chapter 3, I will perform a narrative-rhetorical reading of Susanna and illustrate that the story uses sexual anxiety and desire to set up a moral dilemma for Susanna. That moral dilemma is resolved in two ways: Susanna's refusal to allow herself to be raped, and Daniel's intervention. I argue that although the story has many mimetic features, the thematic function overrides the mimetic, especially after the appearance of Daniel. Put another way, the story's emphasis on Susanna, the Elders, and Daniel as "plausible people" is secondary to its stress on what those characters represent and the message it is relaying through those representations.

Second, in Chapter 5, I will analyze chronologically selected aesthetic interpretations of the story found in the Renaissance period, i.e., from ca. 1450–1650. My intention is to show that the prevailing artistic interpretation during the Renaissance focuses on the mimetic, sexual aspects of the story due to issues of patronage, and sex/gender current at the time. Third and finally, I will argue in Chapter 6 that several Renaissance renderings provide counter-readings, which focus more on the values and themes present in the story. These renderings provide models for readers to resist the sexually exploitative features of both the narrative and its interpretations.[5] In my Conclusion, I reflect on the need for readers to resist potentially harmful interpretations, especially those that focus on the mimetic level of the story's rhetoric.

Put simply, this first-century B.C.E. story is a primarily a thematic one, and many Renaissance interpretations misunderstand or misappropriate the story to suit various needs, with harmful ideological results. Additionally, many commentators on Susanna, including feminists, interpret the story on a mimetic level. In my opinion, these analyses are just as harmful as the sexualizing renderings in the Renaissance because these interpreters view the reader(s) of Susanna as complicit in the text's mimetic emphasis on voyeurism and sexual aggression. As I will show in Chapter 3 and the Conclusion, readers and interpreters do have the ability to resist works and interpretations with which they do not agree. Consumers of various media must recognize the need to counter or resist such interpretations so that their awareness of harmful narratives and images in their own time can be resisted as well.

1.2. *Contribution*

To be sure, many works on Susanna have appeared in the last few years, and some of them have even taken up the subject of aesthetic interpretations of the

5. At the outset I should note that due to circumstances beyond my control, not all the artistic renderings discussed hereafter are reproduced for the reader. I am aware of the negative impact this may have for some readers, and apologize for this omission. However, all the images mentioned can be found easily online.

story.[6] My intention in this monograph is to provide the first such treatment of this topic focused on the Renaissance period that discusses the story at length, using insights from the field of biblical studies.[7] By bringing together information on many of the most important aesthetic interpretations of the Susanna story created during the fifteenth through seventeenth centuries, this project will be making a large contribution to the field of biblical studies by illuminating the power and endurance of this story. Only in the past few years has biblical studies as a discipline begun to acknowledge the validity and value of aesthetic studies concerned with biblical materials. The field has recently experienced a wealth of new works on the subject, as well as groups and seminars conducted at regional and national conferences.[8] These new fields of inquiry are not only necessary, but also vital because they seek to explore the often opaque interplay between text and culture in which all human beings exist. This project will also make a contribution to the fields of art, music, and literary history. That is, by placing these interpretations alongside one another in a diachronic survey, one may see the interaction between various media in a more significant way.

1.3. *Outline of Method*

The issue of method in a project like this one, with many layers, textures, time periods, and, most importantly, many aesthetic representations, is an important and complex one. Because I will be dealing with biblical literature, culture, and history in Part I and literature, art, music, history, and society during the Renaissance in Part II, I will use two different methods. In Part I, I will use what I call

6. The best recent example is the collection of essays in Ellen Spolsky, ed., *The Judgment of Susanna: Authority and Witness* (SBLEJL 11; Atlanta: Scholars Press, 1996).

7. To my knowledge, there exists only one other work on aesthetic interpretations of Susanna during the Renaissance, and it is concerned solely with artistic works. See Andrea Marie Willis, "The Theme of Susanna and the Elders from the Late Fourteenth through the Early Sixteenth Century: A Study of History, Iconography and Societal Interpretations" (M.A. thesis, University of South Carolina, 1998).

8. There now exist several groups within the Society of Biblical Literature devoted to investigating the impact biblical literature has had and continues to have on aesthetic works, e.g., the History of Interpretation Section, the Bible in Ancient and Modern Media Section, and the Use, Influence, and Impact of the Bible Program Unit. Additionally, Blackwell Publishers has launched an important new commentary series devoted exclusively to the reception history of biblical books. Selected examples of works focused on aesthetic interpretations of biblical literature include J. Cheryl Exum, *Plotted, Shot, and Painted: Cultural Representations of Biblical Women* (JSOTSup 215; GCT 3; Sheffield: Sheffield Academic Press, 1996); Alice Bach, ed., *Biblical Glamour and Hollywood Glitz* (Semeia 74; Atlanta: Scholars Press, 1996); eadem, "Calling the Shots: Directing Salomé's Dance of Death," in her *Women, Seduction, and Betrayal in Biblical Narrative* (Cambridge: Cambridge University Press, 1997), 210–62; Larry J. Kreitzer, *The Old Testament in Fiction and Film: On Reversing the Hermeneutical Flow* (The Biblical Seminar 24; Sheffield: Sheffield Academic Press, 1994); idem, *The New Testament in Fiction and Film* (The Biblical Seminar 17; Sheffield: JSOT Press, 1993); and Margarita Stocker, *Judith, Sexual Warrior: Women and Power in Western Culture* (New Haven: Yale University Press, 1998). For more examples, see the various bibliographies contained in these works.

narrative-rhetorical criticism, which I will explain in Chapter 3. In Part II, I will employ a descriptive and comparative method to examine the various aesthetic interpretations of the story. That is, I will describe the interpretation using terminology appropriate to its genre and discuss historical information where available and/or appropriate, and then compare that interpretation with my reading of the story and the story itself. Thus, my method here will be historical in a sense as well, i.e., I must be aware of historical and social trends in a given historical period in order to comment appropriately on an interpretation.

My examination will be informed throughout by feminist values and assumptions. By "feminist," I mean a way of perceiving the world, and the relations within it, in which women are viewed as full members of humanity, and not relegated to a lower class of existence than that of men. Rita M. Gross writes,

> The most basic definition of *feminism* is the conviction that women really do inhabit the human realm and are not "other," not a separate species. Sometimes I wear a T-shirt that proclaims: "Feminism is the radical proposition that women are human beings." This proclamation seems so simple and obvious, but its implications are profound and radical.[9]

In feminist scholarship, this position is usually tied to a critical or negative view of patriarchal or anthropocentric assumptions that women are somehow less than men. The purpose of reading with a feminist hermeneutic, then, would be to expose and critique male-centered assumptions, with the hope that one's reading will lead to some sort of recognition that certain texts (often sacred texts) may reinforce these assumptions, and to empower readers to develop different, perhaps more equitable, ways of viewing texts and gender relations. In the case of biblical or non-canonical religious texts, a feminist reading must be tempered by the recognition that no character can exist in this literature outside of the confines of a patriarchal system and ideology. That is, in this literature one is dealing with thoroughly patriarchal societies, in which the ideology of patriarchy is almost universal and, as such, one should expect a plethora of male-centered assumptions. While this recognition may be beneficial in that one can be assured that feminist readers of the Bible and non-canonical texts will always find materials to engage, the influence of and ideology put forth by these texts has been primarily focused on the heightened status of men, usually to the detriment of women.

In Chapter 3, I will engage narrative-rhetorical criticism. I refer here to the type of analysis introduced by Wayne C. Booth, James Phelan, and others.[10] Rhetoric has traditionally embraced two disparate definitions. On the one hand, it may be taken to mean artful speech or decisions made about the composition of a text. On the other hand, it can mean the art of persuasion. Within the field of biblical studies, such scholars as James Muilenburg and Phyllis Trible have championed the first definition; this definition dominated the discourse of biblical

9. Rita M. Gross, *Feminism and Religion: An Introduction* (Boston: Beacon, 1996), 16–17.

10. See primarily Wayne C. Booth, *The Rhetoric of Fiction* (Chicago: University of Chicago Press, 1961), and James Phelan, *Narrative as Rhetoric: Technique, Audiences, Ethics, Ideology* (Columbus: Ohio State University Press, 1996).

studies in the mid- to late twentieth century.[11] More recently, such scholars as Yehoshua Gitay and George Kennedy have championed the latter definition.[12] The new rhetoric, i.e., the work of Chaim Perelman and Lucie Olbrechts-Tyteca, has influenced Gitay and Kennedy's more general emphasis on rhetoric as persuasive discourse.[13] This new rhetoric is, in essence, a rediscovery of classical Western rhetoric.[14]

This extremely concise sketch of rhetoric as it is viewed in modern biblical scholarship illustrates the elasticity not only of the term but also, by extension, of the method. My method in Part I of this project will draw heavily from Phelan's work, which builds on the pioneering efforts of theorists such as Booth. Basically, a narrative-rhetorical reading pays attention not only to character development and narrative progression, but also to how these tools enable the author to persuade his/her reader(s) to accept the values, norms, and perceptions he/she conveys in their work. Since I argue in Chapter 2 that both versions of Susanna were likely composed in the first century B.C.E., it will be necessary to be familiar with the socio-political and religious conditions of that century. As such, my reading in Chapter 3 will also reflect a more traditional historical-critical reading of the text in that historical and social information of the first century B.C.E. will form an indispensable background to understanding the values, norms, and views associated with sex and gender in that period.

1.4. *Conclusion*

In this work, I intend to investigate and delineate the connection(s) between biblical literature and patriarchal power structures, so as to "open our eyes to the ways we imprison ourselves in our own mythologies."[15] Put another way, by examining the story of Susanna, a story that deals with female sexuality and possible rape, as well as interpretations of that story, I will illustrate not only the relationship(s) between religious structures and larger cultural views and attitudes toward female sexuality, but also the reciprocal influences between the two. It is my contention that many interpreters, both biblical and aesthetic, have not paid close attention to the rhetoric of the story, which I will argue is primarily

11. See James Muilenburg, "Form Criticism and Beyond," *JBL* 88 (1969): 1–18, and Phyllis Trible's, *God and the Rhetoric of Sexuality* (OBT; Philadelphia: Fortress Press, 1978). See especially Trible, *Rhetorical Criticism: Context, Method, and the Book of Jonah* (GBS; Minneapolis: Fortress, 1994).

12. See Yehoshua Gitay, *Prophecy and Persuasion* (Forum Theologicae Linguisticae 14; Bonn: Linguistica Biblica, 1981), and George Kennedy, *New Testament Interpretation Through Rhetorical Criticism* (Chapel Hill, NC: University of North Carolina Press, 1984).

13. Chaim Perelman and Lucie Olbrechts-Tyteca, *The New Rhetoric: A Treatise on Argumentation* (Notre Dame: University of Notre Dame Press, 1969), and Perelman, *The Realm of Rhetoric* (Notre Dame: University of Notre Dame Press, 1982).

14. For a more detailed discussion of the new rhetoric and specifically what aspects of classical rhetoric it has retained/recovered, see The Bible and Culture Collective, *The Postmodern Bible* (New Haven: Yale University Press, 1995), 156–68.

15. Stocker, *Judith, Sexual Warrior*, 2.

thematic. Instead, they have focused on the more sexual, mimetic level of the story, and in so doing have perpetuated harmful messages about women, sexual aggression, meaning in reading, and the power of the reader to resist harmful positions, attitudes, and messages in texts. My hope for this project is that if we can see more clearly the way religious texts have been used in the past to bolster cultural attitudes that might prove harmful to women, we might be more critical of our own cultural attitudes, so that tools for analyzing and altering potentially dangerous attitudes may be developed.

Chapter 2

CONTEXT(S) AND (RE)DATING THE STORY OF SUSANNA

2.1. *Introduction*

In this chapter I will take up the issue of (re)dating the story of Susanna. Being aware of particular cultural and religious presuppositions of the narrator and author will allow us to engage the story more fully.

Almost all commentators agree that determining a date for Susanna is a challenge.[1] For example, as John J. Collins points out, "The story could have been composed at any time in the Hellenistic or even the late Persian period."[2] Carey A. Moore is equally ambiguous in his evaluation:

> No particular century can confidently be assigned as the *terminus a quo* for the story, although some time in the Persian period [538/37–333] is quite possible, that is, a time when the Jewish community in Palestine enjoyed a modicum of independence and self-governance, and, most important of all, when its religion was unthreatened from outside.[3]

Similarly, Michael Heltzer holds that the story was composed during the Persian period, but that it was written in Achaemenid Babylonia due to the similarity between the name Susanna and the city of Susa, as well as the form of self-government found in the story.[4] In his article for the *Anchor Bible Dictionary*, Michal Dayagi Mendels agrees with Heltzer; in his opinion, Susanna was composed in Babylon during the Persian period.[5]

Other scholars argue for a Hasmonean date for the *Vorlage*. In his work, Helmut Engel makes a case for a date of composition sometime between the mid-second and the mid-first century B.C.E.[6] In his 1957 study, R. A. F. MacKenzie notes that the picture of the Jewish community in Susanna agrees with the

1. Much of the argument concerning the date of Susanna will be published in an article entitled "(Re)Dating the Story of Susanna: A Proposal," *JSJ* 34, no. 2 (2003): 121–40.

2. John J. Collins, *Daniel* (Hermeneia; Minneapolis: Fortress, 1993), 438.

3. Carey A. Moore, *Daniel, Esther and Jeremiah: The Additions* (AB 44; Garden City, N.Y.: Doubleday, 1977), 91–92. Moore's statement stems from his observation that external evidence for a date is lacking, and so scholars must rely on internal data, which he sees as being ambiguous. I find both external and internal evidence more available and reliable, as I will show below.

4. Michael Heltzer, "The Story of Susanna and the Self-Government of the Jewish Community in Achaemenid Babylonia," *AION* 41 (1981): 35–39.

5. Michal Dayagi Mendels, "Susanna, Book of," *ABD* 6:246–47 (247).

6. Helmut Engel, *Die Susanna Erzählung: Einleitung, Übersetzung und Kommentar zum Septuaginta-Text und zur Theodotion-Bearbeitung* (OBO 61; Freiburg: Universitätsverlag; Göttingen: Vandenhoeck & Ruprecht, 1985), 175–83.

situation in Palestine under Hasmonean rule "after 150 B.C.," but does not specifically argue for a date of composition.[7] Similarly, Robert H. Pfeiffer observes that since the story is found in the Septuagint (hereafter LXX) version of Daniel, which, along with Moore, he dates to ca. 100 B.C.E., "the story is not later than that date, and probably not more than a half a century earlier."[8] In her 1993 monograph, Marti J. Steussy argues for "a date in the late second century B.C.E., probably in the range of 120–135 for the OG translation of Daniel," with the Theodotion (hereafter Th) version coming in the mid-first century C.E.[9] Finally, Koenen posits a second-century B.C.E. date for Th, while the LXX has more in common with the canonical book of Daniel, including a Hasmonean-period date.[10]

Still another group of interpreters agree with a first-century B.C.E. date for the *Vorlage* of the story. The scholar who first suggested this date was Nehemiah Brüll.[11] According to Brüll, the story of Susanna was composed as a Pharisaic response to the problem of witnesses and justice that arose in the first century B.C.E. The story had its origins in a Midrash on Jer 29:21–32, but was used as an anti-Sadducean polemic. Brüll's theory was enthusiastically accepted by many scholars, including C. J. Ball and David M. Kay, and thus set the tone for Susanna studies for several decades.[12] Recently, though, many scholars including Engel and Steussy have rejected Brüll's setting of the story in the first century B.C.E. because they do not view the story as being concerned with legal issues, but rather theological ones.[13] Even so, I find most of Brüll's argument convincing, and agree with him regarding the date of Susanna. In what follows, then, I will begin with Brüll's general thesis that Susanna was composed in the first century B.C.E. and augment it.

Even though there is no widely accepted date for the story of Susanna, Moore's observation quoted above regarding the situation of Jews in Palestine as portrayed in the story may point us in the right direction. Jews in Palestine enjoyed some independence under the Hasmonean dynasty as well during the

7. R. A. F. MacKenzie, "The Meaning of the Susanna Story," *CJT* 3 (1957): 211–18 (214).

8. Robert H. Pfeiffer, *History of New Testament Times with an Introduction to the Apocrypha* (New York: Harper & Brothers, 1949), 449.

9. Marti J. Steussy, *Gardens in Babylon: Narrative and Faith in the Greek Legends of Daniel* (SBLDS 141; Atlanta: Scholars Press, 1993), 28–37 (31).

10. Klaus Koenen, "Von der todesmutigen Susanna zum begabten Daniel: Zur Überlieferungsgeschichte der Susanna-Erzählung," *TZ* 54 (1998): 1–13 (7–11).

11. Nehemiah Brüll, "Das apokryphische Susanna-Buch," *Jahrbuch für Jüdische Geschichte* 3 (1877): 1–69. See especially p. 63: "Das Susanna-Buch ist somit nich anderes als eine anti-sadducäische Tendenzschrift, in welcher auf nicht ungeschickte Weise ein alter Sagenstoff von einem Processe gegen Frauenverführer so bearbeitet wurde, dass er zu einem belehrenden Zeitbilde sich gestaltete."

12. See C. J. Ball, "The Additions to Daniel II: The History of Susanna," in *The Holy Bible: Apocrypha* (ed. Henry Wace; 2 vols.; London: John Murray, 1888), 2:323–43 (325–31); and David M. Kay, "Susanna," *APOT* 1:638–51.

13. See Engel, *Die Susanna Erzählung*, 68–69 and 76–77; and Steussy, *Gardens in Babylon*, 49–50. Much of their opposition to Brüll's work stems from the important analysis of Walter Baumgartner, especially his "Susanna: Die Geschichte einer Legende," in his *Zum Alten Testament und Seiner Umwelt* (Leiden: Brill, 1959), 42–67.

Hellenistic period. Might the narrative setting of Susanna correlate with a particular time during Hasmonean rule? Or should the story be dated more generally to the Hellenistic period? As I have stated, I believe the story was composed during the first century B.C.E., but we must examine several pieces of evidence before that claim may be accepted.

2.2. *Culture and Society in the First Century B.C.E.*

In the first century, the social and economic situation of Judea was intimately tied to its relationship with foreign powers. Prior to Pompey's invasion of Jerusalem in 63 B.C.E., the Hasmonean rulers were content with maintaining good relations with Greece and Rome. Under Jannaeus, Rome seems to have been content to leave Judea alone, because he considerably expanded the country's borders. Accompanying this expansion were increased taxes as well as other material hardships for both urban and rural areas. However, since Jannaeus seems to have taken several coastal cities, Judea would have had a new access to sea trade and its concomitant benefits.[14] This increased trade would most likely have benefited the agricultural situation in Judea as well. Even so, the distribution of wealth under Jannaeus was still remarkably uneven; almost all of the prosperity his exploits generated was in the hands of a tiny percentage of landed upper class persons. This is mostly due to the pervasive practice of tax farming, which began in the Ptolemaic period and would continue through the first century.[15]

Even though Salome Alexandra's (76–67 B.C.E.) reign brought about a modicum of peace for Judea, there was social unrest both before and after she took control. There were several instances of armed resistance to those in power, and banditry becomes prominent immediately prior to Herod's reign in 37 B.C.E.[16] Much of this unrest probably was a reaction to the economic hardships imposed on the populace by the ruling class. It would be tempting to hypothesize that the lower classes were upset by the increasing Hellenization, or adoption of various Greek practices and ideology.

Following the analysis of Alan F. Segal, I think it best to view Hellenism as a new world-system or ideology that was superimposed on an older, more established one.[17] This superimposition caused the breakdown of traditional life

14. See H. Jagersma, *A History of Israel from Alexander the Great to Bar Kochba* (trans. J. Bowden; Philadelphia: Fortress, 1985), 89–93.

15. For a brief yet informative discussion of tax farming, see John H. Hayes and Sara R. Mandell, *The Jewish People in Classical Antiquity: From Alexander to Bar Kochba* (Louisville, Ky.: Westminster/John Knox, 1998), 34–35.

16. See *J.W.* 1.303–13. For an excellent sociological analysis of peasant banditry during and after this period, see Richard A. Horsley with John S. Hanson, *Bandits, Prophets, and Messiahs: Popular Movements at the Time of Jesus* (Harrisburg, Pa.: Trinity, 1999), 48–87. E. P. Sanders, in his *Judaism: Practice and Belief, 63 BCE–66 CE* (London: SCM Press; Philadelphia: Trinity, 1992), 36–40, lists several examples of internal conflict in Judea from 63 B.C.E.–74 C.E., even though he does not consider the people mentioned above to be "brigands."

17. Alan F. Segal, *Rebecca's Children: Judaism and Christianity in the Roman World* (Cambridge, Mass.: Harvard University Press, 1986), 13–37.

with the result that previously assumed views and practices were now exposed as mere possibilities, not "natural." The pluralism of ideas and practices that followed required the adherents of the more established ideology to become acculturated to the new one.[18] This thesis is one of the strengths of Segal's analysis; in point of fact, all Jews living in Palestine were acculturated to the new Hellenistic ideology. That is, every person living in Palestine who wished to get along in any economic or political capacity had to deal in some way with this new world-system. The issue then becomes not whether to Hellenize or not, but rather how acculturated to become. To be sure, acculturation for some involves secularization, modernization, and/or assimilation, to use Segal's terms. On the other hand, groups can be only marginally acculturated and thus retain most of the practices and views of the previous ideology even while demonstrating a few qualities or practices of the new ideology.

Segal goes on to argue that the roots of conflict between these two symbiotic ideologies lies in the Maccabean revolt (mid-second century B.C.E.), and even then Hellenization itself was not really the problem, for the Hasmoneans openly adopted Hellenistic customs.[19] Rather, conflict arose over the uses to which Hellenization was put. In other words, until those who advocated Hellenism—primarily aristocratic Jews in Jerusalem—began to infringe upon the Torah by altering Jewish worship practices, Hellenists and more conservative Jews did not have much about which to disagree. For their part, many Greeks showed an open attitude and even a respect for the Jews, the "race of philosophers," and Jews displayed an openness to and even a curiosity about Greek customs and thought prior to the mid-second century.[20] However, after the Maccabean revolt and the subsequent Hasmonean dynasty, certain Jews, e.g., the Essenes, displayed a remarkable distaste for the people and the practices that conflicted with their traditional practices, i.e., the Torah.

All of this is to say that while the social and economic situation in first-century Judea was not to everyone's liking, the religious situation was both informed by

18. The situation seems to have been analogous to European Jewry following the *haskalah* movement in the eighteenth century C.E. As Michael A. Fishbane, *Judaism* (Religious Traditions of the World; San Francisco: HarperCollins, 1987), 78, notes in this regard, "No longer was there a traditional, pregiven and predetermined social-religious reality that people incorporated in themselves with mother's milk, as it were. Now the extent and nature of one's own Jewish practice and identity would have to be chosen over against other religious and cultural options available in the society-at-large. This now meant that, for all practical purposes, one's Jewish identity was a matter of personal choice, not just fate."

19. The work of Elias Bickerman is still instructive in this regard. See *The God of the Maccabees: Studies in the Meaning and Origin of the Maccabean Revolt* (trans. H. R. Moehring; SJLA 32; Leiden: Brill, 1979).

20. The quote is from Theophrastus (ca. 370–285 B.C.E.), *On Piety*, one of Aristotle's chief pupils. See Menahem Stern, ed., *Greek and Latin Authors on Jews and Judaism* (3 vols.; Jerusalem: The Israel Academy of Sciences and Humanities, 1974–84), 1:10. For a discussion of Greek views of Jews as philosophers, see M. Hengel, *Judaism and Hellenism: Studies in their Encounter in Palestine during the Early Hellenistic Period* (trans. J. Bowden; 2 vols; Philadelphia: Fortress, 1974), 1:255–61.

and contributed to the larger climate of unrest. If we stay with Segal's view of cultural interaction, i.e., competing or at least interacting worldviews, then I think we can understand better the religious situation in the first century. As Segal explains,

> The process of Hellenization was similar to two contemporary types of cultural contact: modernization, a phenomenon in the third world, or secularization, a phenomenon of religious transformation in Western societies. These transformations are stimulated by the society's need to acculturate a new world system. They also involve a breakdown of the power, wholeness, and appeal of the traditional religion... In both cases, the traditional unity of the culture is broken down. Often this outcome is accompanied by an ideology of pluralism and free competition between varieties of religious expression. The key commonality in the two developments is that the religious establishments can no longer take for granted the allegiance of their populations. As a result, the religious tradition, which was an almost unconscious, self-evident assumption about the world, becomes a set of beliefs that has to be marketed.[21]

Thus, because of the increasing assimilation to Greco-Roman ideologies by those in power, institutions and attitudes in the first century were radically altered. This alteration led to one of the most interesting products of the Hellenistic period; some Jews decided to voice their approval or disapproval of the religious situation through various religious groups, or parties.[22] Those who had the means to support assimilation could find a home in the Sadduccean party; those who wholeheartedly disapproved had the option of joining the Essenes. The other major party of this period, the Pharisees, often appear to be ambiguous in their attitude toward the new ideologies at work in Judea; on the one hand they did not complain when they received political power under Salome Alexandra, but on the other hand, they later refused to take a loyalty oath to Herod.[23] Of course, we should always keep in mind that the vast majority of Jews at this time were not members of any of these parties, but still considered themselves to be Jews.

In addition to the strengthening of parties, the new Hellenistic worldview affected different geographic regions differently; a person's religious identity often had only a marginal impact on this affect. As Segal states,

> The principal factor in determining whether a Jew would Hellenize was neither prejudice nor religion. Rather, Hellenistic sociology and economics affected the decision significantly. Rural people, who had no need of developing international trade or formal education, continued with their native Hebrew and Aramaic languages and distrusted the new cultural forms. The city populations, containing aristocrats, venture capitalists, merchants, and skilled tradesmen, were necessarily more affected. In Judea, as in the rest of the Hellenistic world, Hellenization was largely an urban phenomenon and also a necessary fashion for the wealthier classes.[24]

21. Segal, *Rebecca's Children*, 25.

22. One of the best discussions of religious groups during this period is Sanders, *Judaism: Practice and Belief*, 315–490.

23. *Ant.* 15.368–72. However, see *Ant.* 17.41–45: Herod fines over six thousand Pharisees for refusing to take an oath of loyalty.

24. Segal, *Rebecca's Children*, 27.

This last point is especially important for our understanding of the religious situation in the first century; those religious groups that were able to align themselves with the upper classes, viz., the Sadducees, were able to reap the benefits of cultural interaction during this period in a more substantial way than other groups, most notably the Essenes.

2.3. *Issues of Gender in the Second Temple Period and Susanna*

Given that there was economic disparity between rich and poor, social unrest, and moderate religious factionalism in the first century, the question now becomes: How might these factors have affected the view(s) of women prevalent during this time? Of course, the question of women's social and religious position in Judea during the Greco-Roman period, or in our case the first century, is an enormous one, and one that more than a few scholars have undertaken.[25] However, it will suffice for my purposes to focus on those aspects of women's social and religious identity that figure into the story of Susanna. Thus, I will limit my investigation to the issues of women as daughters and wives, women in public, women's religious devotion, and women as (suspected) adulteresses.

2.3.1. *Daughters*

Jewish daughters in the first century B.C.E. were less valued in a familial sense than male children. First of all, there was a widespread cultural predisposition that viewed male children as more beneficial to the family than a daughter would be, primarily for economic reasons. As Ross S. Kraemer notes,

> While daughters could be expected to leave their mothers at an early age, sons could be counted on to remain in the family sphere. They were expected to provide for their mothers in old age, and to serve as their legal guardians and protectors. These roles were particularly important given the typical great age discrepancy between Greco-Roman wives and their husbands, which vastly increased the likelihood that women who survived childbirth and avoided divorce were likely to end up as widows. Daughters, on the other hand, could be expected to provide little in the way of sustenance and support for their aged mothers.[26]

25. The early discussion of Joachim Jeremias, in his *Jerusalem in the Time of Jesus: An Investigation into Economic and Social Conditions during the New Testament Period* (trans. F. H. and C. H. Cave; Philadelphia: Fortress, 1969), 359–76, has now been greatly supplemented. See, e.g., Léonie J. Archer, "The Role of Jewish Women in the Religion, Ritual and Cult of Graeco-Roman Palestine," in *Images of Women in Antiquity* (ed. Averil Cameron and Amélie Kuhrt; Detroit: Wayne State University Press, 1983), 273–87; eadem, *Her Price is Beyond Rubies: The Jewish Woman in Graeco-Roman Palestine* (JSOTSup 60; Sheffield: JSOT Press, 1990); and especially Tal Ilan, *Jewish Women in Greco-Roman Palestine: An Inquiry into Image and Status* (Tübingen: J. C. B. Mohr, 1995; repr., Peabody, Mass.: Hendrickson, 1996). For an examination of women during this period outside of Judea, see Elaine Fantham et al., *Women in the Classical World: Image and Text* (New York: Oxford University Press, 1994); and Sarah B. Pomeroy, *Goddesses, Whores, Wives, and Slaves: Women in Classical Antiquity* (New York: Schocken, 1975).

26. R.S. Kraemer, "Jewish Mothers and Daughters in the Greco-Roman World," in *The Jewish Family in Antiquity* (ed. Shaye J. D. Cohen; BJS 289; Atlanta: Scholars Press, 1993), 89–112 (108). Also see Ilan, *Jewish Women*, 44–48.

Even though Kraemer's article focuses on maternal preference for sons, the same preference was undoubtedly found in fathers as well. In fact, the relationship between father and daughter seems to have been somewhat tenuous due to the economic burden the daughter brings, as well as the possibility of shame being brought on the father by the daughter.

The most important text in this regard is the second-century B.C.E. book of Sirach.[27] Nowhere else can one find such a vitriolic assessment of the negative characteristics of daughters, as well as women in general. Sirach points out that "the birth of a daughter is a loss" (22:3), and warns his affluent, male audience to keep watch over their daughters so as to prevent them from committing any sexual acts prior to marriage, which would shame their father (26:10–12). In fact, Sirach goes so far as to advise almost total seclusion and control of daughters so that they will not "put you to shame in public gatherings" (42:11). In all this, as I noted above, there is a concern for the economic liability that a daughter poses for the father both prior to and after marriage (in case of divorce). Perhaps even more important is the issue of honor/shame and the effect a daughter could have on her father's honor.[28] Thus, the relationship between a daughter and her father was probably fraught with concern over marriage, sexual chastity, and the maintenance of honor. Of course this is not to say that fathers did not have affection for their daughters, just that that affection was probably tempered by the real social and ideological realities with which a father of a daughter would be faced.

In addition, patrilocality and patrilineality were practiced. That is, a daughter was identified by her association with her father until she was married, and thus brought under the control of another man. At this point, she would leave her natal house and cohabit with her new groom and his family in their home (*4 Macc.* 18:7–9). If a daughter happened to be divorced, she would then return to her father's house. Furthermore, the basic education most daughters received was tailored toward marriage and household duties; only upper class women could afford to receive any further education.

In sum, then, a daughter's social status would have depended on her father's status since she was identified socially by his standing, not her own. Once she was of marriageable age (from about 12–18 years of age), her parents would begin trying to find her a suitable groom, and once she was married, she became part of

27. For Sirach in general, see Patrick W. Skehan and Alexander A. Di Lella, *The Wisdom of Ben Sira* (AB 39; Garden City, N.Y.: Doubleday, 1987); and Richard J. Coggins, *Sirach* (GAP; Sheffield: Sheffield Academic Press, 1998). On Sirach and women, see Pamela M. Eisenbaum, "Sirach," in *Women's Bible Commentary* (ed. C. A. Newsom and S. H. Ringe; expanded ed. with Apocrypha; Louisville, Ky.: Westminster/John Knox, 1998), 298–304. Also see Claudia V. Camp, "Understanding a Patriarchy: Women in Second Century Jerusalem through the Eyes of Ben Sira," in *"Women Like This": New Perspectives on Jewish Women in the Greco-Roman World* (ed. Amy-Jill Levine; SBLEJL 1; Atlanta: Scholars Press, 1991), 1–39; and Warren C. Trenchard, *Ben Sira's View of Women: A Literary Analysis* (BJS 38; Chico, CA: Scholars Press, 1982).

28. Space limitations prevent me from exploring fully this issue. For a succinct summary of honor/shame issues in Sirach, see Eisenbaum, "Sirach," and David Arthur deSilva, "The Wisdom of Ben Sira: Honor, Shame, and the Maintenance of Minority Cultural Values," *CBQ* 58 (1996): 433–55.

her husband's extended family.[29] However, should she divorce or be divorced, she would return to her father's house and become his economic responsibility again.[30] Our sources are obviously androcentric and, as such, reveal the anxiety that daughters caused their fathers, but they do not give us any indication of what it was like to be a daughter prior to marriage. That information simply has not survived.

In general, the details and arrangement of marriage for a daughter was left to her parents. They would attempt to find her a socially and economically suitable groom, if possible from their own extended family (2 Esd 9:47). It may be that the daughter had some input in her potential mate, but it is more likely that they did not. As Ilan notes,

> Throughout the Hellenistic-Roman period, and according to all relevant sources, marriage was a matter to be settled by the parents of the bride and groom, on the basis of social connection and status. When children married they had absolutely no right to choose their partner, especially if such a choice would fall outside the criteria dictated by society.[31]

However, it is likely that only wealthy families practiced this stringent control over their daughters' marriage; in the lower social classes, families most likely allowed their daughters and sons to have some say in the choosing of a mate (Sir 22:4; cf. 7:25). Ilan agrees, and writes,

> Although the marriage of a daughter was theoretically controlled entirely by her father it can be assumed that the reality was somewhat different and that such rigorous control over the marriage of children was exercised more in wealthy families, which had to take into account rather complicated economic and political factors.[32]

Since most of our available sources deal with upper class concerns, we are limited in our evaluation of marriage practices among lower class persons.

Marriage as a social contract also had an economic side as well. First of all, it was the custom for a bride or her family to present the new groom with a dowry, as in Tob 8:21. Also, the prospective groom would present his bride's father with a *mohar*, i.e., a bride price. Eventually, the groom did not have to provide a *mohar* upon marriage, but instead make a contract called a *ketubbah* that stipulated a certain amount of money that would be paid to the bride in the case of divorce or the death of the husband. All of the monetary values of these various

29. With regards to the age of marriage, see Ilan, *Jewish Women*, 65–69.

30. While men had the right to divorce their wives, it also appears that in some cases the wife could divorce her husband. See Ilan, *Jewish Women*, 141–47; and John J. Collins, "Marriage, Divorce, and Family in Second Temple Judaism," in *Families in Ancient Israel* (ed. Leo G. Perdue et al.; The Family, Religion, and Culture Series; Louisville, KY: Westminster/John Knox, 1997), 104–62 (115–21).

31. Ilan, *Jewish Women*, 79.

32. Ilan, *Jewish Women*, 79. Also see Collins, "Marriage, Divorce, and Family in Second Temple Judaism," 107–12. Based on marriage contracts from Elephantine, Collins asserts that a woman's consent was required for marriage, and thus that a prospective bride did indeed have some say in her marriage.

practices depended on the social status of the family, as well as the age of the bride (see Lev 27:4–5).

There seems to have been a change in the way in which the *ketubbah* was viewed during the late Second Temple period. A reform began under the direction of Simeon ben Shetah, possibly the brother of Salome Alexandra (76–67 B.C.E.), in which a husband would write his wife's *ketubbah*, and in it would promise to pay an agreed-upon sum not prior to marriage, as was previously the case, but only in the case of divorce.[33] In addition, Simeon ordered that the husband had to pledge all of his property as part of the *ketubbah*.[34] In effect, this meant that the economic power of the bride's father was now legally tempered because the *ketubbah* contained no money to be held by the father. Also, since the husband had much more to lose in the case of a divorce initiated by him, the wife now held more power within the marriage. The net result of this reform was that the status of married women was at least somewhat improved when compared to the regulations in biblical literature.

2.3.2. *Wives and Women in Public*

Once a couple was married, the woman was expected to be subordinate to her husband, just as she was subordinate previously to her father. In her work, Archer details the ideologies behind this view of women as inferior to men.[35] One of the most important factors she lists is religion; she notes that

> The patriarchal ordering of Jewish life was both expressed and reinforced by the teachings of the nation's religion—itself a cult which centred upon a single male deity and one which was directed exclusively by men. In other words, the authority which men assumed over women was, by our period, viewed in terms of a divine ordering of the universe: woman, created after man and out of him, was by nature inferior, and as the one responsible for man's first fall was deemed to be in need of constant control and supervision.[36]

Thus the patriarchal nature and ideology of Second Temple Judaism(s) affirms that women are, by nature, inferior to men. Along with this religious argument goes the epistemological assertion that women are mentally and rationally subordinate to men, who were "naturally" charged with their care.[37]

The duties of a married woman who is in the care of her husband were numerous, but were all located firmly in the domestic sphere.[38] In addition to the

33. See *t. Ketub.* 12:1 and *b. Ketub.* 82b. Secondarily, see Ilan, *Jewish Women*, 89–94. Also see Archer, *Her Price is Beyond Rubies*, 157–68.

34. See J. Klausner, "Queen Salome Alexandra," *WHJP* 6:242–54 (250–52).

35. Archer, *Her Price is Beyond Rubies*, 207–12.

36. Archer, *Her Price is Beyond Rubies*, 208. Archer bases her claim on interpretations of Gen 3, specifically Josephus's *Ag. Ap.* 2.201 and Philo's *Opif.* 167. Based on these texts, she argues, women were placed in a "position of subordination to and dependence upon men" (p. 109).

37. See, e.g., *Letter of Aristeas* 250–51: "The female sex is…easily liable to change its mind because of poor reasoning powers" (*OTP* 2:29).

38. This brief summary may be supplemented by the following sources: Archer, *Her Price is Beyond Rubies*, 226–39; and S. Safrai, "Home and Family," in *The Jewish People in the First Century* (ed. S. Safrai and M. Stern; 2 vols.; CRINT 1; Philadelphia: Fortress, 1976), 2:728–92 (761–64).

expected familial propagation, she was expected to perform numerous roles related to food preparation and the maintenance of the home. She was not expected to work outside the home, and indeed was generally forbidden to do so, but could labor within the home and sell the fruits of that labor for profit. In addition, she was expected to provide hospitality and to attend to any guests of her husband. Finally, a married woman had to take on the duties of child rearing along with all of her other obligations.[39] Archer sums up the status of the wife as follows: "All in all, therefore, the lot of the married woman was not dissimilar to that of the minor daughter. Both were denied the right to act independently; both were subject to the all-embracing authority of a male overlord."[40]

A wife's duties were almost entirely performed in the domestic sphere of activity, which accords with the more general tendencies of the patriarchal ideology of Judea in the Second Temple period. This confinement of activity is representative of a larger concern found in the first century B.C.E., viz., the proper (physical) place for women to inhabit. In turn, this concern is linked to another issue, that of preserving a woman's chastity, which was a major concern for parents. Ilan spells out the ideological dilemma:

> A woman was the subject of constant worry for her husband [as a daughter was for her father]: another man might meet her, talk with her, look her up and down, and in the end seduce her. Looking and talking, as opposed to sexual relations, were naturally not considered culpable offenses, but since they could very well lead to the sin of adultery, which at least theoretically carried the death penalty, or even worse to pregnancy and the birth of bastard children, a need was felt to "construct a fence around the *Torah*", that is, to institute safeguards against coming too close to the opportunity to transgress. These safeguards fall into two categories: a) the admonition against a man's speaking with a woman not related to him; and b) the more serious admonition against a man's even looking at another woman.[41]

One of the most important and effective ways to enforce such ideological safeguards was to insist that women remain almost totally secluded in their houses, away from the sweet tongues and prying eyes of would-be seducers. This, in my opinion, was more of a prescriptive ideal created by men in positions of authority over women to deal with their own concerns about preserving chastity than an accurate depiction of social reality.[42]

Our sources from this period are particularly emphatic on this point. For example, Sir 9:5–9 strongly discourages looking at or dining with women besides one's wife. Of course, this directly implies that women could be encountered outside of the home, but that is the point: the women one might encounter outside the home are precisely those one should stay away from because they are not adhering to the ideal of seclusion. Likewise, Sir 42:11–14 admonishes fathers to

39. See the exaltation of the mother in *4 Macc*. 14:11–18:5.

40. Archer, *Her Price is Beyond Rubies*, 225.

41. Ilan, *Jewish Women*, 125.

42. The seclusion of women in the domestic sphere was a hallmark of classical Athenian civilization. For an analysis of this phenomenon, see Fantham et al., *Women in the Classical World*, 68–127; and Pomeroy, *Goddesses, Whores, Wives, and Slaves*, 79–92 and passim.

keep their daughters away from both men and lattices in their rooms. Second Maccabees 3.19 mentions "the young women who were kept indoors," and *3 Macc.* 1:18 tells of "young women who had been secluded in their chambers." Pseudo-Phocylides, a work dated to the turn of the era, admonishes its readers, "Guard a virgin in firmly locked rooms, and do not let her be seen before the house until her wedding day."[43] In the book of Judith, probably composed in the early first century B.C.E., Judith is looked upon as being holy due to her self-imposed seclusion following the death of her husband. Even after her (in)famous expedition, she returns to the confines of her home to live out her remaining days in faithfulness. This ideal of virginal confinement for the sake of purity finds perhaps its greatest expression in the pseudepigraphal work *Joseph and Aseneth*. This text, written possibly in the late first century B.C.E., portrays its heroine, Aseneth, as residing in a large and ornate tower, "where her virginity was being fostered" (2:7).[44] Aseneth only forsakes her tower and her virginal status after she sees Joseph, and subsequently converts to Judaism.

Thus, it seems that the ideal for married women, and indeed all women, during this time was to remain in the home, and to have as little contact with males outside the family as possible. Of course, as both Ilan and Archer observe, the ideal did not always match reality, mostly due to economic factors.[45] For example, only wealthy families could afford to construct houses with separate women's quarters.[46] Also, there are several sources which presuppose that women were not only present, but active in the marketplace, which most likely indicates that lower class families needed to have as many people working as possible, including women.[47] Because of this, Ilan writes:

> In this light we may very cautiously offer the suggestion that the moral requirement that men and women be separated was formulated by and for the well-established classes, who could in fact obey such a requirement. This illustrates once again that rabbinic and other sources represent the middle and upper classes, and neither relate to nor show much consideration for the lower classes.[48]

If the ideal of separation of the sexes was not always possible, it was still an important ideological factor with regards to the view of women during the first century B.C.E.

43. P. W. van der Horst, trans., "Pseudo-Phocylides," in *OTP* 2:565–82 (581).

44. The translation used is that of C. Burchard, "Joseph and Asenenth," in *OTP* 2:177–247. On the date of *Joseph and Aseneth*, see Burchard, 187–88; and Randall D. Chesnutt, "Joseph and Aseneth," *ABD* 3:969–71 (970). For this text in general, see the recent work of Edith M. Humphrey, *Joseph and Aseneth* (GAP; Sheffield: Sheffield Academic Press, 2000).

45. See Ilan, *Jewish Women*, 129–34; and to a lesser degree, Archer, *Her Price is Beyond Rubies*, 249–50

46. Again, the presence and maintenance of separate women's quarters in private houses was a widespread practice in Athenian civilization. See Pomeroy, *Goddesses, Whores, Wives, and Slaves*, 80–83; and Fantham et al., *Women in the Classical World*, 103–4, especially Figure 3.17.

47. For these sources, see Ilan, *Jewish Women*, 128–34.

48. Ilan, *Jewish Women*, 134.

2.3.3. *Women's Religious Devotion*

Some of the more important activities that women performed outside of the home were religious in nature. Ilan, based on *m. Qidd.* 1:7, points out that there were no hard and fast rules that prevented women from performing religious commandments, such as the commandments related to Temple worship, wearing the *tefillin*, and even the Nazirite vow.[49] In addition, she observes that women most likely participated in the major pilgrimages to Jerusalem. Related to women's levels of religious observance during the first century B.C.E. is the issue of women's educational instruction and their subsequent study of Torah. Despite Safrai's extremely brief discussion of the matter in his important study of education in Palestine, women seemed to have had access to basic education, sometimes including Torah and even rabbinic materials.[50]

For the most part, the majority of the instruction a girl or woman would have received would have been tailored for domestic duties. However, women would be exposed to various laws and regulations concerning how to keep a *kosher* home, and this minimal instruction conceivably could have led to more general teaching(s). Even if this possibility is granted, though, women had to face an uphill battle with regard to educational issues. First, only upper class women were likely to have been literate enough and to have the requisite amount of leisure time to pursue serious study. Second, since most women were married at a fairly young age, they were saddled with various domestic duties that would have prevented many of them from attending any formal schooling, such as synagogue classes. Third, as Archer observes, there were even more restrictive ideological barriers to women's education that would have prevented the vast majority of women from receiving anything but the most basic education. That is, Archer argues that after the reforms of Ezra and Nehemiah the "nuclear" family model gradually replaced the extended family system, which advocated a more strict set of gender roles.[51] This set of gender roles relegated women to the private sphere, in which they would perform their assigned roles of wife, mother, and homemaker. The same set of roles prescribed that men should be active in the public sphere, where they would work and be active in politics, society, and religion. Over time, Archer claims, women were eventually not exempted from Torah

49. Ilan, *Jewish Women*, 176–84.

50. See Safrai, "Education and the Study of the Torah," in Safrai and Stern, eds., *The Jewish People in the First Century*, 2:945–70 (955). Besides Safrai's otherwise excellent piece, see M. Hengel and C. Markschies, *The "Hellenization" of Judaea in the First Century after Christ* (trans. J. Bowden; London: SCM Press; Philadelphia: Trinity, 1989), 19–29. Archer, *Her Price is Beyond Rubies*, 69–85, provides a useful overview of the development of the educational system in post-exilic and Hellenistic times. For the specific data on women's study of Torah, see Ilan, *Jewish Women*, 190–204; and Archer, *Her Price is Beyond Rubies*, 85–101. The former is much more optimistic than the latter that women were able to study Torah. Ilan cites several Rabbinic texts that allow for the possibility that women might be able to learn Torah, including *m. Ned.* 4:2–3; *t. Ber.* 2:12; and *y. Soṭah.* 1:4, 16d. Finally, for an interesting application of data regarding education and women to Second Temple period literature, see Linda Bennett Elder, "Judith's *Sophia* and *Synesis*: Educated Jewish Women in the Late Second Temple Period?" in *Biblical and Humane: A Festschrift for John F. Priest* (ed. Linda Bennett Elder et al.; Atlanta: Scholars Press, 1996), 53–69.

51. For what follows, see Archer, "The Role of Jewish Women," 273–78.

study because of their household duties and other ideological reasons, they were excluded from it. Archer's thesis has much to commend it, and I agree with almost all of her conclusions. However, the fact remains that there were women who did study Torah, including the famous later examples of Beruriah and Matrona.[52] Thus, while Archer's argument is quite persuasive, she perhaps overstates the force of her data.

If we accept that some women did, in fact, study Torah, how might that study have affected their religious devotion or action(s)? Since Archer categorically denies that women had access to study of Torah, she holds that "about the only privilege left to women in Hellenistic Palestine was that of weeping—in other words, their one official position was that of publicly mourning the dead at funerals."[53] However, it is more likely that women performed numerous religious actions, even if they did not have unrestricted access to study of Torah. E. P. Sanders notes that during the first century B.C.E., "there were three foci of religion: the temple, the synagogue (or house of prayer) and the home."[54] Despite the restrictions placed on women's participation in Temple services due to purity regulations, the Temple did, in fact, contain a Women's Court.[55] As S. Safrai notes, though, this name "does not derive from the fact that this court accommodated only women, for all visitors to the Temple passed through it and often spent some time there; it stems, rather, from the fact that for the most part women did not advance beyond it."[56] According to this view, women were able to attend Temple services and offer sacrifices via male priests, albeit from an outer courtyard.[57]

However, other scholars posit a livelier role for women in the Herodian Temple. After surveying the tannaitic material on this topic, Susan Grossman concludes,

52. For a discussion of these women, see Ilan, *Jewish Women*, 197–204. Also see Tal Ilan, "'Beruriah has Spoken Well' (*tKelim Bava Metzia* 1:6): The Historical Beruriah and Her Transformation in the Rabbinic Corpora," in *Integrating Women into Second Temple History* (TSAJ 76; Tübingen: Mohr Siebeck, 1999), 175–94.

53. Archer, "The Role of Jewish Women," 283. Ilan, *Jewish Women*, 189–90, mentions mourning in her discussion of the various occupations that women might have held in our period.

54. Sanders, *Judaism: Practice and Belief*, 48.

55. This name is found in both Josephus (*J.W.* 5.198–200) and midrashic literature (*m. Mid.* 2.5–6).

56. S. Safrai, "The Temple," in Safrai and Stern, eds., *The Jewish People in the First Century*, 2:865–907 (867). Josephus, *J.W.* 5.198–200, 227; *Ant.* 15.419; and *Ag. Ap.* 2.102b–105, seems to concur.

57. See Sanders, *Judaism: Practice and Belief*, 51–69, for a description of the Temple, and pp. 306–14 for illustrations. Sanders mentions the Women's Court in the Temple on pp. 57 and 61. Gentiles were also allowed limited access to the Temple, provided they ritually purified themselves prior to entry. See Safrai, "The Temple," 877–78. *Contra* the commonly accepted view that the Temple contained a specific court for Gentiles, see Solomon Zeitlin, "There was No Court of Gentiles in the Temple Area," *JQR* 56 (1965): 88–89. Also see Donald D. Binder, *Into the Temple Courts: The Place of the Synagogues in the Second Temple Period* (SBLDS 169; Atlanta: Society of Biblical Literature, 1999), 380–87, for an analysis of the place of Gentile "God-fearers" in Second Temple Period synagogues.

> Women appear to have been present in the Temple and to have actively participated by bringing, and sometimes handling, their sacrifices. Nevertheless, women seem to have been excluded from the central areas of sanctity in the Temple, according to the rabbinic imagination.[58]

Grossman concludes her examination by positing three reasons why women were excluded from further entry into the Temple. First, it is possible that there was a concern over mixing the sexes. Yet, as we have seen, men and women often commingled in the Women's Court. Second, women could have been refused further access to the Temple because of a concern over menstrual impurity. Third, as Grossman notes,

> Women may have been excluded from the most sacred areas of the Temple because, in the patriarchal society of the time, women's roles in sacred areas was defined in such a way as to support the male-defined, largely familial role of women in the greater society; concomitantly, women occupied a lesser status than men in religions in which men comprised the leadership.[59]

According to Grossman, women may have enjoyed an active role at the Herodian Temple, yet still were excluded from certain holy areas to which men had access.

With regards to synagogues, our literary evidence from the first century is meager. That is, most scholars assume the presence of (at most) synagogues and (at least) private houses being used for worship purposes. Implicit in this assumption is that the Jerusalem Temple no longer retained its sole claim on the religious imagination, i.e., the experience of the exile had shown that God is mobile (Ezek 1:4–28a) and thus can worshipped in a variety of settings. Even so, we have no archaeological or literary evidence from the first century B.C.E. for synagogues in Palestine.[60] Thus, all of the assumptions and reconstructions of religion and religious practice carried out in private settings during that century remain conjecture. Of course, by the first century C.E., our evidence, both literary and archaeological, is more secure. Based on those data, and assuming that what first-century C.E. sources such as Josephus and Philo relay can be extrapolated back in

58. Susan Grossman, "Women and the Jerusalem Temple," in *Daughters of the King: Women and the Synagogue* (ed. Susan Grossman and Rivka Haut; Philadelphia: Jewish Publication Society, 1992), 25.

59. Grossman, "Women and the Jerusalem Temple," 26.

60. We do have several inscriptions from the diaspora that attest to prayer houses, or what later would be termed synagogues. The earliest such inscriptions come from Egypt, and are usually dated to the third century B.C.E. They mention "prayer houses" (*proseuche*) specifically. For an analysis of these inscriptions, see Lee I. Levine, *The Ancient Synagogue: The First Thousand Years* (New Haven: Yale University Press, 2000), 75–82. See also Peter Richardson and Valerie Heuchan, "Jewish Voluntary Associations in Egypt and the Roles of Women," in *Voluntary Associations in the Graeco-Roman World* (ed. John S. Kloppenborg and Stephen G. Wilson; London: Routledge, 1996), 226–51; and John M. G. Barclay, *Jews in the Mediterranean Diaspora: From Alexander to Trajan (323 BCE–117 CE)* (Hellenistic Culture and Society 33; Berkeley: University of California Press, 1996), 26–27. There is archaeological evidence as well of a first century B.C.E. synagogue on the island of Delos, although there is some controversy over whether or not this structure was actually a synagogue. See Levine, *The Ancient Synagogue*, 100–105.

time a century, we may make a few general comments on synagogue or private worship.[61]

One of the identifying characteristics of Judaism in general during the first century B.C.E. was Sabbath observance, and for most Jews, this was a time set apart for study of Torah. Synagogues, or perhaps privately owned houses, allowed people to come together, not only for public study, but also for prayer and the general sense of community that public worship affords. In his work on synagogues in the Second Temple period, Donald D. Binder writes,

> While there is no firm evidence for women functionaries in the synagogues of our period, women clearly served as participants within the Sabbath services and at other activities held within the synagogues. In some locales, it is possible that women may have been seated separately from the men or that they may have met at separate times for the weekly services. Epigraphic evidence from the diaspora also portrays women as donors to the synagogues and participants within manumission ceremonies. In general, the climate within the diaspora seems to have been more conducive for allowing women to assume more active roles within the synagogue.[62]

Thus, while it seems that communities in the diaspora were more willing to afford women the opportunity to partake in synagogue services, women in Judea seem to have participated in worship gatherings as well.[63]

Since we know, albeit from later rabbinic sources, that some women did study Torah, as there is evidence that women attended synagogues, and because many scholars feel that women possibly held various leadership positions in synagogues, it seems safe to posit that women might have been welcome at certain synagogues.[64] However, women undoubtedly held the most influence in religious

61. Sanders, *Judaism: Practice and Belief*, 198–99, mentions Josephus, *Life* 277, 280, 290–303; and Philo, *Creation* 128; *Hypothetica* 7.12–14; *Spec. Laws* 2.62–70; *Every Good Man is Free* 81; and *Embassy* 132, 155–58 in this regard. Even though Josephus and Philo are writing in the first century C.E., their information on this issue is useful primarily because both of them assume rather than argue for the existence of synagogues. Thus, they do not seem to have any particular bias at this point.

62. Binder, *Into the Temple Courts*, 379. The epigraphic evidence to which Binder refers comes from Cyrenaica, Delos, Halicarnassus, Sardis, Acmonia, and Gorgippia. See Binder, *Into the Temple Courts*, 377–78.

63. Another example of this view can be found in Hannah Safrai, "Women and the Ancient Synagogue," in Grossman and Haut, eds., *Daughters of the King*, 39–49.

64. For the evidence that women held positions of leadership in synagogues beginning in the late first century B.C.E., see Bernadette J. Brooten, *Women Leaders in the Ancient Synagogue: Inscriptional Evidence and Background Issues* (BJS 36; Atlanta: Scholars Press, 1982). Binder, *Into the Temple Courts*, 372–75, calls attention to the dates of Brooten's data: only one stems from the first century B.C.E., and that inscription is ambiguous. Shaye J. D. Cohen, "Women in the Synagogues of Antiquity," *Conservative Judaism* 34, no. 2 (1980): 23–29, asserts that women played roles in the building, maintenance, and leadership of synagogues. Sharon Lea Mattila, "Where Women Sat in Ancient Synagogues: The Archaeological Evidence in Context," in Kloppenborg and Wilson, eds., *Voluntary Associations in the Graeco-Roman World*, 266–86, argues that women were most likely segregated from men, even though no physical barriers may have been present. Based on these data, my view is close to that of Cohen. That is, based on the available inscriptions and archaeological evidence, I see no reason to deny that women participated in the creation and lives of synagogues. *Contra* my optimistic position, see Archer, "The Role of Jewish Women," 280–83.

observances conducted in the home.[65] From *kosher* laws to the recitation of the *Shema*, from private prayer to Sabbath practices, not only would women have been present, they would have been active participants due to their dominance in the private, domestic sphere.

Thus, women's religious devotion in the first century B.C.E. was hardly monolithic. They participated in both public and private observances, and in some cases held important roles and/or positions in those observances.[66] They undoubtedly prayed privately, just as they undoubtedly worshipped publicly at the Temple.[67] Granted, they were not able to pursue all of the avenues of public religious expression that were open to men, but I certainly think that women were able to express their religious feeling(s) in several manners. In sum, while I agree with Archer's analysis regarding the growth of patriarchal ideology in the post-exilic period, I prefer to view the situation for women in a more positive light. That is, while Archer writes rather matter-of-factly that the influence of purity codes and sexual role differentiation in the post-exilic period served "gradually to exclude women from nearly all public expressions of piety," I would rather focus on and highlight those public and private expressions of piety to which women did have access.[68] I would now like to examine one last issue before moving on to my argument for the date of Susanna, viz., the issue of women as suspected adulterers.

2.3.4. *Women as Suspected Adulteresses*

By definition, a woman committed adultery when she slept with any man other than her husband. However, the only way a man could be guilty of adultery is if he slept with another man's wife since Jewish law allowed polygyny. However, the actual process by which a woman was accused and/or convicted of adultery in the Second Temple period is not clear. In Num 5:11–31, a procedure is adumbrated by which the suspected adulteress, or *sotah*, would be tested to determine if she is guilty. The test involves a priest mixing a solution of water and dust from the Tabernacle floor and making the woman drink it. If she is innocent, nothing will happen to her, but if she is guilty, then "the water that brings the curse shall enter into her and cause bitter pain, and her womb shall discharge, her uterus drop, and the woman shall become an execration among her people" (Num 5:27).[69] Interestingly, classical Athenian law viewed adultery in a slightly different fashion. As Sarah B. Pomeroy notes,

65. Again, see Archer, "The Role of Jewish Women," 283: "In the ritual of the home women also had little role to play."

66. An example of a public ritual is found in Jdt 16:1–17, Judith's public recitation of a psalm.

67. Examples of private prayer by women include Tob 3.11–15; Jdt 9:2–14; and Add Esth C 14:3–19. For an examination of prayer in apocryphal texts, see Toni Craven, "'From where Will My Help Come?': Women and Prayer in the Apocryphal/Deuterocanonical Books," in *Worship and the Hebrew Bible: Essays in Honor of John T. Willis* (ed. M. Patrick Graham et al.; JSOTSup 284; Sheffield: Sheffield Academic Press, 1999), 95–109.

68. Archer, "The Role of Jewish Women," 277.

69. Unless otherwise specified, all quotations from primary sources are taken from the NRSV translation. For a brief yet interesting comment on this passage, see Danna Nolan Fewell and David M. Gunn, *Gender, Power, and Promise: The Subject of the Bible's First Story* (Nashville: Abingdon,

> Whether adultery came about through rape or seduction, the male was considered the legally guilty or active party, the woman passive. The husband of a raped or adulterous woman was legally compelled to divorce her. The accused woman had no opportunity to proclaim her innocence, though, with difficulty, her guardian might do so in her behalf. A woman thus condemned was not allowed to participate in public ceremonies, nor to wear jewelry, and the most severe deprivation was probably that she would be a social outcast and never find another husband.[70]

Thus, in Athens, a woman would not be able to undergo any sort of public test to determine her innocence or guilt unless her male guardian spoke up for her. With regards to the *sotah* test during the Second Temple period, though, it seems to have undergone at least a modification, and at most a drastic alteration.

Ilan mounts impressive evidence to suggest that several rabbis, most notably R. Yohannan ben Zakkai, opposed the *sotah* test, primarily because too many people were committing adultery.[71] It is unclear, though, how accurately Mishnaic materials would reflect pre-70 C.E. events, so any conclusions based on this evidence must remain speculative. Nevertheless, it does seem that the *sotah* test was a subject of controversy in the late Second Temple period; so much so that Ilan feels justified in claiming that "an attempt was made to stop it altogether before the Destruction [of the Temple]."[72] Furthermore, Ilan claims that the controversy surrounding the *sotah* test "seems to have been internal to the Pharisees, and those who objected to the rite...seem to have held the upper hand and may even have succeeded in abolishing it."[73] Even if the controversy were an inter-Pharisaic dispute, the Sadducees would have been involved, at least in part, for as Ilan notes,

> The trial of the *sotah* lay in the domain of the Sadduccean priests, who by all indications retained exclusive control over it during the Second Temple period until its revocation after the destruction of the Temple or perhaps a bit before that.[74]

Thus, the suspected adulteress, or *sotah*, might have fared better during the Second Temple period than previously due to the fact that the test itself was falling out of favor with several prominent Pharisees. As we shall see, the Pharisees were

1993), 109–11. As Fewell and Gunn note, the "test" seems to be heavily slanted toward a guilty finding. See also Katherine Doob Sakenfeld, "Numbers," in Newsom and Ringe, eds., *Women's Bible Commentary*, 49–56 (53); Michael Fishbane, "Accusations of Adultery: A Study of Law and Scribal Practice in Numbers 5:11–31," *HUCA* 45 (1974): 25–45; Tikva Frymer-Kensky, "The Strange Case of the Suspected Sotah (Numbers V 11–31)," *VT* 34 (1984): 11–26; and, more recently, Bonna Devora Haberman, "The Suspected Adulteress: A Study of Textual Embodiment," *Prooftexts* 20 (2000): 12–42.

70. Pomeroy, *Goddesses, Whores, Wives, and Slaves*, 86.

71. See Ilan, *Jewish Women*, 136–41. She cites the *Mishnah*: "'When adulterers became many [the rite of] the bitter waters ceased; and Rabban Yohanan b. Zakkai brought it to an end, for it is written, "I will not punish your daughters when they commit prostitution nor your daughters-in-law when they commit adultery, for they themselves [go apart with whores ...]" (*Hos*. 4.14)' (*m.Sot*. 9:9)" (p. 137).

72. Ilan, *Jewish Women*, 137.

73. Ilan, *Jewish Women*, 140.

74. Ilan, *Jewish Women*, 141.

at the zenith of their power during the reign of Salome Alexandra (76–67 B.C.E.), so it is perhaps during this time or after that we should see the real beginning(s) of this opposition.

2.4. *History of the Reign of Salome Alexandra*

At this point, it would be useful to delineate exactly what was going on the first century B.C.E., paying special attention to the reign of Salome Alexandra, in order to understand more fully Ilan's claim. Undoubtedly, the first century B.C.E. was a turbulent time in the history of Judea. The preceding centuries had witnessed the Hellenizing program of Alexander the Great and his successors, as well as the political push and pull over Judea between the Ptolemies (ca. 301–198 B.C.E.) and the Seleucids (ca. 198–142 B.C.E.). Of course, one of the major events in the preceding centuries had been the conflict surrounding Antiochus IV Epiphanes (175–164 B.C.E.), and the subsequent military revolt conducted by the Maccabees, which eventually resulted in the Hasmonean dynasty in Judea, the first time since the destruction of Jerusalem in ca. 587 B.C.E. that a Jewish party ruled the country. However, what began as a reactionary movement against the perceived excesses of Hellenization and foreign rule eventually took on many of the characteristics it had originally despised.

In the early first century B.C.E., Judea is nation-state trying to come to grips with its past and its future via several groups vying not only for political dominance, but also for an ideological monopoly on identity. I shall begin my discussion with Alexander Jannaeus (103–76 B.C.E.), high priest and the last great Hasmonean ruler, who was faced with both external and internal problems as he was appointed to his positions. Jannaeus began his reign by trying to take the city of Ptolemais (Acco) as soon as he was installed as leader in 103 (Josephus, *Ant.* 13.324). The inhabitants of that city called on Ptolemy IX Lathyrus (116–107; 88–81 B.C.E.) for aid. Ptolemy IX seems to have been popular with the people, but extremely unpopular with his mother, Cleopatra III, who expelled him from Egypt in 107; he eventually settled in Cyprus (*Ant.* 13.328). Ptolemy IX's forces managed to defeat Jannaeus temporarily, after which the former invaded Judea. His appalling treatment of his own soldiers, as well as political ambitions proved his undoing. His mother, Cleopatra III, responded and defeated her son, forcing him back to Cyprus (13.338–44). Following this, Cleopatra III was dissuaded from invading Judea, and even made a favorable treaty with Jannaeus, which allowed him to continue his expansionistic campaigns (13.345–55). His next target was Transjordan, which he took, and thus from ca. 95 onward, Jannaeus had control of all of the coastal plain except Ashkelon (13.356–71; also *J.W.* 1.86–87).

After these campaigns, Jannaeus was forced to turn his attention to his increasing domestic problems. He was first confronted by sedition at the Feast of Tabernacles, which he managed to put down only with the help of his Pisidian and Cilician mercenaries (*J.W.* 1.88–89; *Ant.* 13.372–74). His people rose up against him again after an ill-fated attempt on Jannaeus' part to attack the Nabatean king Obedas I (ca. 93–85). Jannaeus lost his entire army and, upon returning to

Jerusalem, was faced with another civil war. This insurrection lasted six years, during which time approximately fifty thousand Jews were killed (*J. W.* 1.90–92; *Ant.* 13.375–76). Because of the immense losses suffered during this war, the opponents of Jannaeus sent to the Syrian king Demetrius III (95–87) for help. Demetrius arrived in Judea, and promptly defeated Jannaeus' troops. However, it was Demetrius who was defeated in the end; Josephus reports that six thousand Jews deserted Demetrius and joined Jannaeus out of pity for the latter's defeat. Because of this mass desertion, Demetrius fled the country. After this impressive display of loyalty on the part of Jannaeus' subjects, they most likely expected some remuneration or at least a hearty show of appreciation. It appears that they received none, for Josephus reports that they began to wage war on Jannaeus yet again. Jannaeus defeated and killed many of them, but subjected about eight hundred of them to a rather savage death; he crucified them while he had their wives and children killed before their eyes, all the while publicly eating and drinking with his concubines.[75]

Hayes and Mandell note two reasons why Jannaeus' reign was marked by such vehement internal problems: "The transformation of the Jewish state into a monarchy gave the ruler greater opportunity to exercise autocratic power [and] his wars of expansion and the employment of mercenary forces probably produced excessive economic burdens for his subjects."[76] However, the most important issue for my purposes is Jannaeus' problems with the Pharisees. Conflict between the Pharisees and the Hasmonean line was nothing new. During the reign of John Hyrcanus (135–104 B.C.E.), a controversy had arisen over the legitimacy of Hyrcanus' claim to the high priesthood. In his *Antiquities*, Josephus claims that Hyrcanus was himself a Pharisee, and a member of that party named Eleazar asked him to give up the high priesthood in favor of only being monarch. Hyrcanus not only refused to do so, but evidently switched his loyalty to the Sadduccean party.[77] Because of this act, the Pharisees were anything but cordial to the Hasmoneans from this point until the conciliatory policies of Salome Alexandra, his wife, some thirty years later.[78] In fact, Schürer posits that it was the

75. *J. W.* 1.96–98; *Ant.* 13.379–83. This scene is most likely colored by Josephus's rather dim view of Janneus as representing one of the last hopes for the Hasmonean dynasty. Whatever potential Janneus may have had, he failed to restore the house to the glory of Hyrcanus.

76. Hayes and Mandell, *The Jewish People in Classical Antiquity*, 98–99.

77. *Ant.* 13.288–98. This story is suspiciously absent from *J. W.* 1.54–69. Emil Schürer, *A History of the Jewish People in the Time of Jesus Christ* (new rev. English ed. by G. Vermes et al.; 3 vols.; Edinburgh: T&T Clark, 1973–86), 1:213–14, notes that Hyrcanus was most likely motivated to break with the Pharisees because of the "distinctly worldly character of his policies" (p. 213). For the Talmudic version of this story, see *b. Kidd.* 66a.

78. There is some controversy over whether or not the wife of Jannaeus is to be identified with the widow of Aristobulus, whose name is either "Salina" or "Salome" (*Ant.* 13.320). Although this is an interesting an important issue, I will not deal with it here due to space restraints. Schürer, *A History of the Jewish People*, 1:219, 229–30, assumes that the two women are one and the same. However, Ilan, "Queen Salamzion Alexandra and Judas Aristobulus I's Widow: Did Jannaeus Alexander Contract a Levirate Marriage?" *JSJ* 24 (1993): 181–90, argues that the two women are not the same person.

Pharisees who were responsible for most, if not all, of the seditious behavior of the people during the reign of Jannaeus.[79] As D. S. Russell notes, Jannaeus'

> growing unpopularity was matched only by the growing popularity of the Pharisees themselves, who were openly critical of his manner of life. To them it was quite intolerable that a drunkard and profligate like Jannaeus should claim the status of either High Priest or of King; he had wilfully neglected his spiritual office, sacrificing it to that of a rough soldier whose delight was in war; his sympathies, moreover, were with the wealthy and powerful Sadducaean families.[80]

As such, it is no great surprise that the Pharisees objected to Jannaeus and his reign.

Jannaeus was killed in battle in Transjordan at the siege of Ragaba in 76, but not before advising Salome Alexandra, to whom he willed his kingdom, to make peace with the Pharisees. Josephus's report of this scene is suspect in that his account in *Antiquities* has no parallel whatsoever in *The Jewish War*. In the former, Josephus goes to great lengths to portray Jannaeus' wish to appease the Pharisees, even going as far as ordering his wife to allow them to desecrate his corpse if they saw fit.[81] If we assume that the account in *Antiquities* contains some truth—which is not at all clear—it would seem that this tactic paid off; Josephus reports that the Pharisees were so touched by this action that they made several speeches which were so moving that the people gave Jannaeus the most impressive burial any king had ever received (*Ant.* 13.406).

The mere fact that Jannaeus bequeathed his kingdom to his wife should come as no surprise. According to Josephus, John Hyrcanus had evidently left his realm to his wife, who was subsequently imprisoned by her son Aristobulus I (105–104 B.C.E.) (*J.W.* 1.71; *Ant.* 13.302). Thus, there was at least one precedent in Judea for willing one's queen the kingdom. Outside of Judea, there were ample examples of female royalty as well, especially in Ptolemaic Egypt. In the second century B.C.E., two of the most important political figures in Egypt were Cleopatra II and Cleopatra III, mother and daughter respectively. In fact, as Ilan notes, it may have been "under Ptolemaic influence that first John Hyrcanus the Hasmonean,

79. Schürer, *A History of the Jewish People*, 1:222–24. Jonathan A. Goldstein, "The Hasmonean Revolt and the Hasmonean Dynasty," in *The Cambridge History of Judaism*. Vol. 2, *The Hellenistic Age* (ed. W. D. Davies and Louis Finkelstein; Cambridge: Cambridge University Press, 1989), 292–351 (343), agrees, and among other sources cites *b. Kidd.* 66a. However, Lester L. Grabbe, *Judaism from Cyrus to Hadrian* (2 vols.; Minneapolis: Fortress, 1992), 1:304, is more skeptical.

80. D. S. Russell, *The Jews from Alexander to Herod* (New Clarendon Bible; Oxford: Oxford University Press, 1967), 71. For a similar explanation of the animosity between Jannaeus and the Pharisees, see Solomon Zeitlin, "Queen Salome and King Jannaeus Alexander: A Chapter in the History of the Second Jewish Commonwealth," *JQR* 51 (1961): 1–33 (7–8).

81. *Ant.* 13.401–2. Even though this scene in *Antiquities* implies that the Pharisees constituted a major opposition to Jannaeus, it is not certain how much power they actually exerted during his reign. See Grabbe, *Judaism from Cyrus to Hadrian*, 1:304: "one can only conclude that Pharisaic opponents—which most probably existed—were only a part of the opposition to Alexander. One also suspects that the deathbed scene with regard to the Pharisees was an invention by Josephus to explain the influence of the Pharisees over Alexandra Salome during her rule."

and then his son Alexander Yannai, each nominated his wife as his successor."[82] Whether or not this was the case, Salome Alexandra took the reins of command and, at least initially, encountered no opposition.

One of the first actions Alexandra took after assuming political control of Judea was to appoint the older son of Jannaeus, Hyrcanus, to the position of High Priest. It seems as if he was both incompetent to govern and lazy, according to Josephus (*Ant.* 13.407–8; *J.W.* 1.109). One of the most important events during her reign is the Pharisees' gaining of power and influence.[83] Josephus relays how Jannaeus had told her to view them as royal advisers and to do nothing without their consent, but it seems as if their power went even further. Based on Josephus, Schürer (and subsequently Hugo Mantel) holds that during the reign of Alexandra, the makeup of the *Gerousia* was altered in order to include Pharisees as members.[84] If there were one main council in Judea that addressed political and religious issues, which is not at all clear, it likely would have been in Jerusalem and would have been composed of mostly aristocratic members.[85]

The first mention of a *Gerousia* occurs in Josephus and is found in a letter of Antiochus III the Great (223–187 B.C.E.), and most likely refers to a senate-like organization composed of upper-class citizens.[86] Although it is anachronistic to mention Sadducees during the third to second centuries B.C.E., it does appear that over time this party asserted control over the *Gerousia* due to the connections between them and the upper class members of society (see, e.g., *Ant.* 13.297; 18.17). Thus, J. Klausner assumes rather than argues that the Sanhedrin during this period was composed primarily of aristocratic Sadducees.[87] The importance of this information for our purposes is that if the *Gerousia* traditionally had been composed of only aristocrats and Sadducees, then the sudden inclusion of Pharisees into the mix would have caused great consternation in the council as well as

82. Ilan, "'And Who Knows Whether You have not Come to Dominion for a Time Like This?' (Esther 4:14): Esther, *Judith* and *Susanna* as Propaganda for Shelamzion's Queenship," in *Integrating Women*, 127–53 (132).

83. Jacob Neusner, in his *From Politics to Piety: The Emergence of Pharisaic Judaism* (2d ed.; New York: Ktav, 1979), 45–66, analyzes Josephus's portrait of the Pharisees in both his *Jewish War* and *Antiquities*, and concludes that only the material in the former may be relied upon favorably because, according to Neusner, Josephus takes pains to paint a flattering picture of the Pharisees in *Antiquities*, and as such the work cannot be trusted in this regard. In his work, Steve Mason persuasively refutes Neusner's analysis, and argues that Josephus's view of the Pharisees is more constant between the two works. See Mason, *Flavius Josephus on the Pharisees: A Composition-Critical Study* (StPB 39; Leiden: Brill, 1991). Because Mason's work is more responsible in its assessment of Josephus's writings, I agree with his conclusions. I will, then, take a broader view of Josephus's testimony, and thus will include material from both in my examination.

84. *J.W.* 1.111–12; *Ant.* 13.408–15. See Schürer, *A History of the Jewish People*, 1:230–31; Hugo Mantel, *Studies in the History of the Sanhedrin* (Cambridge, Mass.: Harvard University Press, 1961), 30 n. 175 and 96. Also see Jagersma, *A History of Israel from Alexander the Great to Bar Kochba*, 96; and Russell, *The Jews from Alexander to Herod*, 74.

85. See the reasonable caveats regarding any reconstruction of this council espoused by Anthony J. Saldarini, "Sanhedrin," *ABD* 5:975–80.

86. *Ant.* 12.138. See also Schürer, *A History of the Jewish People*, 2:203.

87. Klausner, "Queen Salome Alexandra," 243–44.

political opposition from outside the council. However, while a change in the composition of the *Gerousia* would explain the rise in power the Pharisees experienced, Josephus never mentions it and thus it must remain a hypothesis, albeit a very persuasive one.[88]

Another reason why the Pharisees may have gained prominence under Salome is the possibility that Simeon b. Shetah, a leading member of the Pharisaic party during this time, was reputed to be her brother.[89] Louis Finkelstein goes so far as to claim that Salome appointed Simeon to the position of co-leader of the Temple Tribunal, or the *Gerousia*.[90] Talmudic tradition attributes to Simeon the founding of a school system in Jerusalem that eventually morphed into an educational system for the masses.[91] Education is not the only area in which Simeon inaugurated reform; he also set his sights on the regulations surrounding the *ketubbah* marriage contract.[92] Simeon was extremely concerned with the conduct and treatment of false witnesses, as well. In fact, later rabbinic tradition thinks so much of Simeon that he is referred to as a *nasi* ('prince').[93] Even though most of this information is chronologically problematic in that it stems from rabbinic materials, it seems that Simeon did exert a large influence during or around the time of Salome's reign, and that he did initiate several reforms.

The Pharisees acted as if they were in charge of Judea. They began to execute enemies, free prisoners, and recall exiles; "In short, the enjoyments of royal authority were theirs" (*J.W.* 1.111; cf. *Ant.* 13.409). One of the most important indications of their influence during Salome's reign is that she restored the Pharisaic regulations that Hyrcanus had abolished.[94] Of course, this simply may indicate good diplomatic skills on her part. In fact, Klausner regards decisions like this one as just that—calculated political moves: "she may have deliberately turned over domestic affairs to the Pharisees to preclude their interference in foreign matters which she regarded as much more important and to which she paid much attention."[95] As Klausner notes, Salome was no shrinking violet; she reportedly doubled her army as well as collected a large body of foreign troops to safeguard herself and the country. Even so, with typical disregard for women,

88. Even though Josephus never mentions this event, Klausner, "Queen Salome Alexandra," 243–44, mentions several alterations in Sadducee traditions that he dates to the reign of Salome.

89. Klausner, "Queen Salome Alexandra," 248, cautiously accepts this tradition: "The Talmud [e.g. *Ber.* 48a] regards the queen, Jannaeus' wife, as the sister of Simeon ben Shetah. In any case, there is little doubt that in Jannaeus' days, and even more so during the reign of Salome, Simeon ben Shetah was very close to the Pharisee Queen." Also see Schürer, *A History of the Jewish People*, 1:221–22.

90. Louis Finkelstein, "Pharisaic Leadership after the Great Synagogue (170 B.C.E.–135 C.E.)," in Davies and Finkelstein, eds., *The Cambridge History of Judaism*, 2:245–77 (271).

91. See *y. Ketub.* 8:11, and the discussion of this reform in Klausner, "Queen Salome Alexandra," 252–53. Also see Russell, *The Jews from Alexander to Herod*, 74–75.

92. Klausner, "Queen Salome Alexandra," 250–52, examines the *ketubbah* reform.

93. *T. Hag.* 2:8, quoted in Neusner, *From Politics to Piety*, 106.

94. *Ant.* 13.408. This action is not mentioned in *J.W.* 1.111, although Josephus implies that the Pharisees took advantage of Salome's religiosity.

95. Klausner, "Queen Salome Alexandra," 245.

Josephus states rather glibly, "if she ruled the nation, the Pharisees ruled her" (*J.W.* 1.112).[96]

Of course, this exercise of power by the Pharisees inevitably led to a backlash, which was led by Salome's second son Aristobulus II and his supporters. These supporters are described by Josephus as being the "most eminent of the citizens," as well as fervent supporters of Jannaeus (*J.W.* 1.114; *Ant.* 13.411–12). Both of these descriptions lead me to believe that the supporters of Aristobulus II were most likely Sadducees due to the socio-economic information as well as their loyalty to Jannaeus, who was avowedly anti-Pharisaic.[97] Aristobulus II was given the chance at military success by Alexandra when she sent him on an expedition to Damascus against Ptolemy, the son of Mennaeus. However, the sortie accomplished nothing, and it opened the door for Tigranes, the king of Armenia, to capture Damascus. Tigranes then laid siege to Acco (Ptolemais) in preparation for an invasion of Judea, but Salome was able to allay his campaign by means of several gifts (*J.W.* 1.115–16; *Ant.* 13.418–21). Late in Salome's reign, though, Aristobulus seems to have honed his military skills, because he and his supporters succeeded in occupying twenty-two fortresses in a bid to gain control of the country. Before Alexandra could respond to this threat, she died.[98]

In his *Jewish War*, Josephus ends his account of Salome's reign with a simple notice of her death (*J.W.* 1.119). However, in his *Antiquities*, he provides a long summary of and reflection upon her time in power, as well as her character. His description is worth quoting in its entirety:

> She was a woman who showed none of the weakness of her sex; for being one of those inordinately desirous of the power to rule, she showed by her deeds the ability to carry out her plans, at the same time she exposed the folly of those men who continually fail to maintain sovereign power. For she valued the present more than the future, and making everything else secondary to absolute rule, she had, on account of this, no consideration for either decency or justice. At least matters turned out so unfortunately for her house that the sovereign power which it had acquired in the face of the greatest dangers and difficulties was not long afterward taken from it because of her desire for things unbecoming a woman, and because she expressed the same opinions as those who were hostile to her family, and also because she left the kingdom without anyone who had their interests at heart. And even after her death she caused the palace to be filled with misfortunes and disturbances which arose from the public measures taken during her lifetime. Nevertheless, in spite of reigning in this manner, she had kept the nation at peace. Such, then, was the end of Alexandra. (*Ant.* 13.430–32)

96. For specific examples of Josephus's attitude(s) towards women, see Cheryl Anne Brown, *No Longer Be Silent: First Century Jewish Portraits of Biblical Women* (Gender and the Biblical Tradition Series; Louisville, Ky.: Westminster/John Knox, 1992), especially her general comments on pp. 15–16 and 212–15.

97. Schürer, *A History of the Jewish People*, 1:232; and Klausner, "Queen Salome Alexandra," 245–47, concur.

98. For a succinct, reliable overview of Salome's reign, see Joseph Sievers, "The Role of Women in the Hasmonean Dynasty," in *Josephus, the Bible, and History* (ed. Louis H. Feldman and Gohei Hata; Detroit: Wayne State University Press, 1989), 132–46 (135–40). Zeitlin's assessment, in "Queen Salome and King Jannaeus Alexander," 27–33, is much more critical of Salome's time in power.

There are several points to note in this passage. First, Josephus here reiterates the intimate connection between Salome and the Pharisees, which I believe he indicates by mentioning "those who were hostile to her family"; recall that Jannaeus had been no friend to the Pharisees. Again, there is little doubt that Salome was a supporter of the Pharisees during her reign, and this fact lends weight to the claim that Simeon b. Shetah might have been her brother due to his influence and reforms around the time of her reign. Second, Josephus seems to be of two minds in his assessment. On the one hand, he praises Salome for keeping the peace and the ability to execute her plans, but he also strongly criticizes her for her legacy, which seemingly includes the downfall of the state under Roman rule. This ambiguity most likely stems from Josephus's desire to portray the Pharisees in a negative light, i.e., Salome's domestic policies failed due to her reliance on Pharisaic advice, but her foreign policy was somewhat successful because it was implemented independent of the Pharisees.[99]

Finally, the issue of gender seems to be central in Josephus's analysis of Salome's reign. As Ilan notes, "This text blames the queen for all the misfortunes of the Hasmonean household...for no specific reason except that she was a woman and women should not assume supreme power!"[100] Indeed, the references to Salome's sex are quite prominent, and perhaps point to an attitude that women are not fit to rule. In her work on this subject, Ilan notes the prevailing Greek attitudes found in Plato, Aristotle, and Cato to the effect that women not only should not rule, but are in fact incapable of doing so.[101] This prevailing attitude coupled with the concrete fact that Salome was appointed to rule by Jannaeus instead of her adult male sons most likely generated the need for some actions on the part of Salome's supporters, to justify her position and rule. This justification, according to Ilan, is found in Greek Esther, Judith, and Susanna. Prior to discussing this view and its implications for dating Susanna, though, it would be helpful to discuss the different versions of Susanna and the external evidence for dating the story at our disposal.

2.5. *The Greek Versions of Susanna*

The story of Susanna and the Elders appears in two different Greek versions. One, the Old Greek (OG) version, is a relatively compact morality tale, and seems to have been intended for edification.[102] In this version of the story, the Elders see

99. See Mason, *Flavius Josephus on the Pharisees*, 257–58. Mason explains Josephus's remarks on Salome's death in *Antiquities* as an attempt to implicate the Pharisees in the downfall of the Hasmonean dynasty.

100. Ilan, "'Things Unbecoming a Woman' (*Ant* 13.431): Josephus and Nicolaus on Women," in *Integrating Women*, 85–125 (103). In this chapter, Ilan argues that the passage quoted above derives from Nicolaus and not from Josephus.

101. For this discussion, see Ilan, "'And Who Knows,'" 128–32. Among the works Ilan cites are *Republic* 5.454E–457C; and *Politics* 1.5.1260a; 2.6.1269b; 5.9.1313b.

102. Some scholars have erroneously termed this version the "LXX" version. However, I prefer the term "Old Greek," because the term "LXX" is usually used to designate the Septuagint, i.e., the collection of Greek translations of the Hebrew Bible from Hebrew texts. However, some documents

Susanna and separately lust after her. They then admit their lust to one another, and go immediately to Susanna and grab her. Susanna refuses to acquiesce to their desire, at which point the Elders simply walk away. However, they later summon her, accuse her of adultery, and the people condemn her to death. At this point, the angel of the Lord comes to Daniel, and he publicly cross-examines the elders concerning their testimony. Their stories conflict, thus exposing their deception. The people then gag them and throw them into a ravine. The OG version ends with an endorsement of pious young men.

The other and slightly longer version is that of Theodotion (Θ/Th). This rendering of the story elaborates the intrigue and seems to give a greater prominence to the character of the young Daniel. The Th version contains many of the same elements of the OG version, but also inserts new details into that framework; as a result, most scholars think that the Th version used and adapted the OG version.[103] The major new details in the Th version include a fuller characterization of Susanna (vv. 1–4); a description of Susanna and her garden (vv. 15–18); the immediate reactions of Susanna, the Elders, and Susanna's household to her refusal of the Elders' attempted rape (vv. 24–27); a longer version of Susanna's prayer to God (vv. 42–43); and a more glowing view of Daniel (vv. 50, 64).

The relationship between the two versions is not paramount to this book, but it is necessary to discuss the issue briefly, as it pertains to the possible date of the story. Most scholars posit some sort of literary dependence of Th on the OG version.[104] As Collins notes, the most obvious reason for this position is that there are several instances of verbatim overlap between the two texts, and that Th is a more elaborative story.[105] Moore writes, "of the sixty verses 'shared' by the LXX and Θ, only about twenty-three per cent of them have either total (cf. vss. 29, 33–34, 40, 48, 52, 57–58) or even significant partial verbatim agreement (cf. vss. 5b, 10a, 22b, 23a, 36a, 41a)."[106] Because of these overlaps, Collins and Moore

included in the LXX are thought to have been composed originally in Greek, not Hebrew. To avoid any confusion, then, I will refer to this version as the OG. With regards to the date of both versions, most scholars now agree that the LXX translation was initiated in the third century B.C.E. in Alexandria; see Melvin K. H. Peters, "Septuagint," *ABD* 5:1093–1104.

103. For standard judgments on these and other issues concerning the two versions and their relationship, see Moore, *Daniel*, 78–80, and Collins, *Daniel*, 426–28. The Th version is attributed to Theodotion, who was active in Ephesus in the mid-second century C.E.; see Henry Barclay Swete, *An Introduction to the Old Testament in Greek* (rev. Richard Rusden Ottley; Cambridge: Cambridge University Press, 1914; repr., Peabody, MA: Hendrickson, 1989), 42–49, and Leonard J. Greenspoon, "Theodotion, Theodotion's Version," *ABD* 6:447–48. However, as we shall see, the Th version of Susanna most likely predates the figure of Theodotion. For a side-by-side comparison of the two translations, see Joseph Ziegler, ed., *Susanna, Daniel, Bel et Draco*, in *Septuaginta* (Vetus Testamentum Graecum auctoritate Academiae Scientiarum Gottingensis editum 16, no. 2; 2d. ed.; Göttingen: Vandenhoeck & Ruprecht, 1999), 216–33; for English comparisons, see Kay, *APOT* 1:647–51, and Steussy, *Gardens in Babylon*, 102–15.

104. Contra this position, Koenen, "Von der todesmutigen Susanna zum begabten Daniel," 1–13, argues that both the OG and Th are derivations of a Hebrew or Aramaic original, but that neither version knew the other.

105. Collins, *Daniel*, 426.

106. Moore, *Daniel*, 79.

concede that there exists some sort of relationship between the two versions, but they disagree as to the nature of that relationship. Moore hypothesizes that the *Vorlage* of Susanna was originally Hebrew or Aramaic, both versions represent translations of that *Vorlage*, and the Θ version probably used the LXX version for its translation.[107] In his detailed comparison of the OG and Th versions of Daniel, Tim McLay agrees with Moore's assessment. He holds that "Th did have both proto-MT and OG (or may have been familiar with OG), but that Th translated his *Vorlage* more or less independently and employed OG occasionally or when confronted with difficult passages."[108] On the other hand, Collins posits "that the *Vorlage* of Θ was already a redaction of the *Vorlage* of the OG. Θ would still have had the older Greek version and drawn from it...and could still have made further redactional changes."[109] Either way, all of these scholars implicitly acknowledge that the Th version made use of the OG version. This position of dependence means that the Th version was composed after the OG version. Since most, if not all, aesthetic interpretations of Susanna use the Th version, it is that version on which I will focus.

2.6. *External Evidence: Textual Data*

The textual data for Susanna is of little help. Thus far, no copies of our story have been discovered at Qumran, despite earlier speculation.[110] The OG version of the story is only found in three manuscripts, the earliest dating from ca. 150 C.E.[111] The Th version of Susanna is found in Origen's Hexapla, dating from the third century C.E. Another clue may be gained from the fact that there seems to be little difference between the language and style of the Additions to Daniel and the LXX translation of Daniel itself. This similarity could indicate that the Additions were translated at the same time as LXX Daniel. Thus Moore writes,

> Inasmuch as the literary style and diction of the Additions do not differ from the rest of the LXX of Daniel, we may safely assume that the Additions had the same date and place of translation as the canonical Daniel.[112]

Moore places the date of translation for LXX Daniel at ca. 100 B.C.E. because this text is used in 1 Maccabees, which was translated into *Koine* Greek in the mid-first century B.C.E. As such, it is likely that the LXX version of Daniel was

107. Moore, *Daniel*, 80–84.

108. Tim McLay, *The OG and Th Versions of Daniel* (SBLSCS 43; Atlanta: Scholars Press, 1996), 15.

109. Collins, *Daniel*, 426.

110. J. T. Milik, "Daniel et Susanne à Qumrân," in *De la Tôrah au Messie: Etudes d'exegèse et d'herméneutique bibliques offertes à Henri Cazelles* (ed. Maurice Carrez et al.; Paris: Desclée, 1981), 337–59, argued that 4Q551 represents a portion of an Aramaic *Vorlage* for Susanna. Recently, though, George W. E. Nickelsburg, "4Q551: A *Vorlage* to Susanna or a Text Related to Judges 19?," *JJS* 48 (1997): 349–51, has shown these fragments to be a part of a narrative influenced by Judg 19 rather than a link in the textual history of Susanna.

111. See Moore, *Daniel*, 33. The three MSS are the Kölner Papyrus 967; Codex Chisianus 88; and the Ambrosian Syro-Hexaplar. For a discussion, see Ziegler, *Susanna, Daniel, Bel et Draco*, 9–86.

112. Moore, *Daniel*, 33.

produced at some point in the first century B.C.E., which could shed light on the date of the Additions to Daniel.

In terms of the Th version of Susanna, a date is much more slippery. As I noted above, most scholars hold that Th cannot be dated to the mid-second century C.E., the accepted date for the activity of Theodotion.[113] Some scholars have even posited a predecessor to Theodotion, whose work was included with Theodotion's in Origen's Hexapla. Leonard J. Greenspoon writes,

> Quotations from Theodotion's Daniel and from other material identified with him antedate "historical" Theodotion by as much as a century. This has led to the hypothesis of an "Ur-Theodotion." His work may be described as a thoughtful revision of the Old Greek of some (all?) of the Old Testament towards a Hebrew that closely resembled the text preserved by the Masoretes (the MT). This anonymous individual (or group of individuals) apparently lived in the first century B.C.E. and provided the basis for "Theodotionic" quotations prior to Theodotion.[114]

Other scholars have posited a similar thesis, but with a slight modification. In several texts there is a recension of the LXX that has been termed the *kaige* version by D. Barthélemy.[115] Commenting on this thesis, Emanuel Tov notes,

> In antiquity this anonymous revision was ascribed to Theodotion, who apparently lived at the end of the second century CE. Hence the translational units which are ascribed to Theodotion also belong to this revision. Consequently, the revision is now named *kaige*-Theodotion, though it should be noted that its various attestations are not uniform in character. Its presumed early date, the middle of the first century BCE, solves the so-called proto-Theodotionic problem which has long preoccupied scholars.[116]

If either of these hypotheses is accepted, then once again we are thrust into the first century B.C.E. in our search for a date for Susanna. In sum, our external evidence roughly points to a *terminus ad quem* in the mid-first century B.C.E.

2.7. *Internal Evidence*

Turning to internal evidence, we find that our text contains many clues that could help determine a possible date. The story itself places its narrative setting during the exile: "There was a man living in Babylon whose name was Joakim" (v. 1).[117] However, this setting need not reflect historical verisimilitude, i.e., we need not accept the story's account of its own setting. More clues might be found if we examine some of the most important themes in the work: the issues of witnesses and gender.

113. This date is based on two main sources. The first is Epiphanius (*On Measures and Weights* 17), and the second is Irenaeus (*Against Heresies* 3.24). See Collins, *Daniel*, 10.

114. Greenspoon, "Theodotion, Theodotion's Version," 448.

115. D. Barthélemy, *Les devanciers d'Aquila* (VTSup 10; Leiden: Brill, 1963).

116. Emanuel Tov, *Textual Criticism of the Hebrew Bible* (Minneapolis: Fortress; Assen: Van Gorcum, 1992), 145. Tov also cites the work of A. Schmitt (*Stammt der sogenannte "Θ"-Text bei Daniel wirklich von Theodotion?* [NAWG 1; Göttingen: Vandenhoeck & Ruprecht, 1966]) in connection with the non-uniformity of the attestations of *kaige*-Theodotion.

117. All translations of Susanna are my own from the Theodotion version. A full translation can be found in Appendix 1.

2.7.1. *Witnesses*

We know that issues arose concerning the treatment of witnesses during the first century B.C.E. The great Pharisee leader Simeon b. Shetah was particularly involved with the treatment of witnesses. Simeon was reputed to be the brother of Salome Alexandra (76–67 B.C.E.), and during her reign was probably appointed to the *Gerousia*, in which case he would have had more power to put forth his opinions. Rabbinic literature records several incidents involving Simeon and witnesses. For example, *Avot* 1:9 records Simeon saying "Examine the witnesses abundantly, and be cautious in thy words, lest they learn from them to give false answers."[118] On another occasion, two witnesses testified against a defendant, and the latter was sentenced to death. Before he could be executed, it was discovered that one of the witnesses had perjured themselves. Because of this new information, Simeon had the witness put to death.[119]

However, the most important connection between Simeon and the issue of false witnesses occurred because Simeon's own son was sentenced to death. Right before the execution took place, the witnesses confessed to perjury. According to the prevailing Sadduccean interpretation of the principle of *lex talionis*, if a witness was found to be false, then he or she would suffer the same fate as they had inflicted on their victim. Since Simeon's son had not yet been executed, Simeon wanted him to be set free, but his son refused. The Talmud tells us that Simeon's son then offered to accept the death penalty, so that his accusers would be similarly punished, and that the issue of witnesses would be brought to the fore.[120]

This issue of witnesses and the punishment thereof finds its clearest exposition in *m. Mak.* 1:6:

> False witnesses are put to death only after judgement has been given. For lo, the Sadducees used to say: Not until he [that was falsely accused] has been put to death, as it is written, *Life for life*. The Sages answered: Is it not also written, *Then shall ye do unto him as he had thought to do unto his brother*—thus his brother must still be alive.

118. All Mishnaic quotes are taken from Herbert Danby, *The Mishnah* (Oxford: Oxford University Press, 1933).

119. See Louis Finkelstein, *The Pharisees: The Sociological Background of their Faith* (2 vols.; 3d rev. ed.; Philadelphia: The Jewish Publication Society of America, 1962), 2:697–98. Finkelstein also discusses this story on 2:843–44 n. 76. The citations given in that note are: *Mek.*, *Mishpatim*, ch. 20 p. 327; *t. Sanh.* 6:6, p. 424; *y. Sanh.* 6:5, 23b; and *b. Mak.* 5b. However, see Jacob Neusner, *The Rabbinic Traditions about the Pharisees before 70* (3 vols.; Leiden: Brill, 1971), 1:122–27. Neusner argues that the earliest version of this story, which appears in several variations, is found in R. Ishmael's *Mek. Kaspa* 3:31–41, and probably originally contained a story favorable to Judah b. Tabbai, Simeon's close associate. All of the other versions, according to Neusner, are alterations of this earlier story that place Simeon in a more favorable light. The Midrash here is based on Exod 22:24–23:19, and is tentatively dated to ca. 250 C.E. See Neusner, *Introduction to Rabbinic Literature* (ABRL; New York: Doubleday, 1994), 250, and idem, *Mekhilta According to Rabbi Ishmael: An Analytical Translation* (2 vols.; BJS 148, 154; Atlanta: Scholars Press, 1988), 2:232–35. For an examination of these, and other Rabbinic data about Simeon, see Neusner, *Rabbinic Traditions*, 1:86–141.

120. This story is preserved in *y. Sanh.* 6:3. Curiously, Neusner, *Rabbinic Traditions*, 1:111, makes no comment on this story, except to note that it is a "curious supplement" to the story in *y. Sanh.* 6:6.

> If so, why was it written, *Life for life*? Could it be that they were put to death so soon as their evidence was received [and found false]?—but Scripture says *Life for life*; thus they are not put to death until judgement [of death] has been given [against him that was falsely accused].[121]

In his important work on the Pharisees, Louis Finkelstein discusses this issue, i.e., punishing witnesses *prior* to any sort of sentence being carried out against a victim. Finkelstein argues, based on *m. Mak.* 1:6, that the law against punishing witnesses before the enactment of a verdict is Sadduccean in origin and reflects that party's interpretation of Deut 19:21, which they saw as condoning an action being taken in response to an action already committed.[122] However, he notes that the Pharisees expanded that interpretation to include the *intent* of a false witness, which they backed up with Deut 19:19.[123] Thus, according to the Pharisaic interpretation of *lex talionis*, an overt action is not required before retribution can be sought, merely an intent. In the case of witnesses, this view holds that a defendant does not have to be injured prior to punishing any perjurious witnesses. Presumably, the case of Simeon's son preceded this stance on the part of the Pharisees, and may have even occasioned it.

The overlap between these issues and Susanna is quite interesting. In the story of Susanna, as Finkelstein notes, "the false witnesses are executed, although Susanna had only been convicted, but not slain, on their testimony."[124] This execution would seem to be in accord with the Pharisaic interpretation of the law of *lex talionis*, in that the Elders were put to death because of their perjury before Susanna was executed. In fact, some scholars claim that Susanna was composed to address this very issue, i.e., Susanna can be seen as a piece of Pharisaic legal propaganda.[125] If it was, then we should look to a time when the Pharisaic party was engaged in heated opposition with the Sadduccean party, such as under John Hyrcanus (135–104 B.C.E.) or his successor Alexander Jannaeus (103–76 B.C.E.). The Pharisees play an important role at the end of Jannaeus' reign, and gain almost total power during the reign of Salome, if Josephus is to be believed. Prior to drawing any conclusion about the dating of Susanna, though, we should address one of the other main themes of Susanna: gender.

2.7.2. *Gender Issues: Connection(s) with Judith and Greek Esther*

To write that the story of Susanna is concerned with gender is not a risky stance. The book is concerned with a woman facing possible rape or execution based on a false charge of adultery; of course gender issues play a major role in the story. However, what makes this particular treatment of gender so interesting is two-fold. On the one hand, Jennifer A. Glancy notes that, "the mechanisms of gender

121. See Jacob Neusner, *A History of the Mishnaic Law of Damages*. Part 3, *Baba Batra, Sanhedrin, Makkot* (SJLA 35; Leiden: Brill, 1984), 246, who cites *Tosefta* 1.8.

122. Finkelstein, *The Pharisees*, 2:843 n. 75.

123. Finkelstein, *The Pharisees*, 2:696–97.

124. Finkelstein, *The Pharisees*, 2:843 n. 75.

125. One of the earliest and most influential argument for this position is Brüll, "Das apokryphische Susanna-Buch."

representation render the character of Susanna almost entirely as object."[126] Thus, even though the story centers on Susanna, one could argue the implied author construes her as a flat character.[127] In this view, she never emerges as a complete persona; she functions almost entirely as an agent to further the plot of the story. Ilan even claims that Susanna as a character is not required for the story; she writes,

> In *Susanna*, the story of Daniel's rise to fame by cross-examining false witnesses does not necessarily require a woman falsely accused of adultery. It could be told, for example, against a story similar to that of Naboth the Jezreelite in the biblical Book of Kings (1 Kings 21).[128]

As such, there is a sense in which the story of Susanna does not challenge or provoke any sort of gender code(s). That is, given the fact that Susanna rarely acts and speaks for herself and that she is finally saved by Daniel, the character of Susanna seems to accept her assigned place as a woman in the author's fictional world.

The other interesting point about gender in the story of Susanna is the similarities in content of this nature it shares with other stories such as Judith and Esther. In fact, in the Jacobite Syriac version of the Hebrew Bible, all three books (along with Ruth) are grouped together.[129] Michael P. Carroll, through a structuralist examination, argues that all three stories are linked by several similar examples of "surface content," e.g., in all three books there is an attempted seduction by someone of high social standing which fails.[130] As such, they form a "transformational set," to use Claude Lévi-Strauss's terminology. There are more general similarities between the three books as well. In Judith, even though the title character does act independently and eventually saves her town, many scholars believe that at the end of the story, she re-assumes her given place in a patriarchal

126. Jennifer A. Glancy, "The Accused: Susanna and her Readers," in *A Feminist Companion to Esther, Judith, and Susanna* (ed. Athalya Brenner; FCB 7; Sheffield: Sheffield Academic Press, 1995), 288–302 (301).

127. By "flat," I am referring to the distinction made by E. M. Forster in *Aspects of the Novel* (New York: Harcourt, Brace & World, 1927), 67–78, between flat and round characters. The former are characterized as one-dimensional entities, those only associated with one or two distinguishing character traits. The latter refers to more fully developed characters, those with multiple interests and facets.

128. Tal Ilan, "'And Who Knows,'" 143.

129. See Kay, *APOT* 1:638; André LaCocque, *The Feminine Unconventional* (OBT; Minneapolis: Fortress, 1990), 24; S. P. Brock, "Versions, Ancient (Syriac)," *ABD* 6:794–99. See also Dennis Ronald MacDonald, *The Legend and the Apostle: The Battle for Paul in Story and Canon* (Philadelphia: Westminster, 1983), 90: the *Acts of Paul and Thecla* was also included in a Syrian "Book of Women," that included Ruth, Esther, Judith, and Susanna. It is unclear as to whether the book MacDonald mentions is the same as the Jacobite Syriac version mentioned above.

130. Michael P. Carroll, "Myth, Methodology, and Transformation in the Old Testament: The Stories of Esther, Judith, and Susanna," *SR* 12 (1983): 301–12. Carroll's article is useful in illuminating Lévi-Strauss's methodology. However, his view that the action(s) of the Elders represents an attempted seduction represents a serious misreading of the text, which actually portrays an attempted rape.

system, thus negating any feminist potential the story may have had.[131] While I do not totally agree with this position, it is persuasive. The situation is similar with regard to Esther; while she does act to save her people, it is not clear that she emerges as a feminist heroine. As Ilan writes, "Much like Judith, she does not rise to prominence in order to upset the patriarchal order of the kingdom; her mission is simply to intervene in time of crisis."[132] Thus, all three protagonists ultimately endorse the dominant patriarchal ideology embedded within their respective fictional worlds.

The stories share another thing in common as well, viz., many scholars typically assign them to the Hasmonean period, and more specifically to the first century B.C.E. Unfortunately, almost all scholars agree that neither Esther nor Judith has been found at Qumran yet, which might help significantly in dating the stories. It is not surprising that Judith was not preserved at Qumran, given the work's Pharisaic tone.[133] The situation of Esther at Qumran, however, is more ambiguous.[134]

The case for the Greek translation of Esther, as well as the Additions to that book, being completed by the first century B.C.E. is more secure than dating Judith.[135] This is because of the gross historical inaccuracies in the first seven chapters of Judith, as well as the historical allusion in the colophon to Greek Esther. The colophon reads:

> In the fourth year of the reign of Ptolemy and Cleopatra, Dositheus, who said that he was a priest and a Levite, and his son Ptolemy brought to Egypt the preceding letter about Purim, which they said was authentic and had been translated by Lysimachus son of Ptolemy, one of the residents of Jerusalem.[136]

Even though this colophon is not clear with regards to the identity of the persons it mentions—which would provide us with a definite date—there are two main views on this issue. Moore, following Benno Jacob, views the Ptolemy in ques-

131. See, e.g., Pamela J. Milne, "What Shall We Do with Judith: A Feminist Reassessment of a Biblical 'Heroine'," *Semeia* 62 (1993): 37–55.

132. Ilan, "'And Who Knows,'" 152.

133. See C. A. Moore, *Judith* (AB 40; Garden City, N.Y.: Doubleday, 1985), 86; and Mathias Delcor, "Le Livre de Judith et l'époque grecque," *Klio* 49 (1967): 151–79.

134. J. T. Milik, "Les Modèles Araméens du Livre d'Esther dans la Grotte 4 de Qumrân," *RevQ* 15 (1992): 321–99, has proposed that six Aramaic manuscripts labeled 4Q550 represented sources for the different witnesses to the book of Esther. More recently, Sidnie White Crawford, "Has *Esther* been Found at Qumran? *4Qproto-Esther* and the *Esther* Corpus," *RevQ* 17 (1996): 307–25, after analyzing Milik's work, posits that 4Q550 represents part of a group of tales dealing with the Persian court, and may have influenced both the *Proto-Esther* that lies behind the MT and Proto-Alpha Text versions of the book, and the Additions to Esther as well.

135. While the relationship between Greek Esther, the Additions to Esther, and the other versions of Esther is interesting, it falls beyond the scope of this examination. For discussions of this thorny problem, see Charles V. Dorothy, *The Books of Esther: Structure, Genre and Textual Integrity* (JSOTSup 187; Sheffield: Sheffield Academic Press, 1997); and Ruth Kossmann, *Die Esthernovelle: vom Erzählten zur Erzählung; Studien zur Traditions- und Redaktiongeschichte des Estherbuches* (VTSup 79; Leiden: Brill, 2000).

136. According to Moore, *Daniel*, 252, all the LXX manuscripts contain the colophon, but only one of the three AT texts retains it. He does not specify which texts he mentions.

tion as being Ptolemy VIII Soter II, which would date the colophon, and subsequently the translation of the LXX version of Esther, to ca. 114 B.C.E.[137] However, Moore assumes, rather than argues, for this view. In fact, in his article on the Additions for *The Anchor Bible Dictionary*, Moore notes that the Additions could be dated to the "2d and/or first centuries B.C.," thus adding ambiguity to his earlier claim.[138]

The other view, held by Elias J. Bickerman, is that the Ptolemy mentioned here is Ptolemy XII Auletos, thus dating the work to ca. 78–77 B.C.E.[139] Bickerman bases his conclusion on the fact that the colophon contains a singular form of the word "reign." This, in his opinion, rules out Ptolemy IX Soter II (114–113 B.C.E.) and Ptolemy XIII (49–48 B.C.E.) because in the fourth years of their reigns, Cleopatra (mother and sister respectively) acted as regent for them. Thus, we would expect a plural form of "reign." In addition, the name of Ptolemy stands before that of Cleopatra in the colophon, which Bickerman implies would be unlikely if either of the aforementioned Cleopatras were acting as regents. Thus, Bickerman settles on Ptolemy XII Auletos due to his association with a certain Cleopatra in the fourth year of his reign, as well as the fact that, "beginning with the second year of his reign the name of Cleopatra follows that of her husband in all public or private documents."[140] In my opinion, Bickerman's analysis is more exhaustive and more convincing. Because of this, I agree with his conclusion and date the translation of Greek Esther to 78–77 B.C.E., just one year before Salome Alexandra assumed political power in Judea in 76 B.C.E.[141]

Determining a date for Judith is a tad more difficult due to the numerous historical incongruities in the first seven chapters of the book. Most scholars agree on a date for Judith in the Hasmonean period, i.e., 165–64 B.C.E. More specifically, the narrative probably was written either in the reign of John Hyrcanus I (135–104 B.C.E.) or Alexander Janneus (103–78 B.C.E.). In his work on Judith, Moore argues persuasively for a date of composition late under Hyrcanus or early under Jannaeus, with an early Pharisaic author, and J. C. Dancy contends

137. See Moore, *Daniel*, 250–52; idem, "On the Origin of the LXX Additions to the Book of Esther," *JBL* 72 (1973): 382–93; and Benno Jacob, "Das Buch Esther bei den LXX," *ZAW* 10 (1890): 241–98. Schürer, *A History of the Jewish People* 3:506, 719, agrees with Moore's date. However, there seems to be a chronological difficulty with Moore's proposal. Ptolemy VIII was not surnamed Soter II, but rather Euergetes II, "Physkon," and ruled with his wife Cleopatra II from 145–116 B.C.E. See Alan Edouard Samuel, *Ptolemaic Chronology* (Münchener Beiträge zur Papyrusforschung und antiken Rechtsgeschichte 43; Munich: Beck, 1962), for the chronology of the Ptolemaic period.

138. C. A. Moore, "Esther, Additions to," *ABD* 2:626–33 (632).

139. Elias J. Bickerman, "The Colophon of the Greek Book of Esther," *JBL* 63 (1944): 339–62.

140. Bickerman, "The Colophon of the Greek Book of Esther," 347.

141. Michael V. Fox, *Character and Ideology in the Book of Esther* (Studies on Personalities of the Old Testament Series; Columbia: University of South Carolina Press, 1991), 139 and n. 21, agrees with Bickerman's analysis, although he incorrectly cites 73 B.C.E. as the date proposed by Bickerman. More recently, S. W. Crawford, "The Additions to Esther," *NIB* 3:970–72; and Ingo Kottsieper, "Zusätze zu Ester," in Odil Hannes Steck, Reinhard G. Kratz, and Ingo Kottsieper, *Das Buch Baruch, Der Brief des Jeremia, Zusätze zu Ester und Daniel* (ATDA 5; Göttingen: Vandenhoeck & Ruprecht, 1998), 111–207 (121–24 and 206–7), accept Bickerman's dating scheme.

that Judith was probably composed in the early first century B.C.E.[142] Interestingly, Morton S. Enslin hypothesizes that the characterization of Judith as a widow perhaps reflects a compliment to Salome Alexandra, herself a widow.[143] If this theory is correct, the date of Judith would have to be located in the first quarter of the first century B.C.E, approximate to the reign of Salome. In her work on Judith, Denise Dombrowski Hopkins agrees with Enslin's hypothesis, even though she does not cite his work.[144] Almost all scholars agree that Judith was originally composed in Hebrew, and that the Greek translation found in the LXX must have been completed by the mid-first century C.E.[145] Thus, a general date for Judith in the first century B.C.E. is more than acceptable.

2.7.3. *Susanna, Greek Esther, Judith, and Queen Salome*

Given that Susanna, Greek Esther, and Judith all have female protagonists, deal with gender issues, and so many scholars assign them to the first century B.C.E., the question arises as to a possible connection between the three books. In a recent work, Ilan argues that all three books are, in fact, connected.[146] Her thesis is that all three books were used, if not composed, to serve as propaganda for the reign of Salome Alexandra (76–67 B.C.E.). That is, all three stories have possible dates of composition in the first century, with Greek Esther dated immediately prior to Salome's reign. Furthermore, all three books exhibit what can be termed qualified feminism. As Ilan writes, "The books do not openly promote women's leadership, nor are they revolutionary in nature. Yet they do question some of the suppositions of their day on the 'natural order', in which man should rule over women."[147] Thus, these works could serve to pave the way for a woman to assume political power by showing that even though women could serve in leadership positions, as in Judith, ultimately there would be no threat to male dominance over society.

Ilan posits that some propaganda was needed to defend the abilities of women to perform the actions of royal office, but would also allay the anxieties of men regarding women in positions of political power. In her opinion, Greek Esther, Judith, and Susanna served this very purpose. All three books deal with the issue of male leadership, and all, save Susanna, treat the topic of females in power. In Judith, a widow rises up in a time of crisis, critiques the cowardly male leaders, and undertakes a dangerous mission to save her town. She travels to the enemy camp with only a female attendant, and proceeds to entice the enemy leader until

142. See Moore, *Judith*, 67–70; idem, "Judith, Book of," *ABD* 3:1117–25 (1123); and J. C. Dancy, "The Book of Judith," in *The Shorter Books of the Apocrypha* (ed. J. C. Dancy; CBC; Cambridge: Cambridge University Press, 1972), 67–131 (71).

143. Morton S. Enslin, *The Book of Judith* (ed. Solomon Zeitlin; JAL 7; Leiden: Brill, 1972), 180–81.

144. See Denise Dombrowski Hopkins, "Judith," in Newsom and Ringe, eds., *Women's Bible Commentary*, 279–85 (280–81).

145. Moore, *Judith*, 93–94. The mid-first century C.E. date is due to the citation of Judith in *1 Clem.* 55:4–5.

146. Ilan's argument is found in her "'And Who Knows,'" 127–53.

147. Ilan, "'And Who Knows,'" 153.

she beheads him while he is passed out from too much alcohol. She then returns to her town, displays his head, and rallies their troops. She is praised for her actions, even going to Jerusalem to be lauded. However, at the end of the book, she returns to her status as a widow, and remains unmarried and isolated until her death. Commenting on this return to widowhood, Amy-Jill Levine states that Judith's "ultimate return to the private sphere and consequent reinscription into androcentric Israel both alleviate the crisis precipitated by her actions and discourse and reinforce the norms they reveal."[148] In other words, since at the end of the narrative Judith is somewhat reinscribed into her traditionally assigned role of widow, the potential crisis for and threat to the accepted patriarchal ideology brought on by her mission is avoided. If Enslin's aforementioned hypothesis is correct, then the story of Judith can be seen as an attempt to allay fears about the reign of a widow, as well as an implicit critique to Josephus's denigration of Salome as a female ruler in his *Antiquities*.

In Greek Esther, we find a comparable situation. Esther begins her textual existence as a member of Artaxerxes' harem, in conspicuous opposition to Queen Vashti, who had refused to obey the king's order to appear before him and his friends. Esther eventually is chosen as queen by the king, and the two are married. However, her foster father, Mordechai, angers the king's chief friend, Haman, by refusing to do obeisance to him. Haman then discovers that Mordechai is a Jew, and hatches a plot to destroy all the Jews in the kingdom. Through Esther's piety, and a little help from God, Haman's plot is foiled, and he is executed in the place of Mordechai. This basic story is found in both the Hebrew and Greek versions of Esther, but in the latter there are several additions that augment this rudimentary plot. The most important addition for my purposes is Addition D, in which the meeting between Esther and the king is supplemented. In the Hebrew version of Esther, she faces the king with graceful resolve, saying, "If I perish, I perish" (4:16). However, in Addition D, Esther's character becomes much more rounded. She is changed from a grim, confident character to one who is rightfully fearful of her king:

> She stood before the king. He was seated on his royal throne, clothed in the full array of his majesty, all covered with gold and precious stones. He was most terrifying. Lifting his face, flush with splendor, he looked at her in fierce anger. The queen faltered, and turned pale and faint, and collapsed on the head of the maid who went in front of her. (Add Esth D 15.6–7)

This description of a queen appearing before her king does not portray Esther as more powerful than Artaxerxes; in fact, she faints at the very sight of him. She even faints again after they begin speaking. Here is no danger to the patriarchal order; rather, here we see a queen acting in a manner befitting the grandeur of a king. Even though Esther is an influential queen, this addition paints her as awe-struck by the majesty of the king, clearly placing her own power in a subordinate

148. Amy-Jill Levine, "Sacrifice and Salvation: Otherness and Domestication in the Book of Judith," in Brenner, ed., *A Feminist Companion to Esther, Judith, and Susanna*, 208–33 (209–10).

position to his.[149] This alteration of the Esther story in Hebrew may reflect a need to tone down the powerful and resourceful character of Esther found there, perhaps in light of Salome's impending rule.

Finally, in Susanna there is no discussion of women's leadership, but there is a critique of male figures in positions of authority, especially in the OG. This critique could conceivably raise questions regarding male leaders and some of their practices without offering a specific alternative, i.e., a woman assuming a leadership position. As Ilan writes,

> If this book is not a direct piece of propaganda for women's leadership, it certainly undermines the assumption underlying the opposite point of view, namely that men are made to rule over women. It does so by pointing out the wickedness and high-handed behavior of some male rulers on the one hand, and the righteousness and sexual innocence of some women on the other. The stage is set for a possible role reversal.[150]

Like Judith and Greek Esther, in her story, Susanna seems to give an endorsement to the traditional ideology of patriarchy, i.e., a man saves her and she ultimately resumes her role as a wife, daughter, and mother.

2.8. *Conclusion*

In conclusion, both the OG and the Th versions of Susanna were written in the first century B.C.E. The external evidence shows that both versions were produced during that century if we accept either the "*Ur*-Theodotion" or the *kaige*-Theodotion hypotheses I mention above. The internal evidence found in the story also points to a first-century date due to the similarities with Judith and Greek Esther regarding gender, as well as the theme of witnesses, which parallels the activity of Simeon b. Shetah, also active in the first century.

This date, as well as the more general information regarding women during the Second Temple period, will be of immense help in the next chapter, in which I will examine and discuss Susanna according to the literary-rhetorical method I outlined in Chapter 1. Specifically, my discussion in this chapter will allow for a greater historical and chronological accuracy in my reading, so that the reading will be informed by the milieu and mores of the first century B.C.E.

149. For a wonderful reading of this story, see Erich S. Gruen, *Heritage and Hellenism: The Reinvention of Jewish Tradition* (Hellenistic Culture and Society 30; Berkeley: University of California Press, 1998), 177–86. In his commentary, Jon D. Levenson interprets Addition D as heightening the positive image of Esther by elevating the challenge of confronting the king. See Levenson, *Esther* (OTL; Philadelphia: Westminster, 1997), 87–88.

150. Ilan, "'And Who Knows,'" 149–50.

Chapter 3

A Narrative-Rhetorical Reading of Susanna

3.1. *Method*

I will utilize a rhetorical style of reading in this chapter. Exegetical methods dealing with rhetoric have flourished over time, and in the twentieth century we have seen a revival of sorts of rhetorical methods.[1] Since I am concerned in this project with rhetoric as persuasion, not all of these methods are as useful to me as others. For example, the method(s) articulated by Phyllis Trible and Burton L. Mack in their introductory texts on the topic focus on rhetoric as artful or well constructed speech.[2] While these approaches are interesting, they do not allow one to ask questions about different audiences, ethics, and ideology. In other words, they focus on the level of the text alone and go no further.

Recently in the field of Biblical Studies, the work of Vernon K. Robbins has revitalized interest in rhetoric.[3] Robbins' method, in my opinion, is actually a meta-method that seeks to incorporate the work of numerous other fields under the rubric of "socio-rhetorical" interpretation. That is, Robbins isolates five different textures or levels of meaning in any given text, and posits different methods appropriate to each texture. Thus, if one focuses on the "inner texture" of a text, one will analyze the text itself, including its use of language. For this texture, then, one would utilize the resources of literary and rhetorical criticism, as well as philology. In my opinion, the overriding problem with Robbins' method is that it combines so many methodological approaches that analyze so many different phenomena associated with the text that the combination becomes overwhelming.[4] Thus, the sheer size of Robbins' project outweighs its usefulness as a discrete method.

I have chosen instead to use the method developed by James Phelan, which will allow me to ask more specific questions of my text: the story of Susanna. Phelan's interpretive scheme allows me to isolate different audiences implied

1. For a survey of rhetoric in the twentieth century, see Renato Barilli, *Rhetoric* (Theory and History of Literature 63; Minneapolis: University of Minnesota Press, 1989), 102–29.

2. See Trible, *Rhetorical Criticism*; and Burton Mack, *Rhetoric and the New Testament* (GBS; Minneapolis: Fortress, 1990).

3. See especially *The Tapestry of Early Christian Discourse: Rhetoric, Society and Ideology* (London: Routledge, 1996); and *Exploring the Texture of Texts: A Guide to Socio-Rhetorical Interpretation* (Valley Forge, Pa.: Trinity, 1996).

4. Robbins himself admits as much when he states, "No interpreter will ever be able to use all the resources of socio-rhetorical criticism in any one interpretation" (*Exploring the Texture of Texts*, 2).

by the narrative, as well as determine how character and progression affect the possible responses of those audiences. Because of these foci, I am then able to incorporate the issue of ethics into my reading, which in the case of Susanna is imperative. Perhaps most importantly, Phelan's method is transplantable, i.e., I will use the conclusions I reach in this chapter and apply them to the aesthetic renderings I survey in Chapters 5 and 6. In sum, Phelan's method permits me to integrate the responses of various audiences to various textual phenomena in such a way that will allow me to carry my reading into other types of texts, i.e., the rich aesthetic tradition that has grown up around the story of Susanna. In what follows, I will examine and discuss Phelan's interpretive method, as I understand it. Following and building upon this discussion, I will attempt to formulate several questions to be asked of the text.

I shall begin by describing how Phelan uses the term "rhetoric." In contradistinction to both of the traditional views I mention in Chapter 1, Phelan notes, "viewing narrative as having the purpose of communicating knowledge, feelings, values, and beliefs is viewing narrative as rhetoric."[5] This communication he speaks of is imagined as a dynamic process that occurs because of and in the act of reading:

> When I talk about narrative as rhetoric or about a rhetorical relationship between author, text, and reader, I want to refer to the complex, multilayered process of writing and reading, processes that call upon our cognition, emotions, desires, hopes, values, and beliefs.[6]

Obviously, this process of engagement emphasizes the response(s) of the reader(s), and Phelan attempts to develop what he terms the interpretive practice of "rhetorical reader-response." He defines that practice as follows:

> Rhetorical reading [is] the recursive relationship between authorial agency, textual phenomena, and reader response. Thus, it assumes that the text is a sharable medium of a multileveled communication between author and reader, even as it takes the reader's experience of the text as the starting point for interpretation. Its effort is to link response to interpretation by seeking textual sources for individual responses, while also acknowledging that the construal of those sources is influenced by the reader's subjectivity. In other words, in its way of linking reading to interpretation, rhetorical reader-response maintains both that the text constructs the reader and that the reader constructs the text, with the result that it does not believe that there is always a clear, sharply defined border between what is sharable and what is personal in reading and interpretation. Furthermore, even as the approach starts with response, it does not regard that response as something fixed beyond question but rather as something that may change and develop in the very effort to link reading and interpretation.[7]

Thus, Phelan's approach focuses on readerly responses to textual phenomena, yet refuses to reify those responses. Additionally, this approach attempts to ground those responses in features of the text itself, so that responses are not accepted willy-nilly.

5. Phelan, *Narrative as Rhetoric*, 18.
6. Phelan, *Narrative as Rhetoric*, 19.
7. Phelan, *Narrative as Rhetoric*, 176–77.

This stance seems to advocate a rather rigid view of the text, in that Phelan locates final interpretive authority over readerly responses in the text itself. So, Phelan does not share the view of post-structuralist critics regarding the inherent instability of texts, even though, as we shall see, he does not view the text as an "other" in the process of reading.[8] However, lest one think that Phelan is a traditionalist, he is critical of theorists like Booth who privilege authorial intention. Phelan holds that interpreters cannot divine authorial intention because of the proliferation and malleability of meaning(s) in a text. Instead, he focuses on "the recursive relationships among authorial agency, textual phenomena, and reader response, to the way in which our attention to each of these elements both influences and can be influenced by the other two."[9] In his description of "rhetorical reader-response," Phelan also allies himself with a medial position with regards to the creation of meaning. That is, for Phelan, meaning is a mutual effect that occurs in the interplay between the reaction(s) of reader(s) and the features of a given text. Thus, Phelan seems to occupy a middle ground in his approach between more radical theorists and conservative critics.

Since Phelan is so interested in the response(s) of reader(s), he ensures that his approach will effectively analyze those responses by articulating a particular view of audience(s). Phelan, following the work of Peter J. Rabinowitz, posits two types of audiences implied in narrative, viz., the Narrative Audience (NA) and the Authorial Audience (AA):[10]

> The narrative audience is the one implicitly addressed by the narrator; it takes on the beliefs and values that the narrator ascribes to it, and in most cases it responds to the characters and events as if they were real. Joining the narrative audience is crucial for our experience of the mimetic component of the text and sometimes for the thematic and synthetic components as well. The authorial audience takes on the beliefs and knowledge that the author assumes it has, including the knowledge that it is reading a constructed text. Joining the authorial audience is crucial for our experience of all the invitations offered by the different components of the text. Engaging with the text involves entering both of these textually signaled audiences simultaneously; engaging also means that we bring our individual subjectivities, our flesh-and-blood selves to bear on our experience.[11]

This description also hints at a third audience, assumed in Phelan's work: the real reader who is alive and breathing. This category of real reader will be important for my later discussion of ethics in reading.

The two main foci of Phelan's textual work are character and progression. In fact, a close reading of Phelan's reading(s) gives the impression that it is through character and progression(s) that an author communicates particular values or

8. In his Introduction to *Narrative as Rhetoric*, 1–23, Phelan discusses deconstruction and its view of rhetoric and narrative.

9. Phelan, *Narrative as Rhetoric*, 19.

10. For Rabinowitz's work on this subject, see "Truth in Fiction: A Reexamination of Audiences," *Critical Inquiry* 4 (1976): 121–41. In this article, Rabinowitz argues for the presence of four audiences: the actual audience; the authorial audience; the narrative audience; and the ideal narrative audience. However, as Phelan notes, "in practice, Rabinowitz's third and fourth audiences have been conflated into the single category of narrative audience" (*Narrative as Rhetoric*, 142).

11. Phelan, *Narrative as Rhetoric*, 93.

ideas. Phelan treats these concepts as interrelated, so my discussion of them will be as well. Phelan's model for examining character centers on his division of character into three aspects: mimetic, thematic, and synthetic. Briefly, the mimetic aspect of character "refers to that component of character directed to its imitation of a possible person," i.e., an entity with recognizable traits.[12] The thematic component of character is concerned with the character as a representative of some larger group or idea(l). Finally, the synthetic aspect of character is aimed at the character as an artificial construct. In my analysis of Susanna below, I will focus on the first two components only, as my interest lies in the internal rhetoric of the story.

Along with character, Phelan also privileges analysis of a text's progression. He defines progression as the movement of narrative through time. "In examining progression, then, we are concerned with how authors generate, sustain, develop, and resolve readers' interests in narrative."[13] The way in which these interests are cultivated is through the author's use of what Phelan calls instabilities, the focus of the AA's interests. Phelan defines two main types of instabilities within narrative:

> Authors may take advantage of numerous variables in the narrative situation to generate the movement of a tale. In general, the story-discourse model of narrative helps to differentiate between two main kinds of instabilities: The first are those occurring within the story, instabilities between characters, created by situations, and complicated and resolved through actions. The second are those created by the discourse, instabilities—of value, belief, opinion, knowledge, expectation—between authors and/or narrators, on the one hand, and the authorial audience on the other. To recognize this difference in kind I reserve the term "instabilities" for unstable relations within the story and introduce the term "tension" for those in discourse.[14]

Instabilities, in the sense that Phelan uses the term, must be settled for a given narrative to be resolved, whereas tensions do not have to be reconciled. This resolution of instabilities is also tied to what Phelan terms "closure" and "completeness": the former is concerned with how the narrative indicates its ending, and the latter has to do with the amount of resolution vis-à-vis the instabilities and tensions in a given narrative.[15] The importance of paying attention to a narrative's progression is that it allows one to grasp the way in which the text invites readers to maintain interest in the story.

Progression is also key to the development of character. To explain the impact of narrative progression on character, Phelan distinguishes between a character's dimensions and functions:

> We can usefully distinguish between the thematic elements of a character...by making a distinction between a character's *dimensions* and his or her *functions*. A dimension is any attribute a character may be said to possess when that character is considered in

12. Phelan, *Narrative as Rhetoric*, 218.
13. Phelan, *Reading People, Reading Plots: Character, Progression, and the Interpretation of Narrative* (Chicago: University of Chicago Press, 1989), 15.
14. Phelan, *Reading People, Reading Plots*, 15.
15. See Phelan, *Reading People, Reading Plots*, 17–18. See also *Narrative as Rhetoric*, 89–90.

> isolation from the work in which he or she appears. A function is a particular application of that attribute made by the text through its developing structure. In other words, dimensions are converted into functions by the *progression* of the work. Thus, every function depends upon a dimension but not every dimension will necessarily correspond to a function.[16]

Put another way, dimensions represent the potential a character has to signify and a function would represent the fulfillment of that potential.[17] Recalling Phelan's distinction of aspects within character, the categories of dimensions and functions becomes more useful analytically. In terms of mimetic functions, then, dimensions would be character attributes or traits, and functions would result from the cumulative effect of these traits if they result in the creation of a "plausible person."[18] Phelan then moves on to discuss thematic dimensions and functions:

> Thematic dimensions...are attributes, taken individually or collectively, and viewed as vehicles to express ideas or as representative of a larger class than the individual character (in the case of satire the attributes will be representative of a person, group, or institution external to the work). Just as characters may be functioning mimetically from our first introduction to them, so too may they be functioning thematically, but just as the full mimetic function is often not revealed in the initial stages of the narrative, so too may thematic functions emerge more gradually. In works that strive to give characters a strong overt mimetic function, thematic functions develop from thematic dimensions as a character's traits and actions also demonstrate, usually implicitly, some proposition or propositions about the class of people or the dramatized ideas. Usually, the narrative will then use these functions to influence the way we respond to the actions of the character, and sometimes the progression may make these functions crucial to the work's final effect, even if the work is not organized to convince us of a particular position.[19]

Thus, Phelan's model of character and progression allow for greater analytical clarity by allowing one to distinguish between components of character as well as the way(s) in which a given story moves its action along.

Since Phelan is concerned with the response(s) of reader(s) to a given text, his approach allows for readers—as members of both audiences as well as flesh-and-blood— empathetically to engage and evaluate that text. As a caveat, though, Phelan asserts that the interplay between author, text, and reader is more complex than critics like Booth posit. Whereas in his work, Booth implicitly asserts a solid distinction between the reader implied by/in the text and the real reader, Phelan notes,

> When the shared subjectivity of the reader encounters the otherness of the text, the analyst cannot always definitively locate the boundaries that mark off flesh-and-blood and authorial audiences—or more generally, reader, text, and author—from each other. The synergy among these different elements of the rhetorical transaction is precisely what the rhetorical approach wants to acknowledge.[20]

16. Phelan, *Reading People, Reading Plots*, 9.
17. See Phelan, *Narrative as Rhetoric*, 29.
18. See Phelan, *Reading People, Reading Plots*, 11.
19. Phelan, *Reading People, Reading Plots*, 13.
20. Phelan, *Narrative as Rhetoric*, 128.

The margins between the phenomena involved in reading are, according to Phelan, simply more porous than Booth thinks.

Even allowing for these porous margins, the real audience will inevitably engage in some sort of evaluation of a given text. In his list of characteristics of readers that will be invoked by the reading process, Phelan includes values, hopes, and beliefs. If the feelings and values of the real audience are, in fact, aroused and addressed by a narrative, it is almost certain that they will form ethical opinions and make ethical judgments about the values or beliefs operative in a given narrative. This assumption in Phelan's work is based on the fact that members of the AA are actually real, living persons with ideological baggage. Once this fact is accepted, one may than analyze their reaction to both the thematic and synthetic components of the text in a more realistic manner. This is precisely how and why ethics is so important to Phelan. He writes,

> Just as the authorial audience evaluates the narrator's values, so too does the flesh-and-blood audience evaluate the author's. Entering the authorial audience allows us to recognize the ethical and ideological bases of the author's invitations. Comparing those values to the ones we bring to the text leads us into a dialogue about those values. Sometimes our values may be confirmed by the text, sometimes they may be challenged, and sometimes they may be ignored or insulted. When our values conflict with those of the text, we will either alter ours or resist those of the text (in whole or in part). The ethical dimension of the story involves the values upon which the authorial audience's judgments are based, the way those values are deployed in the narrative, and, finally, the values and beliefs implicit in the thematizing of the character's experience.[21]

Thus, once a given set of values has been ascertained in a given narrative, we may use it to determine not only our own response(s) to it, but also to try and extend our examination to encompass ideological and ethical matters.

This emphasis on ideology also raises an important issue: What is the relationship between ideological commitment(s) and interpretation? Phelan addresses this question at length:

> Having acknowledged the importance of ideological commitments in both the construction and analysis of...narratives, should we conclude that in these matters ideology finally *determines* interpretation? If so, then any genuine adjudication [between interpretations] is impossible, since any judge will simply decide on the basis of her own ideological commitments... To consent to the view that commitments determine interpretation, however, is to deny the existence of facts as anything but the product of interpretation.
>
> Ideological commitments, then, invariably influence interpretation of facts, and to some extent such commitments help shape facts in one way rather than another... But this phenomenon of commitments influencing interpretations that in turn shape facts—let me call this phenomenon a fact—can itself be a reason to question our interpretations. This questioning, of course, will not itself be totally neutral and objective, but it can—and should—come from the commitments of a competing perspective.
>
> In other words, because commitments influence interpretations that in turn shape but do not create facts, the narratives we tell about those facts legitimately make truth claims, but those claims are likely to be highly contested. This contestation is one important means by which we can revise the narratives and refine their truth claims, though our

21. Phelan, *Narrative as Rhetoric*, 100.

> reaching the stage where our narratives are beyond contestation is as unlikely as the eventuality that facts will speak their own interpretations. Furthermore, because the narratives we tell about our world themselves reinforce or revise our ideological commitments and our interpretations of that world, we have a very big stake in the ongoing negotiation of those narratives.[22]

Thus, even though ideology can and does shape they way in which one interprets, that interpretation should not be reified or concretized as the only plausible interpretation. One should, given the tenuousness of ideological commitments as well as the subjectivity of humanity itself, be open not only to contestation of one's interpretation, but also the possibility that one's interpretation could change.

Even so, Phelan discusses the practice of resisting reading. In one of his discussions of Hemingway's *A Farewell to Arms*, Phelan examines Judith Fetterley's analysis of this novel in her work *The Resisting Reader*.[23] Fetterley finds a subtext, or covert story, of misogyny and patriarchy in the novel, centered mainly on the character of Catherine.[24] In her analysis, Fetterley exposes this covert story in an attempt to encourage readers to resist accepting it passively, i.e., to read Hemingway against the grain. Even though Phelan critiques Fetterley's method, her analysis leads him to "question thoroughly the relation between our values and those we are asked to adopt as we enter the authorial audience."[25] Phelan argues in this context that all members of the real audience will not share certain beliefs assumed by the AA. Real readers constantly make evaluations about the beliefs and values they are asked to embrace as members of the AA. These evaluations are, however, underlined by various ethical and moral positions held by members of the real audience.

In the case of *A Farewell to Arms*, Phelan notes "neither Fetterley nor I have hesitated about saying that a sexist presentation of Catherine ought to be judged negatively by all readers."[26] Phelan here is making an ethical or ideological evaluation as a real reader based on his own social location and background, as well as an examination of the text. He then moves on to ask the following questions:

> What are the ethics of reading Catherine as the authorial audience is asked to do? Or, what ethical position must one adopt to enter fully into the authorial audience's expected responses to Catherine's functions? The negative element of my evaluation stems from my conclusion that to enter into the authorial audience is occasionally to participate in and give consent to the deficient ethics of sexism... [Thus] what are the ethical consequences of adopting this world view?[27]

22. Phelan, *Narrative as Rhetoric*, 168–70.
23. See Phelan, *Reading People, Reading Plots*, 165–88. For Fetterley's work, see her *The Resisting Reader: A Feminist Approach to American Fiction* (Bloomington: Indiana University Press, 1978).
24. Of course, Fetterley is not alone in her feminist critique of the novel. For other works of this nature, see Phelan, *Reading People, Reading Plots*, 226–27 n. 2.
25. Phelan, *Reading People, Reading Plots*, 182.
26. Phelan, *Reading People, Reading Plots*, 183.
27. Phelan, *Reading People, Reading Plots*, 184.

In response to these questions, Phelan asserts, "The best way to assess the ethics of Hemingway's world view, I think, is to consider the apparent consequences it has for those characters who share it."[28] In other words, if a real reader has an ethical problem with an aspect of knowledge, value, or action he or she is asked to accept or appreciate as a member of the AA, that reader can test the application of that knowledge, value, or action via the effect it has on characters who participate in or represent it. The effect of this testing can potentially be a transformation or validation of one's own worldview:

> If my analysis...holds up, then we can understand why flesh-and-blood readers whose beliefs about the world are considerably more optimistic than Hemingway's can still adopt his [i.e. the malevolence of the world] and be moved by the narrative. Such readers do not simply give in to the narrative illusion—and they do not end up hating themselves in the morning—because they are very likely not only to accept but to admire (and perhaps even aspire to) the ethical consequences Hemingway draws from that world view. In other words, both existentialists and fundamentalists [i.e. Catholics] can enter Hemingway's authorial audience without compromising their ethical standards. At the same time of course, fundamentalists will find themselves resisting the bald statement of the world view, but the very experience of being moved by the narrative can establish a very productive relationship with it, one arguably more productive than that of the existentialists who will merely have many of their beliefs reinforced. The combination of intellectual resistance and emotional suasion has the potential of making one rethink—and rejustify or reject—one's own world view.[29]

Even though some real readers may object to the values they are asked to recognize and empathize with as members of the AA, in the act of reading and responding to the rhetorical exchange between author, text, and reader, these values may be adopted for a time. This temporary suspension of ethical belief(s), in other words, allows a real reader to enter into dialogue with a narrative, so that beliefs might be questioned or validated, and one can resist a narrative's values or accept them. In his analysis, Phelan offers some concluding thoughts on resisting reading, and whether it is more useful to resist completely a narrative or partially do so:

> The rhetorical consequences of resisting reading will be likely to vary from narrative to narrative. The act of repudiating a narrative more fully [than Phelan does in this chapter] may be relatively empty if the repudiation is easy... The resistance is empty because there is little genuine encounter between the text and the reader...the repudiation may be relatively unsatisfying if the ethical basis of the work is easily rejected... Resistance is more likely to be satisfying and productive when it is partial, when we find ourselves in genuine disagreement with some parts of a work without entirely losing our respect for it. In these cases, we talk with the text and its author more as equals, acknowledging their power, but for that very reason, required to think hard about the nature and meaning of their limits. The dialogue established in these encounters can go on for a long time and can lead us to rethink some of our most fundamental commitments and beliefs.[30]

28. Phelan, *Reading People, Reading Plots*, 185.
29. Phelan, *Reading People, Reading Plots*, 187.
30. Phelan, *Reading People, Reading Plots*, 188.

Thus, a real reader may resist the values or knowledge the AA is asked to accept, but that reader should be open to the possibility that the ideological bases of his or her resistance could be transformed in the process. Additionally, if real readers find themselves in harmony with portions of a work, Phelan thinks that it will be easier and more fulfilling to resist other portions rather than totally resisting a narrative. All the while, one should be aware of the fact that any given narrative is *about* something, i.e., it has something to say, a worldview or value(s) to promote. Put another way, by reading narrative, we are being asked to accept a given worldview in the text, which may or may not cause us to question our values, reinforce our adherence to those values, or abandon them in favor of a more plausible alternative. As Phelan notes, due to the synthetic nature of characters, authors create them "to show us something about the segment of the population to which the created member belongs."[31] As real readers, then, we should be aware of this "showing," and the possible consequences it can have for us as we take our places in both the NA and the AA.

With this admittedly brief discussion of Phelan's approach to narrative behind us, it might be useful at this point to try and summarize the above material in a fashion that will allow me to formulate a set of questions to be asked of a given narrative. That is, I want to try and deduce several queries based on Phelan's work that can be applied to a text, in this case an apocryphal text, so that his work may be used more fruitfully in my reading of Susanna below.

As I note above, Phelan is interested in the interplay or "recursive relationship" between the author, text, and reader. To account for and assess this relationship, he focuses on progression and character. That is,

> To account for the multiple layers of our responses to narrative, I suggest that as we follow the movement of instabilities and tensions, we respond to the text's—and especially the character's—mimetic, thematic, and synthetic components. That is, we respond to the characters as human agents, as representing some ideas, beliefs, or values, and as artificial constructs playing particular roles in the larger construct that is the whole work.[32]

So, we must first be aware of the way in which characters are described and how they speak and act.[33] By paying attention to character(s), we will be able to appreciate the values operative in a given narrative, because it is through character that an author reveals the worldview he or she is advocating.

If character is an essential analytic category of narrative, we should also be aware of the progression of the narrative. That is, how does the story propel itself along, and how does it entice readers to maintain interest? Implicit in analyzing both character and progression is a self-awareness on our part in terms of audience(s). We need to be aware of our observations and which audience we are members of as we make them. For example, if a reader observes a synthetic function for a character, then he or she needs to be aware that they are doing so as a

31. Phelan, *Reading People, Reading Plots*, 14.
32. Phelan, *Narrative as Rhetoric*, 90–91.
33. See Robert Alter, *The Art of Biblical Narrative* (New York: Basic Books, 1981), 116–17.

member of the AA, not the NA. Of course, such awareness is reflective and not immediate, but in order to ascertain how an author structures his or her text and how we respond to it, we need to keep this distinction in mind. As members of the NA, we trust the narrator's comments and judgments and pay attention to the mimetic level of character. Basically, we accept the story at the word of the narrator. When we join the AA, though, we move into a more analytical role in that we begin to ask questions about values and knowledge in the text. We also are able to reflect on the text and the characters at a thematic and synthetic level, and can ask questions of historical background and literary resonances. Finally, we bring all of these observations to bear on ourselves as flesh-and-blood readers, with all of the implications I discuss above.

Before I proceed further, I would like to add a caveat. Given my summary of Phelan, it is dangerous to affirm that a work has a static or only one "meaning" based on a reader's perception of the values an implied author is positing, because that affirmation may then be reified and twisted into a conviction that the work's meaning is "correct." I, along with Phelan and The Bible and Culture Collective, would advocate a more self-critical approach in which the critic acknowledges that any meaning he/she may find in a text as well as his/her interpretation of that meaning is contingent on many social and political factors and that their reading may not be either correct or permanent.[34] This caveat suggests nothing more than the need for readers to be honest concerning their own ideological baggage; this self-criticalness will allow the exegete to be open to a sense of play with the text. In other words, if an exegete reveals his/her social, political, racial, and educational background, then readings may become more diverse because of the different lenses each critic wears by dint of their individuality. This broadening of interpretations just might lead to an acceptance of a text's meaning as constructed in the interplay between text and reader, thus liberating readers from "traditional" interpretations or readings which have been used in the service of oppressive practices. Such is the ideal I have set forth for my own reading of the story of Susanna.

3.2. *Reading of Susanna*

In what follows, I will adhere to the rhetorical reading style of Phelan, but will also attend to literary resonances as they arise. In my opinion, the AA cannot help but notice textual or more subjective indicators of echoes between the story of Susanna and other biblical materials. Thus the awareness of literary reverberations will be treated as a response of the AA to the story, and will factor into its overall view of the narrative. In addition, following Phelan's lead, I will not focus

34. See The Bible and Culture Collective, *The Postmodern Bible*, 166, 182: "A rhetorical criticism that is not radically self-reflexive can too easily be harnessed to an ideologically conservative program of reaffirming classical texts and values… The potential for rhetorical criticism to be in the service of a conservative [or oppressive] agenda is even greater for the Bible than for other classic texts. To exhibit the rhetorical strategies of the Bible easily passes over into demonstrating the success of the strategies, and hence finding yet another way to prove that the Bible is true."

on the synthetic component of character in my reading of Susanna.[35] Instead, I will try to illuminate the way I sense the narrator and author using the mimetic and thematic aspects of character to make a rhetorical point within the story. These categories will be of paramount importance in my reading of Susanna, because, according to Phelan, it is through character that an author seeks to put forth certain propositions. Thus, the analysis of character is of central concern for the understanding of a narrative's rhetoric. I will argue that the story's thematic function is much more pronounced than its mimetic function, and will note the ways in which the author of the story emphasizes the former function.

3.2.1. *Introduction of Susanna and Her Family (Verses 1–4)*

> (1) There was a man living in Babylon whose name was Joakim. (2) He took a wife whose name was Susanna, daughter of Hilkiah. She was exceedingly beautiful and fearful of the Lord. (3) Her parents were righteous and had taught their daughter according to the law of Moses. (4) Joakim was extremely wealthy; he even had a garden bordering his house. The Jews would flock to him because he was the most honored of them all.

In v. 1, Joakim is introduced and named. The reference to Babylon functions as an indicator to the AA of the exilic setting of the story. Susanna is introduced and named in v. 2 as the wife taken by Joakim as well as Hilkiah's daughter. The NA would expect this, i.e., a woman being identified by her association with men. For the AA, this identification will have a significant impact on their view of Susanna. Also, the description of Susanna as beautiful might heighten her status to the NA, and the AA would connect her to other women in the apocryphal corpus, viz., Judith (Jdt 8:7–8 and 10:4), Sarah (Tob 6:12), and Esther (Esth 2:7 and Add Esth D 15:5). This connection will be important because it also serves as a thematic dimension of her character, as it identifies her metonymically with other "heroines." The fact that she is painted as "fearful of the Lord" signals the NA that the narrator is ascribing to her a fairly impressive religious identity. Given the first-century B.C.E. context of the story, Susanna's being religious would imply that she possessed certain general beliefs and particular patterns of behavior. The AA would also connect this mimetic dimension with religiosity on Susanna's part and perhaps try to anticipate why the narrator selected these particular attributes for mention as opposed to, say, her height or hair color.

The signaling of Susanna's parents as righteous in v. 3 again serves as a wink to the AA that something specific is being implied, i.e., Why would the narrator specify righteousness as a quality of the parents? The NA, of course, would count on the reliability of the narrator and simply accept the characterization. The fact that the narrator specifically states that Susanna's parents had taught her "according to the law of Moses," would pique the curiosity of both audiences as well as

35. Phelan, *Reading People, Reading Plots*, 3–8. Phelan critiques structuralist analyses of character as focusing almost exclusively on the synthetic, constructed aspect of character. In his view, this focus ignores the importance of the mimetic and, to an extent, the thematic. For an example of the structuralist analysis of character, see Jonathan Culler, *Structuralist Poetics: Structuralism, Linguistics, and the Study of Literature* (Ithaca, N.Y.: Cornell University Press, 1975), 230–38.

heighten the mimetic and thematic dimensions of Susanna's character. Given my earlier discussion of women's access to Torah study, one may wonder what Susanna's parents actually taught her. Did her teaching consist of just *kosher* regulations, or did it contain other, more "advanced" information? The only hint of an answer in the story itself comes from Susanna's own personal piety. She is unwilling to sin before God, and her prayer at the trial indicates some knowledge of biblical lore, but it might just as easily have originated from an indirect source as well, i.e., her parents or husband.[36] Again, the NA would accept the description as reliable, but would perhaps recognize the religious implications of such a description, i.e., that for a woman to be taught the Torah was both extraordinary and a luxury. The AA, though, would connect this description with the previous depiction of Susanna in v. 2 and begin to ask questions regarding the thematic dimensions and possible function(s) of Susanna as a character. That is, given that the author has chosen to portray Susanna in a very precise way, as overtly religious, there must be some point to the use of these mimetic dimensions.

The mimetic dimension of Joakim's character is fleshed out in v. 4. To begin with, he is extremely wealthy, which would raise his socio-economic status in the eyes of the NA. The mention of the garden here is meant both to heighten his status as well as serve as an indication to the AA that this piece of information will be important later. The final clause in this verse solidifies Joakim's social status to the NA and signals to the AA that perhaps social and religious statuses will be important in this story. Otherwise, why would the author take the time to mention them? There is also some thematizing going on here with the character of Joakim: he represents the honored rich, those who are admired for their wealth and influence. However, unlike his wife, Joakim's character never acquires a thematic function, i.e., the dimensions of Joakim's character never amount to a statement or proposition on behalf of a particular group.

In the first four verses of the work, then, the narrator provides the reader with a wealth of information concerning Susanna's identity and status. Both Susanna's husband and father are named and she is explicitly associated with both of them. Given the patrilocal and patrilineal nature of Israelite society, this is not surprising. On the basis of this description, one can posit that the narrator is attributing an impressive social status and religious identity to Susanna. Since she is mentioned specifically in connection with her husband and father, and since the narrator names them, her status is connected to their wealth and religious background. By virtue of her husband's wealth and honor, as well as her father's righteousness and religious instruction, the narrator is portraying Susanna as a religiously righteous woman with a high social status. However, Susan Sered and Samuel Cooper observe that, as a woman, Susanna has

> no access to socially recognized power. She is female in a society in which the community leaders (including her husband) are male. She is young in a society in which being an "Elder" is a rank of community leadership. She is isolated and alone: no one in the

36. For an examination of prayer in Susanna, see Craven, "'From where Will My Help Come?'" 103–4.

> community—including her own natal family—comes to her defense. She is inarticulate—she is either unwilling or unable to defend herself when accused. She is vulnerable to sexual attack. And most of all, she is simple—she devises no plan to contest the Elders' sophisticated and intricate accusation.[37]

We shall see below exactly why Susanna both does not concoct a plan to save herself from the elders and why she is unwilling to defend herself against their accusation.

3.2.2. *Introduction of the Elders (Verses 5–6)*

> (5) Two Elders of the people were appointed as judges that year, concerning whom the Master had said: "Lawlessness came out of Babylon from Elders who judge, who were supposed to guide people." (6) These Elders were spending much time in Joakim's house and all the people who were to be judged came to them there.

In v. 5, the Elders are introduced and seem to have a high social and religious status initially due to their appointment as judges by the people; Betsy Halpern-Amaru adds that, "by virtue of both sex and age, the elder judges represent the socially empowered."[38] The mention of "judges" might signal to the AA that a crisis may be impending due to the intertextual connection(s) with the book of Judges, i.e., in that book, judges are raised up by God to deal with certain crises. This connection actually is an ironic one due to the nature of the crisis as well as Daniel's later role, which more accurately parallels that of a judge. In any case, the NA is made aware of the Elders' status in the narrator's eyes because of the unattested quote from the Master identifying them as lawless, although their power remains a constant throughout the story save the very end. This quote explicitly inaugurates a thematic dimension to the Elders' character and indicates an instability in the narrative due to the opposition of thematic dimensions between Joakim and Susanna on the one hand and the Elders on the other with regards to the Law and, by extension, religious identity. It is this instability that sets up the main progressions of the narrative because, by definition, an instability must be resolved prior to the end of a narrative. Thus, this instability serves as an indication to the AA that a conflict or crisis is looming. In the narrative setting, though, none of the other characters know about this aspect of the Elders' character; presumably they would still accord them the respect their social status warranted. This irony establishes a tension between both audiences and the characters themselves that technically does not have to be resolved, even though it is.

By explicitly connecting the Elders and Joakim in v. 6, the instability is heightened and thus the progression is furthered. That is, the narrator places the two characters, Joakim and the Elders, in mimetic contiguity by means of placing them both in the same space, but at the same time the author places them in direct thematic contact as well. Thus, both audiences would see the crisis emerging,

37. Susan Sered and Samuel Cooper, "Sexuality and Social Control: Anthropological Reflections of the Book of Susanna," in Spolsky, ed., *The Judgment of Susanna*, 43–56 (44).

38. Betsy Halpern-Amaru, "The Journey of Susanna among the Church Fathers," in Spolsky, ed., *The Judgment of Susanna*, 21–34 (22).

either because of the conflicting mimetic dimensions (good Joakim and his house vs. the bad Elders) or rival thematic dimensions (Law and religiosity vs. lawlessness). This instability is further heightened by the notice that all the Jews "who were to be judged came to them there." This phrase again reeks of irony due to the information both audiences have, which the characters in the narrative do not.

3.2.3. *The Beginning of the Conflict (Verses 7–12)*

> (7) When the people would run off at the middle of the day, Susanna would go into her husband's garden and walk around. (8) And every day, the two Elders would watch her entering and walking, for they were lusting for her. (9) They had perverted their minds and turned their eyes away from Heaven and were not remembering the duty of doing justice. (10) Both of them were deeply moved by her, but neither disclosed his pain to the other, (11) for they were both ashamed to disclose their lust, their desire to be with her. (12) So, they watched eagerly each day to see her.

In v. 7, we move into a new section of the narrative in which the characters of Susanna and the Elders take on new dimensions. The prefatory note describing the people running off at the middle of the day establishes a chronological bearing in the narrative, viz., when the various people at Joakim's house would disperse for lunch. The notice of Susanna going into the garden and walking around raises several issues. First, and rather simplemindedly: Did she not eat? Second, the mention of the garden reminds the NA of Joakim's wealth and status, and, by extension, Susanna's. Similarly, the AA would recall the mention of the garden in v. 4 and wonder why this repetition might be important. Third, both audiences would ask why Susanna would wait until everyone had left to walk in the garden. The narrative provides no answer. Fourth and finally, the mimetic dimension of Susanna's character is being fleshed out here, but is the thematic dimension of her character receiving any attention? There is a possible answer in the response the AA might have to this verse. That is, the AA might connect a religiously identified woman walking in a garden with the story of Eve in the Garden of Eden in Gen 2:8–3:24, and thus expect a conflict to be centered in the garden or even draw parallels between Susanna and Eve, as some scholars have done.[39]

It is in v. 8 that the Elders' character really comes into its own. The opening clause, "and every day," establishes a chronological regularity for the Elders' actions as well as Susanna's time in the garden. Here also we see the first mention of the Elders' voyeuristic behavior. The NA probably would not connect the issue of voyeurism with the Elders' action; instead it would serve as a heightening of their mimetic dimension. The AA, on the other hand, would certainly view their behavior as voyeuristic, with all of the connotations that conduct brings with it. The AA might also connect this activity with legal issues of looking at women as well. One of the most important issues surrounding women in the Second Temple Period was the preservation of chastity. One of the ways in

39. See George J. Brooke, "Susanna and Paradise Regained," in *Women in the Biblical Tradition* (ed. G. J. Brooke; Studies in Women and Religions 30; Lewiston, N.Y.: Edwin Mellen, 1992), 92–111; and Sarah J. K. Pearce, "Echoes of Eden in the Old Greek of Susanna," *Feminist Theology* 11 (1996): 11–31.

which this issue was addressed was to limit or even prohibit males looking at women. Sirach, a second-century B.C.E work, is adamant that looking at a woman can damage one's honor: "Turn your eyes away from a shapely woman, and do not gaze at beauty belonging to another; many have been seduced by a woman's beauty, and by it passion is kindled like a fire" (Sir 9:8). In the second-century B.C.E. work, *Testaments of the Twelve Patriarchs*, looking at women is often associated with moral danger.[40] Various rabbinical sources note this danger, and in some cases even equate voyeurism with adultery.[41] Given these sources and their attitudes, as well as the actions of the Elders, the AA could interpret this verse as the author adding another negative thematic dimension to the Elders' character: voyeurism is bad. The rhetorical implication is that on both a mimetic and thematic level, the Elders are to be viewed negatively.

The final phrase of v. 8 only reinforces this negative portrayal by noting that the Elders were "lusting for her" (ἐγένοντο ἐν ἐπιθυμίᾳ αὐτης, literally "were in heat for her"), and that this is why they watched her. Both audiences would recognize the connection between the Elders and animals because of the phrase "to be in heat." The NA would make a mimetic connection and the AA a thematic one. That is, the NA would compare the Elders' desires and self-control to that of animals and the AA would add another thematic dimension to the Elders' character, viz., the loss of human reason.[42] This negative connotation of "lust" or "heat" is also found in other texts from the Second Temple period. For example, the noun ἐπιθυμίᾳ is found in Sir 5:2, and is used as a measure of shame, i.e., if one pursues "the desires of your heart," one will be acting shamefully. Sirach also mentions "evil desire" in his prayer for self-control in 22:27–23:27 and links it with "haughty eyes" in 23:5. The first-century B.C.E. text the Wisdom of Solomon notes, "roving desire perverts the innocent mind" (4:12).[43] Perhaps most importantly, in *4 Maccabees*, a text dated from the centuries either side of the turn of the era, a distinction is drawn between reason (good) and emotions (not so good), with pleasure being part of the latter.[44] In 1:22, the author tells us specifically "desire precedes pleasure." Later, in 3:2, the author posits that no one can be rid of desire, but that "reason can provide a way for us not to be enslaved by

40. Ilan, *Jewish Women*, 127. She specifically cites *T. Reu.* 3:10–4:1; *T. Jud.* 17.1; and *T. Benj.* 8:2. For a translation of this text, see H. C. Kee, "Testaments of the Twelve Patriarchs," *OTP* 1:775–828.

41. See Ilan, *Jewish Women*, 127. The most interesting source she notes is *y. Ḥal.* 2:4, 58c: "He who looks at a woman's heels…it is as if he had intercourse with her." This sentiment seems to be shared by Matthew's Jesus in 5:27–28: "everyone who looks at a woman with lust has already committed adultery with her in his heart."

42. For this issue, see Eleonore Stump, "Susanna and the Elders: Wisdom and Folly," in Spolsky, ed., *The Judgment of Susanna*, 85–100.

43. David Winston, *The Wisdom of Solomon* (AB 43; Garden City, N.Y.: Doubleday, 1979), 20–25, argues for a date anywhere from 30 B.C.E. to the reign of Caligula (37–41 C.E.). In his examination, Grabbe agrees broadly with Winston's dating, but prefers to place the Wisdom of Solomon in the reign of Augustus, i.e., 27 B.C.E.–14 C.E. See Lester L. Grabbe, *Wisdom of Solomon* (GAP; Sheffield: Sheffield Academic Press, 1997), 87–90.

44. For a good examination of the philosophic vision presented in *4 Maccabees*, see David A. deSilva, *4 Maccabees* (GAP; Sheffield: Sheffield Academic Press, 1998), 51–75.

desire." Thus, by connecting the Elders' activities and their lust for Susanna, our author is drawing on a widespread theme in Hellenistic Judaism and using it to add yet another thematic dimension to the Elders' character which might lead the AA to view them negatively.

The negative rhetorical presentation of the Elders by both the narrator and author continues in v. 9. To begin with, the statement that "they had perverted their minds," would signal yet another mimetic dimension to the NA, as well as reinforce the thematic dimension established in v. 8 regarding the loss of reason. The second phrase, which tells us that the Elders "turned their eyes away from Heaven," also bolsters the earlier thematic dimension established in v. 5, viz., an opposition between the religiosity of Joakim, Susanna, and Susanna's parents and the Elders. That is, by not looking at Heaven, with its religious connotations, in favor of looking at Susanna, which in the minds of the Elders is connected with lust, that opposition is furthered, especially when, in v. 35, Susanna looks to Heaven for assistance. The mimetic impact of this description is once again to lower the NA's view of the Elders.

The final phrase in v. 9 contains two key terms for the AA: "duty" and "justice." With these two obligations being ignored by the Elders, the thematic dichotomy between the Elders and Joakim's family is almost complete. "Justice" in this story is intimately related to religion, which is exactly where the Elders falter. "Justice" is only finally accomplished by the actions of Daniel, in many ways a perfect counterpart to the Elders. "Duty" here also connotes a certain social status, i.e., the status of the Elders in the community is based on the assumption that they will perform their religious duties, which includes the dispensing of justice. Both audiences now know that the Elders are incapable of doing so, but again, none of the characters in the narrative do. Thus, the irony is again building. In sum, if the Elders now have a low religious status and their social status in the community is dependent on their religious status, the AA begins to suspect at this point that a common plot device will be on the horizon, i.e., the power-full will soon be the power-less.

In v. 10, the description of both Elders being "deeply moved" by Susanna rings hollow for both audiences, given the earlier mimetic and thematic descriptions of them. The verb I render as "deeply moved," κατανενυγμένοι, can also mean "stupefied" or more commonly "stabbed" or "wounded" by or over Susanna. All of these other possible translations indicate the sort of impact Susanna had on the Elders.[45] The fact the neither Elder told the other about his "pain" is the first time in the narrative that the two characters are dissociated and, as such, initiates another instability in the plot, viz., Why has the narrator/author suddenly separated these two? The answer lies in the specific way that the narrator develops the mimetic dimensions of both characters, especially in v. 14.

Both audiences discover in v. 11 why neither Elder told the other about his "pain" over Susanna: "they were both ashamed to disclose their lust." This datum accomplishes two contradictory purposes with regard to the NA: on the one hand,

45. In his commentary, Moore (*Daniel*, 96) discusses this verb.

it reinforces the presence of lust on the part of the Elders, but on the other hand it states that they were ashamed of this lust, which is an entirely appropriate and even expected response, given the Elders' religious office. Since the author has connected lust to a loss of reason thematically, both audiences could be confused at this inclusion of shame as a mimetic dimension of the Elders' character. However, the shame language here can also be seen as a further indictment of the Elders, since their private shame indicates that they know their lust for Susanna is wrong. In v. 14, this shame and its implicit regulatory functions will disappear with the collusion of the Elders. As such, one can view the inclusion of shame language in this verse as a tool to further the instability created in the previous verse with the dissociation of the Elders. That is, we have a conflict in the progression of the narrative due to the inclusion of shame language because that language opposes the mimetic and thematic characterization of the Elders thus far. It is an instability in the progression of the narrative that must be resolved, and it will be in v. 14.[46] One could just as easily read the shame language in v. 11 as yet another negative thematic dimension added to the Elders' character. The final phrase of v. 11, "their desire to be with her," is simply an elaboration on the quality of the Elders' lust, and thus an addition to the mimetic dimension of their character.

We find more verbs relating to the Elders' voyeuristic activities in v. 12. They "watched" every day "to see her," still, presumably, in the garden. Thus the author here reinforces the negative thematic dimension found in v. 8 for the AA. The adverb "eagerly" here emphasizes the mimetic aspect of their watching, which again recalls the notice in v. 9 that they had stopped looking to Heaven. This would allow the NA to draw a negative parallel between the Elders' looking at Susanna and their non-looking to Heaven, as well as allow the AA to set up a more complete thematic dimension.

3.2.4. *The Elders' Confession and Plan (Verses 13–14)*

> (13) One day they said to one another, "Let us go home, for it is time for a meal." So they went out and separated from one another. (14) But returning, they came upon each other; when each examined the other for the reason, they both confessed their desire [for Susanna].[47] As a result [of this confession], together they arranged a time when they would be able to find her alone.

46. Another question that can be raised here is whether the AA might detect an instance of unreliable narration (to use Wayne C. Booth's term) or double-voiced discourse (to use James Phelan's term). That is, is there a discrepancy between the values of the author and the narrator here? Given the thematic dimensions of the characters so far, as established by the author, is the narrator opposing those values by including shame language related to the Elders? Put another way, the author has been unabashedly negative in his/her portrayal of the Elders, and yet in this verse the narrator attributes a positive quality to them: shame at their lust. For an in-depth analysis of this phenomenon, see Mikhail M. Bakhtin, "Discourse in the Novel," in *The Dialogic Imagination: Four Essays* (ed. Michael Holquist; trans. Caryl Emerson and Michael Holquist; Austin: University of Texas Press, 1981), 259–422 (301–31).

47. The square brackets indicate that "for Susanna" is not in the text. This practice will be continued below.

In v. 13 the mimetic dimension of the Elders' character is magnified due to their first instance of quoted speech. Presumably, it is the middle of the day because of the reference to eating, and thus we assume that it is the same time when Susanna usually walks in her garden. This places the Elders among those Jews who "run off at the middle of the day," as was noted in v. 7. This connection, added to the shame language in v. 11, might be an attempt on the part of the narrator to complicate the mimetic dimension of the Elders. After all, if they are ashamed of their lust for Susanna *and* are leaving at midday like everyone else instead of watching Susanna, then they cannot be "bad" people, can they? The second phrase of this verse even depicts them leaving—though we are not sure from where—and separating from each other, which mimetically parallels the thematic dissociation of the two in v. 10. Thus, this verse adds yet another instability to the progression of the story because we expect there to be a confrontation between the evil, Law-less Elders and the more religious, Law-full characters in the story, and this verse is prolonging it.

The instability created thematically in v. 10 and mimetically in v. 13 is resolved in v. 14. After each Elder leaves, they both return and discover each other, presumably in the secluded place from where they watch Susanna daily. They then "examine" each other to determine what he is doing. The verb here translated as "examine," ἀνετάζοντες, carries a judicial meaning, along the lines of giving someone a hearing (cf. Judg 6:29), although in Acts 22:29 it carries some corporal implications as well.[48] As a result of this examination, both Elders "confess" their desire or lust for Susanna. The effect of this legal language should not be overlooked. It adds to the mimetic dimension of their character by showing them engaging in the very activity for which the people appointed them. At the same time, due to the location of the action and the subject(s) of their examination, the legal language also adds a thematic dimension to their character by emphasizing both their immersion in legal discourse as well as their lack of attention tothe religio-moral aspect of the Law. Thus, the author has given them another negative thematic dimension, which hearkens back to their description in v. 9.

The second sentence in this verse, "As a result [of this confession], together they arranged a time when they would be able to find her alone," partially resolves the first thematic instability in the story by paving the way for the conflict between Susanna and the Elders. It also creates another wrinkle in that instability because now both audiences can infer that the coming crisis might be a violent one due to the repetition of the Elders' lust and the fact that they are planning "to find her alone," and thus potentially vulnerable. It also seems that in this verse, the shame the Elders feel in v. 11 is implicitly negated due to their collusive agreement to seek out Susanna while she is alone based on their lust. Not only have they overcome any barriers with regards to admitting their lust, it seems as if now they are ready to act upon it. One could argue that the Elders are,

48. For a discussion of this verse and its social background, see Ernst Haenchen, *The Acts of the Apostles: A Commentary* (trans. Bernard Noble et al.; Philadelphia: Westminster, 1971), 634.

by their actions, foregoing their ascribed status as respected Elders in the eyes of both audiences. As Eleonore Stump notes,

> What they [the Elders] do is made considerably worse by their role in society. As elders, they are people who have (or should have) a special understanding of religion and morality and who have a special duty to uphold both.[49]

Again, none of the characters are aware of the Elders' lust and shame; they have no reason so far to distrust the elders. Thus, the social restraints accompanying their position no longer serve as a barrier to their desire. The rhetorical impact of this negation is important: by their collusion the Elders have now created a privileged, private space for themselves in which they feel safe from the public realm of shaming and where they are free to use the Law as they see fit. In effect, the thematic dimension of lust, as highlighted in v. 8, is prioritized in both the mimetic and thematic arenas of their character.

3.2.5. *Susanna Prepares to Bathe (Verses 15–18)*

> (15) Later, when they were watching for a suitable day, Susanna entered as [she had done] before, alone with two maids. She desired to bathe in the garden because it was very hot. (16) There was no one there save the two Elders, hiding and watching her. (17) Then she said to the girls, "Bring me olive oil and ointment, and shut the doors of the garden so that I may bathe [in private]." (18) They did as she said: they shut up the doors of the garden and went out through the side doors to bring what had been commanded of them. They did not see the Elders because they were hiding themselves.

An indeterminate amount of time later in v. 15, the Elders are portrayed as "watching" for a "suitable day," presumably to find Susanna alone so that they could act upon Susanna their lust. In the same sentence, the narrator tells us "Susanna entered as [she had done] before" (literally, "she entered as ever, yesterday and the day before"). Thus the temporal setting of the scene must be midday, and so we are to assume that all the people have left and that the Elders are covertly watching Susanna as they usually do. We would also assume that Susanna is alone in her husband's garden. However, the narrator toys with that expectation; we are told that Susanna entered "alone with two maids." As a result, an instability is created because the Elders are waiting to find Susanna alone, and we expect her to be alone as she was before. Also, since she is not alone, the impending conflict is postponed again. As we shall see, when this instability is resolved, the conflict will finally take place.

The next sentence is possibly the most suggestive in terms of its ramifications for the progression of the story. Susanna, we are told, "desired" (ἐπεθύμησε: the same word used to denote the "desire" of the Elders for Susanna) to bathe in the garden because it was very hot."[50] This note regarding bathing affects both audiences, but in quite different ways. The NA would recognize the increased

49. Stump, "Susanna and the Elders," 86.

50. See Steussy, *Gardens in Babylon*, 110. Steussy argues for a rendering of "to take a swim" instead of "to bathe," because "outdoor bathing is so risqué in our culture that readers quickly conclude that Susanna is 'looking for trouble.'"

opportunity for the Elders' voyeuristic activities, as well as expect the Elders' lust for Susanna to increase, perhaps leading to complications. Moore agrees:

> Inasmuch as there is no parallel in the LXX for vss. 15–18, the bath scene in Θ must have been a later addition. If so, from a literary point of view it is a most welcome one: the bathing scene not only excites the elders, thereby enabling them to attempt their dastardly deed, but it can also fire the imagination of some readers. Of such considerations are good stories made![51]

This sort of focus on the mimetic level of the story, with its emphasis on the importance of the bath scene for the Elders *and* readers, exemplifies the importance of an attentive analysis of the story's rhetoric. That is, if we as readers "welcome" the voyeuristic opportunity provided by the bath scene, then we are both providing fodder for the eroticizing trend of interpretation of Susanna I will discuss in Chapter 5 as well as ignoring the overwhelming thematizing occurring in the story.

On the other hand, the AA might recognize the extra-narrative or intertextual parallels between this scene and other bathing scenes, most notably the story of Bathsheba in 2 Sam 11.[52] In both stories, a beautiful woman either bathing or preparing to bathe is being gazed upon by a male or males who hold more power than she does.[53] David sends for Bathsheba, has sex with her, and she becomes pregnant (2 Sam 11:4–5). In our narrative, the Elders try to extort rape by threatening Susanna with almost certain death, yet, she refuses. The outcomes of both episodes are significant as well: Bathsheba eventually gives birth to Solomon, and Daniel is prepared for his later textual existence by saving Susanna from death. For both audiences, the stage is being set for the expected conflict.

The narrator emphasizes the solitariness of the scene in v. 16 by noting, "There was no one there save the two elders, hiding and watching her." That is, "no one" was there except the Elders who are again hiding and watching her. By the repeated notice of the Elders hiding and watching for Susanna, the narrator and the author would be adding yet another negative mimetic and thematic dimension to the Elders' character.

51. Moore, *Daniel*, 97.

52. On this story in general, see P. Kyle McCarter, Jr., *II Samuel* (AB 9; New York: Doubleday, 1984), 277–91. For a feminist narratological reading of 2 Sam 11, see Mieke Bal, *Lethal Love: Feminist Literary Readings of Biblical Love Stories* (Indiana Studies in Biblical Literature; Bloomington: Indiana University Press, 1987), 10–36. J. Cheryl Exum, "Bathsheba Plotted, Shot, and Painted," in her *Plotted, Shot, and Painted*, 19–53, offers an excellent reading of this story with an emphasis on artistic interpretations of Bathsheba. Engel, *Die Susanna Erzählung*, 157–58, also mentions the connection between Susanna and Bathsheba. Following Engel, Collins (*Daniel*, 431) notes, "Such erotic motifs became more commonplace in the Hellenistic period. Thus Reuben's desire for Bilhah, which is unexplained in Gen 35.22, is occasioned by the sight of Bilhah bathing in *Jub* 33.1–9a and *T. Reu.* 3.11, and in *Vis.* 1.1.1–9, Hermas sins in his heart when he sees Rhoda bathing, even though he does not do anything." Collins also notes the bathing scene in the *Acts of Peter* 132 as conforming to this *topos*. For this scene, see Wilhelm Schneemelcher, "The Acts of Peter," in *New Testament Apocrypha* (ed. Wilhelm Schneemelcher; trans. R. McL. Wilson; 2 vols.; rev. ed.; Louisville, Ky.: Westminster/John Knox, 1991–92), 2:27–321 (285–86).

53. J. Cheryl Exum, *Fragmented Women: Feminist (Sub)Versions of Biblical Narratives* (Valley Forge, Pa.: Trinity, 1993), 174–75, delineates the use of the gaze on the reader(s) of the 2 Sam 11.

Another mimetic dimension is added to Susanna's character in v. 17 due to her first instance of direct speech. She speaks to the two maids, here called girls, and orders them to bring her olive oil and ointment to be used for bathing purposes.[54] She also tells them to shut the doors of the garden, presumably so that she can bathe in private. Thus, the instability created by the presence of the maids in v. 15 is partially resolved here. When they leave in the next verse, Susanna will finally be alone with the Elders and the anticipated conflict will finally be possible. Ironically, Susanna wants to be alone as much as the Elders want her to be alone. An important issue in this verse for the AA concerns the oil and soap Susanna asks the maids to bring her. The word I have rendered as "ointment," σμῆγμα, can also be translated as "soap" or perhaps "cosmetics."[55] If the word is, in fact, meant to indicate "cosmetics," the AA might draw a parallel between Susanna's use of bodily enrichment products and similar uses of comparable products found in other stories circulating during the first century B.C.E. For example, in Jdt 10:3, Judith "anointed herself with precious ointment" in preparation for her journey to the Assyrian camp. Similarly, in Esth 2:3, 9, and 12, special ointments are mentioned which are provided to the young virgins to be brought before Artaxerxes, and Esther specifically receives these ointments in 2:9 and 12. These connections would be important for the AA because they would connect Susanna thematically to other "heroines" in the literature of the Second Temple Period.

However, an important question is raised as well: If σμῆγμα is used to indicate a beauty product, and in both Judith and Esther it is used in preparation for a (possibly sexual) rendezvous with a man, then how are we as members of both audiences as well as flesh-and-blood readers meant to take its use in the context of Susanna's story? Are we to think that Susanna is preparing for a similar encounter with her husband? This seems unlikely given the repetitive behavior of Susanna in the garden, and her seemingly spontaneous decision to bathe because of the heat.[56] However, would the Elders (if they were aware of Susanna's speech) take this as an indication that Susanna is preparing for a romantic meeting, and thus become more excited? Could it be that Susanna simply wants to look and/or feel a certain way for herself? Or, could the narrator/author be trying to entice the audience(s) with Susanna's bathing preparations as the Elders have been enticed by her beauty all along? One could argue that, by presenting Susanna preparing to bathe and by mentioning oil and ointment, with their connotations of romantic

54. For an examination of Susanna's maids in the OG and in the context of ancient slavery, see Jennifer A. Glancy, "The Mistress–Slave Dialectic: Paradoxes of Slavery in Three LXX Narratives," *JSOT* 72 (1996): 71–87.

55. Moore, *Daniel*, 97, translates the word as "cosmetics," while Collins, *Daniel*, 431, uses "ointments."

56. Interestingly, in one of the most influential dramatic re-tellings of the Susanna story, Susanna does decide to bathe after a long walk before Joachim comes home. See the 1544 work of Paul Rebhun, "Susanna: A Miracle Play about the God-Fearing and Chaste Lady Susanna, for Entertaining and Profitable Reading," in *German Theater before 1750* (ed. Gerald Gillespie; The German Library 8; New York: Continuum, 1992), 29–97 (50–52).

encounters, the narrator/author is attempting to make the audience(s) understand why the Elders found Susanna so irresistible.

The reason this question of the Elders' motive(s) is so important is that several scholars argue that we, as readers, must comprehend that motive to understand the story. As Amy-Jill Levine notes,

> For the story to function, their [i.e. the Elders'] desire must be comprehensible to the reader, and thus Susanna must be a figure of desire to us as well. And once we see her as desirable, we are trapped: either we are guilty of lust, or she is guilty of seduction.[57]

In connection with this point, Susan Sered and Samuel Cooper note that, "the significance of Susanna's beauty is quite simply to 'seduce' the reader into thinking that rape is a consequence of male sexual arousal precipitated by female beauty, rather than a product of culturally condoned patriarchal control of female autonomy."[58] That is, readers have to find Susanna desirable to comprehend the Elders' lust for her, and, to some degree, to understand why they are willing to forfeit their social and religious status in exchange for raping her. The narrator assists us in this comprehension by describing Susanna as beautiful and alluding to her bathing, thus attempting to account for the Elders' interest in and actions against Susanna.

These scholars feel that this comprehension of the Elders' motives places us in a precarious situation as flesh-and-blood readers. After all, the story has made painfully clear that the Elders are attracted to and subsequently tempted by Susanna because of their voyeuristic gazing. We are made aware of the consequences, both moral and physical, of such voyeurism due to the execution of the Elders in vv. 61–62. Because of this, scholars argue the author places real readers in a position of moral superiority over the Elders because we are aware of the shame that the Elders should be feeling due to the rhetoric of the story in general as well as the shame language in v. 11. The question thus becomes: Because of this supposed position of moral superiority, are we as real readers allowed to gaze (textually) upon Susanna without feeling guilty due to our double position of readers and judges?[59]

The answer to my question is a qualified yes. On the one hand, if we are going to become members of the AA, then we must encounter the mimetic characterization of the Elders and be aware of their lust for Susanna. On the other hand, we must recognize that this mimetic encounter is but a step in the analysis of the story. Since I view this narrative as being a thematic one, the dangers noted by feminist scholars of participating with the Elders and proliferating the text's gender ideology are unfounded. The claim of these scholars that the narrative forces readers into complicity with the Elders is an incomplete interpretation

57. Amy-Jill Levine, "Hemmed in on Every Side: Jews and Women in the Book of Susanna," in Brenner, ed., *A Feminist Companion to Esther, Judith, and Susanna*, 303–23 (313).

58. Sered and Cooper, "Sexuality and Social Control," 50.

59. In addition to the scholars I specifically mention, much of this position is bolstered by scholarship on Bathsheba, which has many affinities with Susanna. See especially Exum, *Fragmented Women*, 196–97.

focused solely on the mimetic level of the text. As such, these scholars are as guilty of focusing on the sexual, voyeuristic elements in the story as are the artistic interpreters I will discuss in Chapter 5. Put differently, if I read Susanna as a strictly mimetic story, then the voyeuristic activities and lust of the Elders could conceivably cause me to allow the dangerous connection between the male gaze, the woman-as-object, and uncontrolled sexual longings to proliferate in our own social context. However, since I read Susanna as a thematic narrative, my conclusions regarding the effects of reading the story vary considerably from these concerns. That is, readers see the behavior of the Elders and what that behavior gets them in the end. As I will discuss below, we as readers can resist aspects of that behavior we find harmful without simply asserting that merely by reading Susanna we become more prone to guiltless gazing.

Verse 18 finally resolves the instability created by the presence of the two maids by showing them leaving the garden and shutting the doors behind them, thus sealing Susanna inside alone, or so they thought. The narrator again tells us that the Elders were hiding themselves and thus the maids did not see them. Of course, this emphasis on the hiding of the Elders once again adds negative dimensions to both their mimetic and thematic aspects of their character. It is at this point that the stage is finally set for the conflict between Susanna and the Elders to take place, both mimetically and thematically.

3.2.6. *The Attempted Rape and Susanna's Response (Verses 19–25)*

> (19) As the girls were going out, the two Elders stood up and ran to Susanna. (20) They said, "Look, the doors of the garden have been closed and no one can see us. We are lusting for you; agree to be with us! (21) But if [you do] not, we will testify against you, that a young man was with you and because of this you sent the girls away from you." (22) Susanna sighed deeply and said, "It is narrow for me on all sides! For if I do this, it is death for me, but if I do not, I will not escape your hands. (23) It is chosen for me: I cannot do it; I will fall into your hands rather than sin before the Lord!" (24) Then Susanna cried aloud with a great voice, and the Elders, opposite her, cried out [as well]. (25) One of them ran and opened the doors of the garden.

Verse 19 begins the much-anticipated conflict. The Elders stand up—presumably because they had been crouching in the attempt to hide themselves—and run up to Susanna at the same time the maids are departing to fulfill her orders.[60] This physical description would suggest to the NA the Elders' overriding lust; they cannot even wait for the girls to leave before approaching Susanna. Thus, the negative thematizing performed previously by the narrator continues here. The NA might even ask: What if one of the attendants had turned back to ask what kind of oil Susanna wanted and discovered the Elders? Their lust has driven the Elders beyond such worries now, which would only reinforce their loss of reason, initiated in v. 14, which, in turn, could lead the AA to enlarge their negative view of them.

60. Moore, *Daniel*, 97, renders ἐπέδραμον as "accosted" due to the parallel account in the LXX.

At last the conflict comes to a head; the Elders address Susanna. Verse 20 comprises the first part of their threat to Susanna, as well as their second piece of quoted dialogue. It represents their "confession" to Susanna, in the same way they confessed their desire to each other in v. 14. They tell her first, "Look, the doors of the garden have been closed and no one can see us." This is an ironic declaration; the masters of voyeuristic behavior are positive that no one is spying on them? This, another repeated instance of "sight" language, continues the theme of vision in the story, as well as adds another negative thematic dimension to an increasingly long list. That is, the Elders, presumably more than anyone else in the community, know they are doing something wrong. Given their decision to turn "their eyes away from Heaven" in v. 9, it seems they have forgotten that God is traditionally characterized as one who can see all, as in Sir 17:19; 39:19–20; and 42:20. It is no accident that when Susanna prays to God in vv. 42–43, she characterizes him as "the one who knows hidden things" and the one who can see "all things before their beginning." Thus, the Elders still do not quite get it; they still cannot grasp the nature of God and what their own "vision" should be, and this again serves to distinguish them thematically from Susanna and her family. Finally, as if the status of the Elders was not negative enough, they tell Susanna bluntly: "We are lusting for you; agree to be with us!" For the Elders, this initial confession to Susanna is now complete. It should be apparent to both audiences now that the Elders are seeking sexual gratification from Susanna, which, again, has explicitly negative connotations for the thematic and mimetic dimensions of their characters.

The initial confession of the Elders is concluded in v. 21. They tell her that if she does not agree "to be" with them, they will "testify" against her. Once again, as in v. 14, the narrator and author add a mimetic and thematic dimension, respectively, to the Elders' character. That is, by using legal language (καταμαρτυρήσομέν, literally "to bear witness against") both the narrator and the author are again showing the Elders radically misusing their knowledge of the Law. Their promised testimony, in this case, consists of an allegation of adultery, i.e., Susanna was with another (young) man and this is why she sent her maids away. It is important here to look more closely at this threat, for that is what it is; the elders are trying to blackmail Susanna into acquiescing to rape.[61] The nature of their extortion is not only physical, but also social. That is, if the Elders go to the Jews living in Babylon, specifically those congregating around Joakim's house, and publicly tell them their story, Susanna loses her social status. She would be shamed in front of her community and her family, thus relinquishing any claim to honor she or her husband may have.[62] In addition, since the story is set in the

61. In contrast to this statement, it is intriguing to note how many interpreters view the actions of the elders as attempts at seduction. For example, Collins, *Daniel*, 430, entitles his section on vv. 7–27 "The Attempted Seduction." For further comments, see Glancy, "The Accused," 297–99.

62. The categories of honor and shame are of paramount importance for Mediterranean persons in antiquity and late antiquity. One of the best summaries I have found is in Bruce J. Malina and Jerome H. Neyrey, *Portraits of Paul: An Archaeology of Ancient Personality* (Louisville, Ky.: Westminster/John Knox, 1996), 176–82: "Mediterranean society has traditionally employed the

sixth century B.C.E., Susanna would have been subject to the *sotah* test, in which case, if she was found guilty, she would not only be socially shamed, she would be physically harmed and executed as well.[63]

This threat establishes one of the main progressions of the entire story, for now there exists both an instability (albeit a short-lived one) as well as a tension. The former is created due to the conflict generated by the threat, as well as the suspense produced by the temporary absence of the maids, i.e., if the maids were simply leaving to gather a few things for Susanna, they might return at any moment, thus begging the question: Did the Elders expect Susanna to "be with" them right then or later? The tension here is formed out of the disparity between the knowledge of Susanna's situation both audiences possess vs. the knowledge possessed by the characters in the story. As we will see, the threat also re-presents one of the overarching thematic oppositions in the narrative as well: the Law-less and lustful Elders over against the Law-full and honorable Susanna and her family. However, this threat raises an important question: How can the Elders explain *how* they saw Susanna with this young man without admitting that they were watching her? Given the NA's trust in the narratorial voice, this might not be a problem for them, but for the AA it might represent another tension in the narrative that is (partially) resolved in vv. 36–41.

In the next two verses, we hear Susanna's response to the Elders' threats, coincidentally only her second instance of quoted speech as well. She first sighs deeply, and then proclaims the "Catch-22" nature of her dilemma: "if I do this, it is death for me, but if I do not, I will not escape your hands." Her latter statement is clearer initially than her first. After all, if convicted of adultery, which, given the nature of the Elders' social and religious status as well as the nature of the *sotah* test, would almost certainly happen, she would be stoned in accordance with the Law (Deut 22:20–24; Lev 20:10). However, her former statement is more enigmatic, i.e., Why does/should Susanna regard rape as death? Sexual abuse in the form of rape is obviously a violent and terrifying experience, but Susanna has a chance of surviving the ordeal, at least physically. In v. 23, both audiences are clued in as to Susanna's metaphoric identification of rape and

experience of shame deriving from public disapproval as social sanction. Alternately it awards public praise as reward for laudable behavior. This reward of positive public acknowledgment constitutes a grant of honor. Honor and shame are the anthropological terms used to express the core native values of praise and blame; they mark the general pathways of praiseworthy and censurable behavior" (p. 176). For the specific effect I am discussing here, see p. 181: "public criticism produced shame."

63. Susanna's trial appears to me to be a form of the *sotah* test due to the charges, as well as the actions of the elders, i.e., in v. 32 they order her to be uncovered, probably implying veiling, which corresponds to Num 5:18, in which the priest is ordered to dishevel the *sotah*'s hair. For an early, yet tentative exposition of this view, see Frank Zimmermann, "The Story of Susanna and its Original Language," *JQR* 48 (1957–58): 236–41 (236–37). Interestingly, in Nicodemus Frischlin's 1577 Latin drama, Susanna's mother Anna tries to convince Susanna that if she drinks "bitter water," then all suspicion will be removed. See Paul F. Casey, *The Susanna Theme in German Literature: Variations of the Biblical Drama* (Abhandlungen zur Kunst-, Musik-, und Literaturwissenschaft 214; Bonn: Bouvier Verlag Herbert Grundmann, 1976), 109.

death: "I will fall into your hands rather than sin before the Lord!"[64] This datum not only reinforces the earlier mimetic and thematic descriptions of Susanna as a religiously identified woman, it also explains why she would rather let herself be executed for something she did not do rather than let herself be raped by the Elders. That is, Susanna is so immersed in her religious identity that for her to abandon that identity in order to survive would be tantamount to sinning before God.

For the AA, the question might arise at this point: Why would the narrator and author have chosen to construct this scene in this fashion? Why show Susanna's willingness to die rather than to sin? The answer might lie in an intertextual connection. In Gen 39, Joseph fends off the sexual advances of Potiphar's wife, who certainly has more social power than he does. Before the famous ripping of the robe, Joseph tells her, "How then could I do this great wickedness, and sin against God?" Of course, the outcome of the scene in the Joseph novella is not especially good for Joseph: he is thrown into prison. However, God is with him and eventually will make him immensely prosperous. Thus, Joseph remains steadfast in his loyalty to God's Law and his own sense of ethics and prospers in the end because of it. Likewise, in the story of Susanna, a young woman refuses the advances of those in power, and will eventually be rewarded for doing so by the God whom she trusts. This connection may or may not have been intended, but it certainly one possibility for the way in which the author constructs this particular scene.[65]

In vv. 24–25, the instability created in the previous four verses expands to encompass the whole community. Susanna "cried aloud with a great voice," although no one is quite sure why; she did, after all, just agree to "fall into" the hands of the Elders. So, why cry out now? Perhaps to attract attention or to gather witnesses so that someone could "see" the absence of the hypothetical young man?[66] Or, as Collins notes, Susanna may simply be following "the letter of the law," in that "According to Deut 22:24, a young woman who is molested within the city is guilty and subject to stoning if she does not cry out."[67] If this is true, then it seems that once again the author is performing some thematizing; Susanna here knows the Law and follows it, while the Law-less Elders are simply following their lust. In any case, as soon as Susanna cries out, the Elders begin to shout as well. Just as we are unsure as to why Susanna is crying out, we are also unsure as to why the Elders shout. However, two things seem certain. One, the Elders panicked when Susanna began to shout and, two, since there are two of them,

64. Collins, *Daniel*, 431, notes a similar phrase in 2 Sam 24.14: "Then David said to Gad, 'I am in great distress; let us fall into the hand of the Lord, for his mercy is great; but let me not fall into human hands.'"

65. For brief examinations of these parallels, see Bach, *Women, Seduction, and Betrayal*, 65–72; and LaCocque, *The Feminine Unconventional*, 23. For an intertextual reading of the story of Potiphar's wife, see Judith McKinlay, "Potiphar's Wife in Conversation," *Feminist Theology* 10 (1995): 69–80. McKinley mentions a possible connection with Susanna (p. 79).

66. See Moore, *Daniel*, 98.

67. Collins, *Daniel*, 431.

they were probably trying to drown out her shouts. Thus, the shouting of the Elders reveals more than at first glance. They perhaps recognize the tenuousness of their "case" and are continuing to do what they have done all along, to subsume Susanna's voice, her identity to their own. In other words, they dominate her. To further this domination, one of the Elders goes and opens the door of the garden so that the community (of which they are leaders) could hear and "see" their story.

3.2.7. *Susanna and the Elders are Discovered (Verses 26–27)*

> (26) When the people in the house heard the shouting in the garden, they rushed in through the side door to see what had happened to her. (27) After the Elders told their stories, the servants were intensely ashamed, for no such story had ever been told about Susanna.

The process of expanding the instability created in the previous two verses continues in vv. 26–27. The "people in the house" hear shouting in the garden and rush in to "see" what is transpiring, what "had happened" to Susanna. Presumably, these people would be servants (as specified in v. 27) and Susanna's maids might be among them. The shouting heard in the garden would most likely have initially been Susanna's, since she shouted first, thus increasing their cause for worry. Upon arriving in the garden, the Elders relate to them their false allegations; their threat is now partially fulfilled. Curiously, though, the Elders tell "stories," not a singular story. Did the Elders each relate their own story, as Daniel will later force them to do in vv. 52–59? If so, then the thematic dissociation in v. 10 is revisited, thereby possibly creating an instability for the AA that will be resolved in vv. 36–41, only to be revisited again in Daniel's cross-examination.

In any case, the "stories" produce their desired effect: "the servants were intensely ashamed, for no such story had ever been told about Susanna." This comment reinforces the social nature of the threat I mentioned above, as well as heightening both the thematic and mimetic aspects of Susanna's character. Mimetically, the NA learns that no malicious gossip or scandalous tale had ever circulated about Susanna. Thematically, the constancy of Susanna's virtue is emphasized, thus strengthening the thematic opposition between her and her family and the Elders. The Elders, for their part, are trying to undercut that opposition by attempting to shame Susanna publicly by their false testimony, and thus once again to dominate her.

3.2.8. *The Pre-Trial Setting (Verses 28–33)*

> (28) The next day, when the crowd came together to Joakim her husband, the two Elders came forth, full of unlawful intent against Susanna, to put her to death. Before the crowd they said, (29) "Send for Susanna, daughter of Hilkiah, Joakim's wife!" [The crowd] sent for her (30) and she came [with] her parents, her children, and all her relatives. (31) Susanna was exceedingly effeminate and beautiful to the sight. (32) So that they might have their fill of her beauty, the evildoers ordered her to be uncovered, for she was covering herself. (33) Those with her and all those seeing her were weeping.

A new section of the narrative is initiated with v. 28, viz., Susanna's trial. It begins "The next day, when the crowd came together to Joakim her husband." This chronological notation also provides an interesting twist in that this is exactly what the Jews in the story routinely do, as we are told in vv. 4 and 6. The Jews would come to Joakim's house because of his honor and people who were to be judged came there as well because the Elders were usually there. Thus, the setting of Susanna's trial is perfectly familiar to the crowd, but now it is not only Joakim's honor as stake, but also, and more importantly, Susanna's life.

The Elders come forth, presumably in their capacity as judges, "full of unlawful intent against Susanna, to put her to death." Yet again, both the mimetic and thematic dimensions of the Elders' character are enlarged, and, again, for the worse. For a judge to have any intent toward the accused was not a good thing, but here the Elders have "unlawful" intent against Susanna. Of course, this description resonated perfectly with their overall view of God and the Law, as we have seen in vv. 5 and 9. Finally, the Elders wish "to put her to death" before the trial even begins! However, the outcome of the trial was never in doubt given the status of the Elders.

In vv. 29–30 the Elders order the crowd to " 'Send for Susanna, daughter of Hilkiah, Joakim's wife!' " Susanna is again identified by her association with men as in vv. 1–2, but now the Elders seems to be attempting to associate Hilkiah and Joakim with Susanna's shame. After the crown summons her, Susanna presents herself along with "her parents, her children, and all her relatives."[68] The mimetic dimension of her character is once again fleshed out, for only now do we know that Susanna has children, that she is a mother. Interestingly, Joakim is not mentioned, although his presence is implied. If he is present, it might signal his belief in Susanna's innocence, which, given that he was considered the injured party, would speak volumes.[69] The effect of these data, along with the familial procession, probably intended to elicit support for Susanna's innocence, is to situate Susanna firmly in the community. She has a family, her parents and relatives support her, and while this does not *prove* her innocence, in the social context of the first century B.C.E it would help.

The next three verses provide both audiences with a description of the pre-trial setting. Verse 31 tells us that Susanna was "exceedingly effeminate (or 'luxurious,' 'voluptuous') and beautiful to the sight" (τρυφερὰ σφόδρα καὶ καλὴ τῷ εἴδει). Since the same basic information has already been related in v. 2, why mention it here again? This seemingly mimetic description might serve as yet another reminder of why the Elders lusted after Susanna, and as such serves to set up the next verse as well. If so, then we, as members of both audiences, are again faced with a dilemma similar to that found in v. 17. That is, can we understand the lust of the Elders without falling prey to it ourselves? As with my discussion of v. 17, the answer is a qualified yes. We can understand the lust and

68. Interestingly, the OG version here reads "The woman arrived, accompanied by her father and mother; also there came her servants and maids (being five hundred in number), as well as Susanna's four children." All OG quotes are taken from Moore, *Daniel*.

69. See Levine, "Hemmed in on Every Side," 312–13.

behavior of the Elders on a mimetic level, but because the story is a thematic one, the comprehension of their activities is not paramount to my interpretation. Put another way, the main point(s) of the story is built upon the thematic functions of its various characters, and so their mimetic activities are not privileged.

The description in v. 31 might mean something more to the AA, who, given my comments on v. 2, might recall the thematic similarities between Susanna and other "heroines" like Judith and Esther, both of whom were considered beautiful. If this is the case, the physical description of Susanna, along with the presence of her entourage in v. 29, might provide a wink to the AA that the thematic opposition we have seen in the story is still operative. This would, in turn, function as a bit of foreshadowing, partially illuminating the potential outcome of the trial.

The pre-trial description continues in vv. 32–33. The Elders, here explicitly called "evildoers" order Susanna to uncover herself so they can "have their fill of her beauty." This description not only overtly identifies the Elders as evil (as if there were any doubt left), but also tells the NA that Susanna was probably veiling herself. In her work, Ilan makes it clear that during the Second Temple period, if women did go out in public they covered their heads.[70] The Elders, who would have had full knowledge of the legal requirements and social mores for women, are attempting to shame Susanna publicly yet again by ordering the removal of her head covering. Ilan comments on this verse, "Unbound hair on a woman is depicted as compromising her modesty. The worst of Susanna's humiliations occurred when the elders, who were accusing her of adultery, demanded that her head be uncovered."[71] She also notes that ordering a woman's head covering to be removed is not looked upon favorably in Mishnaic materials.[72] The Elders' order to remove Susanna's covering, then, would seem to be excessive, and might serve as another thematic indicator of their abandonment of the Law.

There is another interesting point to be made with regards to v. 32. The OG version of the story here agrees with Th, in that the Elders order Susanna to be uncovered. However, unlike Th, the OG does not include any the phrase, "for she was covering herself." Thus, most commentators assume that the verb in the OG, ἀποκαλύψαι, implies that Susanna was to be stripped naked.[73] This assumption is based in part on texts like Ezek 16:37–39 and Hos 2:3 and 10. These texts, though, speak metaphorically of adultery, and thus, in my opinion, do not constitute good analogies. More on point is the testimony of the Mishnah, specifically *m. Soṭah* 1:5, which prescribes the following scenario:

> A priest lays hold on her garments—if they are torn they are torn, if they are utterly rent they are utterly rent—so that he lays bare her bosom. Moreover he loosens her hair. R. Judah says: If her bosom was comely he did not lay it bare; if her hair was comely he did not loosen it.

70. See Ilan, *Jewish Women*, 129–32.

71. Ilan, *Jewish Women*, 130.

72. Ilan, *Jewish Women*, 130: "According to *halakhah*, 'if a man loosened a woman's hair...he is liable to pay her 400 zuz' (*mBQ* 8.6)."

73. See Collins, *Daniel*, 431; and Moore, *Daniel*, 102–3.

Frank Zimmermann makes the following comment regarding this passage:

> In light of this information, the wickedness of the elders becomes more manifest. In order that their desire be satiated (v. 31), they had her exposed. Now Susanna was very beautiful (Theod. v. 1), and v. 31 takes pains to re-iterate about her beauty. In common decency therefore, the elders should have refrained (comp. R. Judah's statement) from submitting her to that indignity.[74]

Zimmermann views the order of the Elders to strip Susanna not only to represent their lust, but also their attempt to prejudice the verdict against her, "thereby further compounding their villainy."[75] Thus, in the OG, the Elders are portrayed even more vilely than in Th, while Th tones down their negative portrayal.[76]

However, their attempt to shame Susanna publicly seems to be partially successful, because in v. 33 we hear that "Those with her and all those seeing her were weeping." The mimetic impact of this information could lead the NA to assume that everyone was weeping at the indignity forced upon Susanna by the Elders. The potential thematic impact on the AA by vv. 32–33 would consist of reaffirming the aforementioned thematic opposition. The AA could also infer some intertextual connections between these verses and, to mention but one example, the trial and punishment of Jesus in the New Testament Gospels. Jesus, too, is brought before a powerful figure to determine his fate. He, too, is stripped of his clothes in preparation for punishment, as well as having an entourage present at his execution. Obviously, though, Jesus is found guilty and punished for apparent theological reasons in the Gospels. However, this and other discrepancies did not deter some thinkers and artists from looking upon Susanna as a prefiguring of Jesus.[77]

3.2.9. *Susanna's Trial, Part One: The Elders' Testimony (Verses 34–41)*

> (34) Standing in the middle of the people, the two Elders laid [their] hands on her head. (35) Weeping, she looked up to Heaven, for her heart trusted in the Lord. (36) Then the Elders said, "While we were walking about in the garden alone, [this] woman entered with two maids, shut up the doors of the garden, and dismissed the maids. (37) Then a young man, who was hiding, came to her and lay with her. (38) We, being in a corner of the garden, saw the lawlessness and ran to them. (39) Even though we saw them embrace, we were not able to be in control because he was stronger than us. He opened

74. Zimmermann, "The Story of Susanna," 236–37 n. 2. See also Collins, *Daniel*, 432: "The situation addressed by the Mishnah is one where a suspected adulteress is being tested. In the case of Susanna, however, the stripping is a prejudicial punishment."

75. Moore, *Daniel*, 103.

76. For a possible explanation regarding this issue, see Richard I. Pervo, "Aseneth and Her Sisters: Women in Jewish Narrative and in the Greek Novels," in Levine, ed., *"Women Like This"*, 145–60 (148). Pervo implies that Th is more in line with ideal Greek novels than the OG, which is more realistic. Thus, Th may have altered the OG out of artistic concerns.

77. For this issue, see Catherine Brown Tkacz, "Susanna as a Type of Christ," *Studies in Iconography* 20 (1999): 101–53. In early Christian funerary art as well as catacombs, Susanna is often portrayed as a cipher for the virtuous and pious sufferer. For an excellent examination of this issue, see Kathryn A. Smith, "Inventing Marital Chastity: The Iconography of Susanna and the Elders in Early Christian Art," *Oxford Art Journal* 16, no. 1 (1993): 3–24.

> the doors and rushed out. (40) We seized this woman and asked who the young man was, (41) but she did not wish to disclose [his identity] to us. These things we testify." The assembly believed them, as [they were] Elders of the people and judges; they condemned her to die.

Beginning in v. 34, the actual trial scene begins. The Elders stand "in the middle of the people," i.e., those who are mentioned in vv. 4 and 6. They then lay their hands on Susanna's head. Why is this act important, and what might it imply about the Elders and/or Susanna? That is, why is it included in the story? In his commentary, Collins notes three possibilities:

> The ritual of placing hands on the head occurs in three contexts in the Bible: in the preparation of animals for sacrifice (Lev 8:14, 18, 22; Exod 29:10, 16, 19); in the ritual of the scapegoat (Lev 16:21–22); and in the condemnation of blasphemers (Lev 24:14).[78]

Collins hypothesizes that the third option provides the best parallel for what occurs in the story, yet mentions that the second possibility might fit as well. Lawrence M. Wills elaborates on this hypothesis, and in connection with the prescriptions in *m. Soṭah* 1:5 notes the following:

> Ritual shame is evidently the motive behind this practice... One might speculate that the woman also becomes a sort of sexual scapegoat, a permissible object of male erotic attention who is then stoned by the community (according to the provisions of *Leviticus* 20:10), taking away, as it were, the sexual sins of desire of the community. The story of *Susanna*, in that case, would be a narrated expression of this same psychological need to play out sexual tensions and desires in a permissible fashion. The author makes use of a common technique in psychologically oriented narrative. The two elders act upon their forbidden desires (male desires that are extrapolated as normative and "shared" with the audience) and are punished with death. Once the evil trait is released and threatens Susanna, it is discovered and slain.[79]

Wills' argument is quite persuasive; the figure of Susanna at her trial might very well serve as an acceptable object of sexual desire, which is most likely to be found among both audiences as well. The Elders are willing to offer her up for execution to protect themselves from accusations, but they could be trying to vanquish the object of their obsession. Thus, I see no need to make a specific choice from among the latter two possibilities. Both contain elements of the story, and as such may all serve as useful data. Put another way, the laying of hands on Susanna could serve as an echo of both Lev 16:21–22 and 24:14 for the AA, and might function both mimetically and thematically to identify her as a sacrifice and a scapegoat, both for the Elders and readers.[80]

In any case, Susanna's response to this action is to weep and look towards Heaven, "for her heart trusted in the Lord." The mimetic impact of this information would probably cause the NA to recall v. 9, where the Elders "turned their

78. Collins, *Daniel*, 432.

79. Lawrence M. Wills, *The Jewish Novel in the Ancient World* (Myth and Poetics Series; Ithaca, N.Y.: Cornell University Press, 1995), 57.

80. For a survey of opinions regarding the laying of hands on heads, see Engel, *Die Susanna Erzählung*, 137–41.

eyes away to not look to Heaven." It would also increase the NA's view of Susanna's religious identity, given the fact that she will offer no defense on her behalf, but instead trusts in the Lord. The thematizing taking place in this verse is hard to overlook: the Elders are once again being denigrated in comparison to Susanna. Whereas they turned away from Heaven, she looks to it; while Susanna trusts in the Lord almost totally, they seem to have no real conception of God. Moore remarks,

> The story...[is] thoroughly religious in character. God is mentioned or alluded to fifteen times in 'Susanna's' sixty-four verses. In fact, with the exception of the two villains, *everybody in the story* mentions God...it is no coincidence that it was only the wicked elders who did not mention God. *That*, after all, had been their problem all along: they themselves were not at all concerned about him.[81]

It is here, then, that the thematic opposition between Susanna and the Elders reaches its pinnacle. Only in Susanna's prayer in vv. 42–43 and Daniel's comments in vv. 49, 52–53, 55, 56–57, and 59 does the author supplement this opposition. Thus, the net effect of this verse is to solidify the alienation of the Elders from God and the Law, while at the same time indicating Susanna's immersion in both.

Verses 36–41 comprise the testimony of the Elders and the people's response to it. Their testimony is filled with irony, because we, as members of both audiences, recognize that much of their fraudulent testimony is true, but the characters in the story (save the Elders and Susanna) do not possess that knowledge. There is also a preliminary technical question raised by their testimony, i.e., Was it proper for judges to also act as witnesses? Certainly the way in which the two (simultaneously?) testify is not in keeping with the Law. Both Deut 19:15–20 and *m. Sanh.* 5:1 prescribe intense examination of witnesses, and the former also mentions the necessity of having *two* witnesses. However, in the story, the Elders simply give their joint account, thus acting in effect as one witness, without any examination, and the people are convinced based upon their testimony. Thus, given this knowledge on the part of the AA, this scene could be read as a farce or a satire of proper judicial procedure.

The testimony begins in v. 36, ironically with an almost entirely accurate statement of the events. The Elders were indeed in the garden alone (though hardly walking around) when Susanna entered with her maids and then dismissed them. The omitted details thus far are obvious: the Elders were, in fact, spying on Susanna and she only dismissed the maids to bring her bathing paraphernalia. The Elders consciously leave out any mention of a bath so as to diminish any suspicion that they might have been watching Susanna prepare to bathe, which is exactly what they did! Thus, the comments in v. 36 are somewhat accurate, albeit in a muted fashion.

The statement given in v. 37, however, is totally false yet in keeping with the threat made in v. 21: the Elders say they saw a hiding young man come to Susanna and "lay with her." This forms a fanciful counterpart to the actual events

81. Moore, *Daniel*, 89.

in the narrative. Susanna refused the old Elders who were hiding, but here they (re)speak of a young man, hiding as well, who accomplishes the purpose they set for themselves. In her examination of Susanna, Mieke Bal raises the following question: Could this fabricated testimony represent a sexual fantasy of the Elders? Given that the Elders enjoy (almost pathologically) watching Susanna, could this evidence be an instance of projectionism to make up for their age and lack of success with Susanna? Bal notes that the imagined young man here "represents for the elders the other side of voyeurism: the danger and attraction of exhibitionism."[82] In other words,

> They saw her while they were hiding, and, as viewers of pornography, desired/fantasized the act. They hallucinated the act, performed by procuration in their stead, by someone young, *stronger than they*.[83]

Of course, the suggestion that the Elders experienced a hallucination must remain hypothetical, even though it is in keeping with their voyeuristic activities. Even though this line of thought is interesting, it is focused entirely on the mimetic level of the story, and it provides no substantive addition to the rhetoric of the narrative. In any case, as in v. 36, the testimony in the next verse contains some truth: the Elders might have been in a corner of the garden hiding themselves. They indeed witnessed or "saw" a Law-less act: their very own! Finally, they did run (ἐδράμομεν), just as they had run (ἐπέδραμον) to Susanna in v. 19. As we saw in v. 36, though, the omitted details and embellishments are quite easy to notice.

In v. 39, the Elders provide a character endorsement for themselves. After seeing Susanna and the young man "embrace" or "come together" they tried to stop them, to "be in control" of the situation like good conscientious Elders should be, but the young man was simply too strong for them.[84] They, being too weak to stop him, were unable to catch him as he rushed out of the doors. This bit of self-deprecation reinforces the possible fantasy I alluded to above, i.e., not only was Susanna with a young man, he was a strong, vibrant young man as well. Given that this hypothetical young, brawny man escaped, the old, weak (impotent?) Elders did what they could. In v. 40, they testify that they seized Susanna and asked or interrogated (ἐπηρωτῶμεν) her as to his identity.[85] Again, this interrogation is entirely in keeping with the Elders' expected duties. According to the Elders' testimony in v. 41, Susanna did not want to reveal the young beefcake's

82. Mieke Bal, "The Elders and Susanna," *BibInt* 1 (1993): 1–19 (8).

83. Bal, "The Elders and Susanna," 8.

84. As Collins, *Daniel*, 432, notes, "The voyeurism of the Elders is more explicit in the OG." In the OG version, the Elders' testimony highlights their visual and erotic interest in the scene: "turning the corner, we saw this woman sleeping with a man. Stopping, we saw them having sexual intercourse; but they did not know we were standing there. Then we agreed on it, saying, 'Let's find out who they are!' " It seems that the Elders here testify that they were letting themselves get an eyeful of the sexual tryst prior to stopping it, thus heightening their carnal interest in Susanna. This reading of this passage also accords with Bal's interpretation of the Elders' testimony as representing the vocalization of some kind of sexual fantasy. See Bal, "The Elders and Susanna," 8.

85. Interestingly, in the OG version, when the Elders first approach Susanna to confess their lust, they "grabbed" (ἐξεβιάζοντο) her as well.

name, so (they imply) they took her into custody. They then conclude their evidence by saying solemnly, "These things we testify."

All in all, the Elders' testimony is a pack of half-truths and delicate omissions, with a pinch of sexual fantasizing.[86] The thematic impact of vv. 36–41 is hard to miss: by showing the Elders providing false testimony in front of the people who appointed them to dispense justice, the author is taking pains to increase the negative thematic dimensions of the Elders' character. Mimetically, the testimony of the Elders would have a similar impact on the NA, in perfect opposition to the reaction of the people: "The assembly (συναγωγὴ) believed them, as [they were] elders of the people and judges." Evidently the people had little concern for the lack of proper jurisprudence, for "they condemned her to die." This death would probably imply stoning, as specified in Deut 22:21–22 and John 8:5. Thus, the trial would appear to be "officially" over; the witnesses have testified and the verdict has been passed. However, in vv. 42–44 we learn that Susanna's ordeal is far from over.

3.2.10. *Susanna's Prayer (Verses 42–44)*

> (42) Susanna cried aloud with a great voice and said, "O God, the eternal, the one who knows hidden things, seeing all things before their beginning, (43) you know that they [the Elders] have borne false witness against me. Now, I am about to die even though I have done none of these [things] of which they wickedly accused me." (44) And the Lord heard her cry.

In the next section of the story, vv. 42–44, we find Susanna's only response to the false testimony of the Elders: her prayer to God. This, her third and last piece of quoted speech, is really the capstone of the narrator's mimetic portrait of Susanna. Not even after the trial concludes will she perform any action or speak any dialogue. Thus, it is important to pay close attention to her speech in this section, for it will be the last mimetic dimension added to her character.

She begins her prayer by crying aloud, exactly as she had done in v. 24 in response to the Elders' threat; the Greek is even the same: καὶ ἀνεβόησεν φωνῇ μεγάλῃ in v. 24 and ἀνεβόησεν δὲ φωνῇ μεγάλῃ in v. 42. Her characterization of God in vv. 42–43 is very important not only to the NA, as I noted above, but also to the AA, who would probably see it as yet another attempt by the author to dissociate Susanna's religiosity and its concomitant ethical and moral systems with that of the Elders. She addresses her supplication to God, whom she characterizes as "eternal," as well as "the one who knows hidden things, seeing all things before their beginning."[87] This view of God is of utmost importance in the story, because it supplements her sentiment in v. 35 as well as complements the Elders' "blindness" to religious matters, as evidenced in vv. 9 and 20.

Susanna continues her prayer in v. 43 by reminding God, "you know that they [the elders] have borne false witness against me." Thus, it now becomes clear

86. Steussy, *Gardens in Babylon*, 138, lays out the Elders' version of events in comparison with the narrator's version in a table.

87. For the form of Susanna's prayer, see Collins, *Daniel*, 432.

why Susanna offers no defense on her behalf, but instead trusts in the Lord (v. 35). Her trust stems from her view of God as omniscient and able to act in history and time to save those faithful to God. While this is hardly a radical theology, it seems to have evaded the Elders, and so once again the AA might sense the strengthening of the thematic opposition between Susanna and the Elders. Curiously, though, neither Susanna nor the story ever engages the question of theodicy.[88] This lack of engagement has much to do with the theological vision of the story. Daniel J. Harrington, S. J., in his recent survey of apocryphal literature, uses the theme of suffering as a hermeneutical device to read each text in that corpus. He notes, "The message of the Susanna story is that God will vindicate the innocent sufferer. The episode illustrates the power of trust in God and of prayer in the midst of suffering."[89] Indeed, the story itself never waivers in its endorsement of God's saving action on behalf of the virtuous. This lack of speculation into the issue of theodicy only reinforces Susanna's religiosity. Hers is a "blind" faith, unlike the Elders' faith in an unseeing God.

Susanna concludes her prayer by noting, "Now, I am about to die even though I have done none of these [things] of which they wickedly accused me." Susanna knows her fate if God does not intervene will be death, yet it is significant that she does not ask God for help. Again, Susanna's view of God assumes that God will act to save the faithful, and thus she does not deem it necessary to request such assistance. This theological vision is verified in the curt notice provided in v. 44: "And the Lord heard her cry." Again, the story and Susanna herself seem unconcerned with the possible question of why God did not act before the trial, i.e., why God did not hear her earlier cry in v. 24. For the NA, such speculation would most likely not arise, given their reliance on the narratorial voice. However, the AA can indulge in such guesswork, and could possibly find an answer in the presence and content of Susanna's prayer compared with other prayers by women in the apocryphal corpus.[90]

In the Greek Additions to Esther, Esther prays to God (Add Esth C 12–30) and addresses God as having "knowledge of all things," and "Master of all dominion." She prays to God for courage so that she may appeal to Artaxerxes to foil Haman's genocidal plan. In her prayer, she appeals to God:

> Do not let them laugh at our downfall; but turn their plan against them, and make an example of him who began this against us...save us by your hand, and help me, who am alone and have no helper but you, O Lord... O God, whose might is over all, hear the voice of the despairing, and save us from the hands of evildoers.[91]

Thus, Esther finds herself in a dangerous, fearful situation in which she has no helper, no one to plead her case, and so she turns to God. Similarly, in the story of Judith the title character also faces a dangerous situation in which she could

88. For a brief introduction to this issue, see James L. Crenshaw, "Theodicy," *ABD* 6:444–47.

89. Daniel J. Harrington, S. J., *Invitation to the Apocrypha* (Grand Rapids: Eerdmans, 1999), 116.

90. For this topic, see Craven, "'From where Will My Help Come?'".

91. For a discussion of this prayer, see Moore, *Daniel*, 208–15; and Levenson, *Esther*, 84–86.

perish and, having no one else to turn to, turns to God. In 9:2–14, she cries out to God with a loud voice (ἐβόησεν φωνῇ μεγάλῃ):

> O God, my God, hear me also—a widow. For you have done these things and those that went before and those that followed. You have designed the things that are now, and those that are to come... Look at their [i.e. the Assyrians] pride, and send your wrath upon their heads... For your strength does not depend on numbers, nor your might on the powerful. But you are the God of the lowly, helper of the oppressed, upholder of the weak, protector of the forsaken, savior of those without hope. Please, please, God of my father, God of the heritage of Israel, Lord of heaven and earth, Creator of the waters, King of all your creation, hear my prayer![92]

In both cases, the view of God found in the respective prayers dictates the actions and speech of Esther and Judith. Also, in both cases, the women survive their dangerous situation, and even prosper.

If the AA again connects Susanna with stories of other "heroines" like Esther and Judith, then two effects would likely result. First, the AA would treat this connection as foreshadowing, and expect Susanna to be delivered, just as Esther and Judith were. Second, her thematic significance would again be elevated. That is, her connection with these women possibly will serve to place her in a similar thematic category, viz., the heroic woman standing for all oppressed peoples who trust in the Lord. In any case, the story has now taken on a new progression created by the instability in v. 44. Put another way, both audiences would recognize the suspense and foreshadowing initiated in v. 44, and wait with baited breath the resolution of the instability, viz., the fate of Susanna.

3.2.11. *Introduction to Daniel and His Challenge (Verses 45–51)*

> (45) And as she was being carried off to be killed, God awakened the holy spirit of a young man whose name was Daniel. (46) He cried aloud with a great voice, "I am clean of this woman's blood!" (47) All the people turned to him and said, "What did you say?" (48) Standing in the midst of them, he said, "Are you idiots, O Israelites? Would you condemn a daughter of Israel without closely examining or discovering the clear truth? (49) Return to the court! For these men have given false evidence against her." (50) So, all the people hastily returned. The [other] Elders said to [Daniel], "Come, sit down in our midst and report to us. For God has given you the right of an Elder." (51) Daniel replied, "Separate them far from one another and I will examine them."

The instability caused by Susanna's prayer and God's hearing of that prayer is resolved partially in the next section, viz., vv. 45–51. In v. 45, we hear the introductory phrase "And as she was being carried off to be killed," which might cause the AA, and possibly the NA, to recognize the allusion to Deut 22:24, where it states that a convicted adulteress will be taken to the gates of the city to be stoned. This initial phrase leads into what the NA could constitute as proof of Susanna's faith, her view of God: "God awakened the holy spirit of a young man

92. For an examination of this prayer, see Moore, *Judith*, 187–97. Moore's examination is especially useful because he compares Esther's prayer in Addition C with Judith's in Jdt 9. See also Craven, "Judith 9: Strength and Deceit," in *Prayer from Alexander to Constantine: A Critical Anthology* (ed. M. C. Kiley; London: Routledge, 1997), 59–64.

whose name was Daniel."[93] For the NA, this action on the part of God might simply validate Susanna's trust in God, which the narrator mentions in v. 35. A whole set of questions could arise for the AA, though. First, who is this Daniel? The name is obviously appropriate; it means "My judge is God," which fits the story perfectly.[94] Yet the AA might pursue the question further and ask if this Daniel is the same Daniel of the book in the Hebrew Bible. In the context of this story, this Daniel is young and unknown. Also, in v. 64 there is a note concerning his growing fame and reputation. This internal data, along with external historical and canonical connections could lead to an affirmative answer, but in the fictional world of the story, he is but an unknown young man whom God has chosen to aid Susanna.

Obviously, Daniel's character gets off to a good start. The information in v. 45 would cause the NA to recognize that Daniel already had "the holy spirit" within him, and that God acts to rouse it. The mimetic force of such data is strong; Daniel is painted as a spirit-filled youth whom God chooses to be God's instrument. The AA, too, might be impressed by this initial thematic dimension of Daniel's character. It is possible that the AA, based on v. 45, might even include Daniel in the thematic opposition created by the author in the story prior to v. 45. As we will see, this inclusion is more than merited; as I mentioned above, Daniel is in many ways the perfect mimetic and thematic counterpart to the Elders.

The narrator wastes no time in fleshing out the mimetic dimensions of Daniel's character. In v. 46, Daniel speaks his first piece of quoted dialogue. He first cries "aloud with a great voice," just as Susanna has done twice so far in the story, in vv. 24 and 42. This repetition may signal the AA that there is either an important connection between Susanna and Daniel, or that there is something significant in what the characters say following their cry. However, unlike Susanna, it seems that Daniel's voice is heard by those surrounding him, as we will see in v. 47. Daniel shouts, "I am clean (or 'innocent') of this woman's blood!" Thus, Daniel here is disagreeing with the guilty verdict passed in v. 41, which is exactly what the NA would expect him to do, given his status as God's instrument. For the AA, Daniel's words might ring yet another intertextual bell. In Matthew's Gospel, after Jesus appears before Pilate, Pilate tells the crowd, "I am innocent of this man's blood" (27:24).[95] Interestingly, though, in Matt 27:25, the people agree to accept responsibility for the execution, whereas in our story, they are more than willing to redress any errors. This echo of Matthew would only reinforce the aforementioned thematic connection between Susanna and Jesus.

In response to the people's query in v. 47 ("What did you say?"), Daniel makes an important statement in vv. 48–49. He begins by "standing in the midst

93. The OG here reads, "An angel of the Lord appeared just as she was being led away to be put to death. And the angel gave, as he was ordered, a spirit of understanding to a youth named Daniel."

94. See Collins, *Daniel*, 433: "this is the only story where Daniel has a role that matches his name."

95. Robert H. Gundry, in his *Matthew: A Commentary on His Handbook for a Mixed Church under Persecution* (2d ed.; Grand Rapids: Eerdmans, 1994), 564–65, mentions this connection.

of them," just as the Elders had done in v. 34 prior to giving their false testimony. He then asks what the NA has probably been asking since v. 27: "Are you idiots, O Israelites?" Following this bit of ingratiation, Daniel proceeds to lay out his real concern: "Would you condemn a daughter of Israel without closely examining or discovering the clear truth?" The question here raises two issues. The first issue is what Daniel is implying by the term "daughter of Israel." He may here simply be trying to raise the sympathy of the crowd for Susanna by identifying her ethnic background with their own.

The second issue has to do with implication(s) of "closely examining" and "discovering the clear truth." The NA would probably connect these phrases with Susanna's lack of defense and assume that Daniel has now arrived to provide "the clear truth" to the crowd, a truth which Susanna, the Elders, and God presumably already know. The AA, on the other hand, might connect Daniel's comments with the lack of proper judicial procedure at Susanna's trial. In *m. Sanh.* 6:1, a provision is made for a last-minute acquittal:

> If then they found him innocent they set him free; otherwise he goes forth to be stoned. A herald goes out before him [calling], "Such-a-one, the son of such-a-one, is going forth to be stoned for that he committed such or such an offense. Such-a-one and such-a-one are witnesses against him. If any man knoweth aught in favour of his acquittal let him come and plead it.

Thus, since Susanna was not afforded this right, the AA might see Daniel's comment regarding "the clear truth" as an indictment of the way in which the Elders officiated the trial. Also, as Brüll and subsequently Kay have suggested, Daniel's words could also echo those of Simeon b. Shetah in *Avot* 1:9: "Examine the witnesses abundantly, and be cautious in thy words, lest they learn from them to give false answers."[96] Thus, the AA might indeed connect Daniel's words with Mishnaic literature, or they may simply agree with Collins when he writes, "Daniel's question [in v. 48]...suggests that the Israelites are neglecting common procedures or even common sense."[97]

In v. 49, after ordering all present (including the Elders) to "Return to the court!", Daniel finally reveals the secret that, up to this point, only Susanna, the Elders, and God knows: "these men have given false evidence against her."[98] Of course, both audiences also shared in this knowledge as well. By exposing this secret, Daniel not only shatters the ironic tension caused by the difference in knowledge, but also established one of the final instabilities of the story. That is, by announcing the Elders have perjured themselves, Daniel initiates the narrative progression that will carry this instability to its resolution in vv. 61–62. In addition, this announcement heightens both the thematic and mimetic aspects of Daniel's character. The NA might recall the information provided in v. 45 and now recognize that, based on his revelatory knowledge, Daniel is truly an instrument of God. Likewise, the AA could view this open challenge to the Elders as a

96. See Brüll, "Das apokryphische Susanna-Buch," 64; and Kay, *APOT* 1:644.
97. Collins, *Daniel*, 433.
98. Daniel's order to return to the court is in keeping with *m. Sanh.* 6:1.

validation of their inclusion of Daniel in the thematic opposition in the story between the Elders and Susanna, her family, and now Daniel.

The people obey Daniel's command in v. 50 and thus betray their fickleness; earlier in vv. 29 and 32 they had obeyed the Elders and now they act on Daniel's behalf. The other Elders then speak to Daniel. It seems obvious in the story that these Elders have little or no judicial power.[99] They invite Daniel to "sit down in our midst and report to us." Why would Daniel be allowed to enter into a group or council of Elders at his young age? The other Elders provide an answer: "God has given you the right of an elder." Thus, the Elders here seem to share the NA's view of Daniel as God's chosen instrument.[100] The AA might notice an intertextual allusion here between Daniel and Jesus in the Temple (Luke 2.46). Both are young men: Daniel is traditionally said to be twelve, and Jesus is referred to in Luke 2:43 as a παῖς, i.e., a pre-pubescent boy. Also, both are demonstrating incredible discernment for their age and are exhibiting that knowledge in front of wise or important persons much older than they.[101] Thus, Daniel could be seen as a savior figure not only mimetically but also thematically. However, Daniel neither sits in the midst of the Elders nor reports to them; instead he proceeds with the retrial process. He tells the other Elders: "Separate them far from one another and I will examine them," just as the Elders had examined one another in v. 14.[102] The AA might recognize in Daniel's intention an awareness of and wish to fulfill *m. Sanh.* 5:2: "The more a judge tests the evidence the more he is deserving of praise… [I]f they [the witnesses] contradict one another, whether during the inquiries or the cross-examination, their evidence becomes invalid." As we will see, the Elders' testimony is indeed tested in Daniel's cross-examination.

3.2.12. *Susanna's Trial, Part Two: Daniel's Cross-Examinations (Verses 52–59)*

> (52) When they were separated one from the other, [Daniel] called one of them and said to him, "You old man of wicked days, your sins which you committed in the past have now returned: (53) making unjust judgments, condemning the innocent and acquitting the guilty while the Lord said, 'An innocent one and a righteous one shall not be killed.' (54) Therefore, if you indeed saw this woman, tell me, under which tree did you see them having intercourse with each other?" He answered, "Under the mastic tree." (55) Daniel replied, "Appropriately, you have lied and it will affect your own head! For already an angel of God has received the sentence from God and will split you in two!"

99. In fact, the OG version does not include these other elders. Instead, after the Elders are separated, Daniel remarks "Now don't take into consideration that these are elders, saying (to yourself), 'They would not lie.' I, however, will interrogate them as things occur to me." The Th version removes this phrase, and thus makes sure that at least some persons of authority in the narrative are honorable. Moore, *Daniel*, 110, comments that this may be a reason why the early Church had a preference for Th.

100. This awareness on the part of the other elders could serve to ease the critique of those in power in Th.

101. For this episode in Lk, see Joseph A. Fitzmyer, *The Gospel According to Luke I–IX* (AB 28; New York: Doubleday, 1970), 434–48.

102. The verb here is ἀνακρινῶ, and carries a legal connotation.

> (56) After [the first Elder was] removed, [Daniel] ordered the other to be brought. He said to him, "Seed of Canaan and not of Judah! Beauty has deceived you and lust has twisted your heart! (57) You have done this to the daughters of Israel and they, fearful, were having intercourse with you, but a daughter of Judah would not submit to your wickedness. (58) Now, therefore, tell me, under which tree did you catch them having intercourse with each other?" He answered, "Under the evergreen oak." (59) Daniel responded, "Appropriately, you have lied and it will affect your own head! For the angel of God is waiting with a sword to cut you in two, so that you both will be destroyed!"

The next section, vv. 52–55, contains Daniel's cross-examination of the first Elder, although he hardly cross-examines him. In fact, Daniel only asks one question. First, though, I should call attention to the first phrase of v. 52, "When they were separated one from the other." This separation parallels the previous mimetic separation in v. 13, as well as the thematic separation in v. 10. It was only with the collusion of the Elders in v. 14 that the plot to rape Susanna came together, and now that collusion has been terminated. This separation builds on the instability created in v. 49, i.e., now that the Elders have been separated in preparation for questioning, the progression begun in v. 49 is furthered.

Prior to Daniel's only question to this Elder, he engages in a rather vitriolic attack on his character in vv. 52–53. Daniel begins by referring to the Elder as an "old man of wicked days," which for the AA could reinforce the thematic opposition between Daniel (young, godly, wise boy) and the Elders (old, God-less men). The reference to "wicked days" could signify the Elder's own life and activities or, given the story's narrative setting, it could refer to the generation that lived prior to the Babylonian Exile. Some biblical sources, primarily the Deuteronomistic History (DH) judge that generation to be wicked, which then caused the destruction of Judah and Jerusalem, as well as the second deportation by Nebuchadnezzar.[103] Daniel then expounds on the Elder's bad character: "your sins which you committed in the past have now returned: making unjust judgments, condemning the innocent and acquitting the guilty while the Lord said, 'An innocent one and a righteous one shall not be killed'."[104] This short catalog of vices is important for several reasons. First, it demonstrates Daniel's revelatory knowledge of the Elder's past, and thus might serve to heighten the NA's view of Daniel as an instrument of God. Second, it reveals the Elder's true character and values, which are in opposition to God's Law(s). This revelation, while not a surprise to either audience, would certainly be a shock to the other characters. Ironically, Daniel seems to be prejudicing the view of the crowd and the other elders with regards to the Elder's testimony, much in the same way that the Elders tried to influence the verdict against Susanna in vv. 32 and 34. Third, Daniel's comment regarding the Elder's past sins returning sounds like the view of retributive justice adumbrated in the Deuteronomistic History, and thus would shed some light on the meaning of "wicked days" in v. 52.[105]

103. See 2 Kgs 24–25, as well as the parallel material in Jer 52.

104. This quotation from the Lord seems to be an allusion to Exod 23:7.

105. See Martin Noth, *The Deuteronomistic History* (trans. Jane Doull et al.; 2d ed.; JSOTSup 15; Sheffield: JSOT Press, 1991), 134. The Deuteronomistic Historian (Dtr.) was seeking "the true

In v. 54, Daniel finally asks his one and only question of this witness, "Therefore, if you indeed saw this woman, tell me, under which tree did you see them having intercourse with each other?" This, in my opinion, is a baffling question; why would Daniel ask about a tree? In their testimony in vv. 36–41, neither Elder mentions a tree, so why would Daniel choose this particular question? It certainly is not in accordance with proper legal procedure, at least as found in the Mishnah. In *m. Sanh.* 5:1, examiners are expected to "prove witnesses with seven inquiries." Here, though, Daniel only asks one, and a seemingly inexplicable one at that. However, it could be that Daniel's revelatory knowledge mentioned in v. 45 might include the awareness, made clear in the coming testimony, that the Elders did not bother to get their stories straight. In any case, this Elder answers, "Under the mastic tree [σχῖνον]." In addition to being his last instance of quoted speech, this response also sets up the famous wordplay that will be concluded in the next verse, and which has fascinated exegetes since the time of Julius Africanus (ca. 160–240) and Origen (ca. 185–254).[106] Curiously, though, Daniel rushes to condemn his testimony (and subsequently his life) without offering any proof of perjury. Daniel responds, "Appropriately, you have lied and it will affect your own head![107] For already an angel of God has received the sentence from God and will split you in two!" The verb used for "split" here, viz., σχίσει, completes the wordplay begun in v. 54. Even though the NA and the AA would probably recognize and even trust Daniel's judgment here, the characters in the story must be a tad baffled. After all, Daniel has just sentenced an Elder to death based on one question. As we will see in the next section, Daniel again passes judgment on the other Elder, and the crowd seems to have no problem with carrying out Daniel's guilty verdict.

In vv. 56–59, Daniel moves on to interrogate the second Elder. The first Elder is removed and after the second is brought forth, Daniel launches into an inflammatory invective, just as he did previously in vv. 52–53 with the first Elder. He first addresses the second Elder as "Seed of Canaan and not of Judah!" This is a curious description, especially given the aforementioned possibility that the Elders were of the generation alive during the destruction of Jerusalem. "Canaan" here probably refers to Noah's grandson who is cursed in Gen 9:25–27 for not

meaning of the history of Israel from the occupation to the destruction [of Judah in 587 B.C.E.]. The meaning which he discovered was that God was recognizably at work in this history, continuously meeting the accelerating moral decline with warnings and punishments and, finally, when these proved fruitless, with total annihilation. Dtr., then, perceives a just divine retribution in the history of the people." See also John H. Hayes, *An Introduction to Old Testament Study* (Nashville: Abingdon, 1979), 215: "The author intended to demonstrate why such calamity [i.e. the destruction of Jerusalem] had befallen God's people by showing that Israel and Judah had constantly been confronted with the law at every stage of history but had constantly not lived in accordance with the Deuteronomic demands. The calamity was not a tragedy; it was judgment."

106. See Moore, *Daniel*, 110–11. For the correspondence between these two figures, see Julius Africanus, "A Letter to Origen from Africanus about the History of Susanna," in *ANF* 4:385; and Origen, "A Letter from Origen to Africanus," in *ANF* 4: 386–92.

107. This phrase is difficult to translate and to understand. Literally, it means: "Correct, you have lied in your own head."

covering Noah's naked body.[108] In the context of the Genesis story, Canaan evidently did not display enough sexual modesty because he did not cover Noah, so he is cursed.[109] Walter Brueggemann discusses Canaan's offense and concludes that the larger intent of the passage is to

> sharpen the theological contrast between Israel and Canaan. The prohibitions of sexual violation and indignity [found in Lev. 18.7–8, a passage related to the Genesis account] embody a rejection of Canaanite ways of life and self-securing. Israel understands that life is premised on grace and not on the manipulation of the powers of life and well-being. *In such a polemical context, Canaan is not to be understood as an ethnic grouping but as a characterization of all those who practice alternatives to obeying the sovereignty and trusting the graciousness of Yahweh.*[110]

In our story, neither Elder was concerned enough about the social and religious shame their act might bring to control themselves. In sum, Moore seems to agree with Brueggemann when he notes, "All things considered, we should probably understand the phrase to mean, not that the second elder was literally a descendant of Canaan, but that he had *acted* like Canaanites."[111]

Of course, the books of Joshua and Judges provide us with ample "evidence" that Canaanites were sexually immoral, at least by Yahwistic standards. This connection of the second Elder with the Canaanites is intriguing, and it could remind the AA of the description in v. 5 of the Elders as judges. In my discussion of v. 5, I noted that to label the Elders as judges is ironic, because they do not conform to the model of a judge as we find it in the book of Judges. However, Daniel does fit the pattern of a judge nicely, and as such adds another component to the already large thematic and mimetic opposition between Daniel and the Elders. Indeed, if Daniel is seen as a judge figure, not only does my above connection of Daniel to the DH make more sense, but also his address to the second Elder ("Seed of Canaan and not of Judah!") makes perfect sense. That is, Daniel here is relegating this Elder to the same level as the Canaanites in the book of Judges, which hammers home the point that "this Jewish leader is no true Jew."[112] In sum, Daniel is attacking this Elder's Jewishness, his belief in God, and God's Law(s), which, as both audiences know, is sorely lacking.

Daniel continues in v. 56 by telling the second Elder, "Beauty has deceived you and lust has twisted your heart!" Again, this is old news to both audiences. The AA in particular has been aware of the connection between lust and self-control since v. 8. The fact that Daniel is again voicing what both audiences have noticed throughout the story would only lend credence to his information and judgment. Daniel's revelatory knowledge of past events is exhibited again in

108. Even though 9:22 states that Ham saw Noah's nakedness, it is Canaan who is cursed. Interestingly, in the OG this Elder is linked with Sidon, the firstborn of Canaan (Gen 10:15). Moore, *Daniel*, 111–12, discusses the implications of this identification.

109. For this passage generally, see Gerhard von Rad, *Genesis* (OTL; Philadelphia: Westminster, 1972), 137–39.

110. Walter Brueggemann, *Genesis* (IBC; Atlanta: John Knox, 1982), 90–91 (italics mine).

111. Moore, *Daniel*, 112.

112. Collins, *Daniel*, 434.

v. 57, as it was with the first Elder in vv. 52–53. Here Daniel states, "You have done this to the daughters of Israel and they, fearful, were having intercourse with you, but a daughter of Judah would not submit to your wickedness." Thus, Daniel is compounding the guilt of the Elder by noting this is not the first time he has extorted sex from women. Here again, Daniel's remarks prior to his one question seem like an attempt to sway the crowd by introducing "prior bad acts" into the record. There is, of course, a problem with Daniel's statement. Given that he himself characterized Susanna as a "daughter of Israel" in v. 48, how are we to take his description of the daughters of Israel here? I think the usage of "daughter of Israel" has more to do with the context of the utterance and its contiguity to Daniel's address of "O Israelites" to the crowd. Here, however, Daniel makes a distinction between the daughters of Israel and the daughters of Judah. Given the story's narrative setting, i.e., after the exile of Judeans to Babylon, it is likely that more characters would identify with the title of "daughters of Judah" than "daughters of Israel." Both Moore and Collins note that this issue may also be reflective of later tensions between Palestinian Jews and Samaritans, "who considered themselves the heirs of North Israel."[113] In either case, Shaye J. D. Cohen's assessment sums up the matter nicely:

> Susanna has behaved as a true daughter of Judah; daughters of Israel have succumbed to the elders' threats, but not Susanna. The contrast between "Israel" and "Judah" is stark and somewhat puzzling, but what is clear is that a son or daughter of Judah behaves virtuously, even in the face of temptation (unlike the Elders) or compulsion (like Susanna).[114]

Cohen's remark would most likely ring true for the NA, i.e., what matters is that Susanna has acted virtuously.

Following this tirade, Daniel finally asks the second Elder the same question he asked of the first: "Under which tree did you catch them having intercourse with each other?" Again, I can offer no good explanation why Daniel decides to inquire about a specific tree. Even so, the second Elder answers, "Under the evergreen oak [πρῖνον]." Here again, we have the beginning of a wordplay as we did in vv. 54–55. More importantly, this answer seals the verdict; the Elders' testimony does not coincide within permissible parameters, and thus is rendered invalid.[115] Daniel, who knew their testimony was false from the start, responds accordingly, "Appropriately, you have lied and it will affect your own head! For the angel of God is waiting with a sword to cut [πρίσαι] you in two." Here the wordplay begun in v. 58 is completed. Unlike the verdict for the first Elder, Daniel now passes a sentence on both Elders: "you both will be destroyed!" Thus,

113. Moore, *Daniel*, 112. See also Collins, *Daniel*, 434.

114. Shaye J. D. Cohen, "Ioudaios: 'Judaean' and 'Jew' in Susanna, First Maccabees, and Second Maccabees," in *Geschichte–Tradition–Reflexion: Festschrift für Martin Hengel zum 70. Geburtstag*. Vol. 1, *Judentum* (ed. Peter Schäfer; Tübingen: J. C. B. Mohr [Paul Siebeck], 1996), 211–20 (213).

115. In *m. Sanh.* 5:3, various examples are given of acceptable variations in testimony that may still be considered valid.

Daniel exposes the deception and malicious behavior of the Elders. In so doing, he not only validates the NA's and the AA's view(s) of him, but partially resolves the instability he created in v. 49. That is, the Elders have now been sentenced to death and Susanna will undoubtedly be exonerated.

3.2.13. *The Response of the Crowd and the Execution of the Elders (Verses 60–62)*

> (60) [After this,] the whole assembly cried aloud with a great voice and praised God, who saves those hoping in him. (61) They rose up against the two Elders because out of their own mouths, Daniel convicted them of bearing false witness. The assembly then did to them the same wicked thing [they were going to do] to their neighbor; (62) acting according to the law of Moses, they killed them. Thus, innocent blood was saved in that day.

In v. 60, the assembly (συναγωγὴ) responds to Daniel's verdict against the two Elders. In fact, "the whole assembly cried aloud with a great voice," just as Susanna had done in vv. 24 and 42, and as Daniel did in v. 46. However, unlike these previous instances, the assembly here is not shouting a cry for help or voicing a protest. Instead, they "praised God, who saves those hoping in him." This praising of God and narratorial note regarding God's character functions to concretize Susanna's view of God. In other words, the story itself has now adopted Susanna's view of God as its own norm, as part of its accepted world-view. This adoption is likely the result of Daniel's action(s), i.e., the only alternative (or competing) view of God and religiosity in the story is represented by the Elders, who have been proven to be liars. Thus, we are told in v. 61 that the assembly "rose up against the two elders because out of their own mouths, Daniel convicted them of bearing false witness." By this action, then, the assembly has definitively turned against the Elders.

Of course, the assembly does more than turn on the Elders: "The assembly then did to them the same wicked thing [they were going to do] to their neighbor; acting according to the law of Moses, they killed them."[116] These data is important for a number of reasons. First, it shows that the assembly obeys the Mosaic Law, which is a further indication of the story's move away from the Elders and towards Susanna's conception of God. Throughout the story, Susanna, her family, and Daniel are identified with the Law, while the Elders consciously dissociate themselves from it. Second, and more importantly, this action on the part of the assembly might provide the AA with a clue as to the background of the story itself. The fact that the assembly did the same thing to the Elders that the Elders were going to do to Susanna is the key point for this issue. This type of retribution is mentioned in Deut 19:18–21:

> If the witness is a false witness, having testified falsely against another, then you shall do to the false witness just as the false witness had meant to do to the other. So you shall purge the evil from your midst. The rest shall hear and be afraid, and a crime such as

116. In comparison with the OG, the Th version here seems tame. The former paints the death of the Elders in a more descriptive manner: "So they silenced [or muzzled] them, led them off, and pitched them into a ravine, whereupon, the angel of the Lord hurled lightning [fire] in their midst."

> this shall never again be committed among you. Show no pity: life for life, eye for eye, tooth for tooth, hand for hand, foot for foot.[117]

During the Second Temple period, a controversy arose over the interpretation of this passage. To summarize briefly, the Sadducees felt that an overt act was required in order to carry out the prescription in the above passage, while the Pharisees held that the intention of a person should carry equal weight. With regards to perjurious witnesses, this dispute is exemplified in the Talmudic tale of Simeon b. Shetah's son, in which the son was convicted by false testimony, and agreed to die so that his accusers could be punished.[118] The fate of the Elders in our story, though, is different; they are punished *prior* to Susanna's sentencing. This sequence is in agreement with the Pharisaic position on this issue. Suffice it to say here that the AA could recognize this connection, and possibly see Daniel and the assembly acting in a more procedurally correct fashion than the Elders.

Another possible reading for the AA of the connection between Susanna and Deut 19:18–21 could be an intertextual echo of Judith. That is, the Deuteronomic language in 19:20 ("The rest shall hear and be afraid, and a crime such as this shall never again be committed among you") could resonate with the last line of the book of Judith ("No one ever again spread terror among the Israelites during the lifetime of Judith, or for a long time after her death"). The AA might make a (tenuous?) connection between the enactment of the Deuteronomy passage in Susanna and the ending of the book of Judith, thereby establishing yet another link between the stories of Susanna and Judith. For the NA, of course, the execution of the Elders is seen as simply the logical outcome of the story. After all, the Elders are almost always presented in a negative light, so it is little wonder that they perish in an end of their own making. In fact, the narrator ends this section not by commenting on the Elders, but by stating, "Thus, innocent blood was saved in that day." As Collins notes, "this statement is the first conclusion of the story, reflecting the original emphasis on the motif of judgment."[119] At this point, the plot of the story is complete: God/Daniel has delivered Susanna and the Elders have been destroyed by their own lust.

3.2.14. *The Epilogue (Verses 63–64)*

> (63) [Following this,] Hilkiah and his wife gave praise for their daughter together with her husband Joakim and all [their] relatives because [Susanna] was found innocent of a disgraceful deed. (64) [Because of this,] Daniel was great among the people from that day and beyond.

However, this is not the last word. In v. 63, we hear that, "Hilkiah and his wife gave praise for their daughter together with her husband Joakim and all [their] relatives because [Susanna] was found innocent of a disgraceful deed." We have

117. For this passage in general, see A. D. H. Mayes, *Deuteronomy* (NCB; Grand Rapids: Eerdmans, 1981), 288–91; and Gerhard von Rad, *Deuteronomy* (trans. Dorothea Barton; OTL; Philadelphia: Westminster, 1966), 129.

118. This story is preserved in *y. Sanh.* 6:3.

119. Collins, *Daniel*, 435.

come full circle; in vv. 1–4, we are introduced to Joakim, Hilkiah and his wife, and Susanna, and here they are all mentioned again. The AA could see this as a restatement of the opening verses of the story, where Susanna is firmly placed in a patriarchal context as wife and daughter. The effect of bookending Susanna as wife and daughter in the story might be taken as an attempt to remind both audiences that Susanna always acted appropriately, i.e., she never questioned or challenged the prevailing expectation(s) of her as a woman. That is, much like Judith, Susanna seems to be ultimately affirming of her patriarchally assigned station(s). In this regard, Marti J. Steussy remarks,

> The story does not tell us that [Susanna] desires self-determination, only that she resists determination by the elders. Susanna's response to the elders suggests that she is content to be controlled by the Lord; the characterization of her as virtuous daughter, wife, and mother suggests that she also acquiesces to control by her husband and parents.[120]

Of course, unlike Judith, Susanna never experiments with the porous nature of gender code(s), even going as far as accepting the help of a young boy rather than publicly aiding in her own defense. This could be one of the few instances in which the story of Susanna is not complementary with that of Judith. On the other hand, given the honor/shame issues in the story, Steussy's comment on this verse proves illuminating: "Susanna's family celebrates her innocence (or perhaps the recognition of such), rather than her survival."[121]

In fact, the Th version gives the impression that the story is finally not about Susanna at all. In the final verse of the story, we hear that "[Because of this,] Daniel was great among the people from that day and beyond." Collins notes that this verse in Th probably serves as a transition to ch. 1 of Daniel, which immediately follows the story of Susanna in Th.[122] However, in the context of the story, such an ending is unsettling because it seems to be an etiological appendix, having little to do with the story itself. It certainly does not cohere with the previous judge-like portrayal of Daniel, which would necessitate Daniel's withdrawal from the story after the delivery of Susanna.

3.3. *Conclusion*

I would now like to offer some concluding observations on the story of Susanna and the rhetoric I detect in it as a member of both audiences, as well as a real reader. First, I will briefly analyze the ways in which the author provides different dimensions and/or functions for the characters in the narrative before commenting on the story as a whole. I will begin with the mimetic aspect of Susanna's character. She is described as beautiful, fearful of the Lord, educated in the Law, a daughter, a wife, and a mother. She also speaks and performs a few actions. On

120. Steussy, *Gardens in Babylon*, 118 n. 48.

121. Steussy, *Gardens in Babylon*, 115.

122. Collins, *Daniel*, 435. See also J. W. van Henten, "The Story of Susanna as a Pre-Rabbinic Midrash to Dan 1:1–2," in *Variety of Forms: Dutch Studies in Midrash* (ed. A. Kuyt et al.; Publications of the Juda Palache Institute 5; Amsterdam: University of Amsterdam Press, 1990), 1–14.

the basis of these data, does the narrator provide a portrait complete enough to create the illusion of "a plausible person"? That is, does the NA have enough information about Susanna to constitute her as real? Some scholars think not. However, this issue is complicated, and Phelan notes that flexible criteria are more useful in this regard than fixed ones. He writes, "Since my goal is to understand the principles upon which a narrative is constructed, I shall seek to make my judgments according to what I know or can infer about the conditions under which a given author is operating."[123] For my interpretation of the mimetic component of Susanna's character, this means that I need to evaluate the way in which other Jewish writers of the first century B.C.E. portray female characters mimetically.

Esther, Judith, and Sarah are all described as beautiful, yet they are never described in detail. We are simply told of their beauty with no physiognomic information as evidence. In fact, in none of these works are we given any extensive physical descriptions or even many images of physical surroundings. Given these portrayals, Susanna does indeed have a mimetic function, i.e., Jewish narrative literature during this period does not foreground the mimetic aspect of character. This should come as no surprise; Hebrew Bible literature in general is not overly concerned with the mimetic aspect of character.[124] It is the thematic component of character that receives the lion's share of attention during this period. It is to this issue I will now turn.

Given the mimetic portrait of Susanna in the story, the thematic dimensions of her character are easily identified. Susanna is described as beautiful, religious, and God-identified in explicit contrast to the Elders. Because Susanna's attributes, speech, and actions all point to her religious identity, it is likely that the author is using her to make a comment on righteous, religious persons who suffer. That is, Susanna can be seen as standing for all of the righteous Jews who suffer. In that capacity, the outcome of the story would be an incentive for continued belief; if Susanna can keep her faith in God throughout her trial and ultimately be vindicated, then the readers of her story can as well. Put another way, the story develops the thematic dimensions of Susanna's character and the progression of the narrative ultimately develops a thematic function for her character. The proposition put forth by the thematic function of Susanna's character seems clear. Her refusal to be affected by social shame, her unwillingness to be a passive participant in her own rape because of the resultant sin, and her willingness to allow God to defend her highlights her religious identity in contrast to the Elders' (mis)conception of God. Because of Susanna's ultimate acquittal and the Elders' execution, the author is using Susanna's character to persuade the reader(s) that Susanna's faith and idea of God is better than that of the Elders. Thus, the thematizing in the story that centers on Susanna's character leads the AA to identify with and wish to imitate Susanna's religiosity.

If the character of Susanna has few mimetic dimensions, the Elders would seem to have even fewer. They do speak and perform actions, but are never

123. Phelan, *Reading People, Reading Plots*, 12.
124. See Alter, *The Art of Biblical Narrative*, 114.

physically described. However, the narrator does provide us with information surrounding their motive(s) for acting they way they do, and it is this information that makes up for the lack of physiognomic data. That is, by showing and telling us *why* the Elders pursue Susanna, we are in a better position to comprehend their actions, and thus they seem more "real" to us. Thus, while the Elders' character is given less mimetic coloring than Susanna, both audiences could still imagine them as "plausible persons."

In terms of the thematic component of their character, there is decidedly less ambiguity. As my above reading indicates, the Elders are associated with evil and God-less actions and views. From the outset of their textual existence, they are identified as wicked and duplicitous (v. 5). They abuse their position and influence, and even try to rape Susanna, who they most likely have known for some time, as she is Joakim's wife and they usually passed judgments at his house (v. 6). However, the Elders are only momentarily prevented from acting on their lust (v. 11), which, as I note above, seems to cloud their reason and thus their judgment. In fact, as Stump notes,

> Each elder presumably...supposes that God sees his evil... But neither elder is moved to any remorse or sorrow by the knowledge that his evil is known to others who see it as the evil it is. Neither elder shows any internal anguish or moral pain...the shame of having their evil known generated no moral sorrow in them [the elders].[125]

Thus, almost all of the thematizing associated with the Elders' character is negative, i.e., the author uses the Elders as a discordant example to the religiosity of Susanna's character. Put another way, the character of the Elders achieves a thematic function in the story in that the negative thematic dimensions of their character finally merge into a proposition that could be rendered: Lawlessness and lust corrupt, but God "saves those hoping in him" (v. 60). If there is any doubt that the Elders' actions and conception of God are not endorsed by the narrative, I need only point out that those actions and that view of God ultimately gets them executed.

Of the main characters in our story, Daniel receives the least mimetic development. This is because the synthetic aspect of Daniel's character is more foregrounded than it is with the other characters. That is, the character of Daniel is, in my opinion, the most obviously constructed character in the narrative. The author needs Daniel to fill a role established by the progression of the story. Put another way, the character of Daniel is little more than a plot agent, serving to exonerate Susanna and indict the Elders. In this role, Daniel reinforces the thematic functions of both Susanna and the Elders in that his actions underscore and, in a sense, establish the narrative's endorsement of Susanna and its condemnation of the Elders. Thus, Daniel's character also serves somewhat of a thematic purpose as well, even though I do not believe his character achieves a fully operational thematic function. Namely, Daniel's character reiterates the thematic assertion(s) of Susanna's character because his role in the narrative is occasioned by her faith in God. Because of the efficacy of his actions, the AA is being asked again to

125. Stump, "Susanna and the Elders," 94–95.

identify with and perhaps imitate Susanna's religiosity. Furthermore, due to the incredibly convenient appearance of Daniel, as well as his miraculous knowledge and courtroom acumen, the character of Daniel effectively removes all doubt that this story is not a mimetic tale. Rather, the presence of Daniel and his role in the narrative serves to highlight the thematic nature of the story.

One of the most interesting effects of the story on the AA is that the progression of the story leads the reader to draw the conclusion that it is not simply the voyeuristic activities of the Elders and their subsequent lust that lead to their death. This view is only plausible if one focuses one's analysis on the mimetic level of the text and ignores the thematizing in the narrative. It is not the behavior of the Elders that leads to their death; rather it is their lack of proper religiosity, which is evidenced by their voyeuristic actions. Put another way, the voyeurism and lust of the Elders are mimetic indicators of a thematic assertion the narrative wants to make, viz., the Elders' religious deficiencies as a foil for what it sees as a better example, Susanna's faith in God. Because of this, according to Phelan, flesh-and-blood readers that encounter the text are likely to assess and possibly re-evaluate their own behavior and attitudes based on this conclusion.

However, the artistic tradition (and to some extent the musical and literary) that has grown up around the story of Susanna addresses this problem in two main fashions. On the one hand, the dominant rendering of the Susanna topos in Renaissance art specifically asks viewers to assume the position of watcher or voyeur. That is, when we view interpretations of this story by such artists as Tintoretto and Guercino, which I will discuss in Chapter 5, we are being asked to take on the very role and perform the very action that we are asked to condemn when we read about the Elders and their actions. Thus, there is cognitive dissonance in the act of interpretation between what we know of the story, and what we are being asked to do when we view artwork based on the story. The reason for the dissonance is that these eroticizing interpretations focus only on the mimetic level of the story's rhetoric, i.e., they are concerned solely with portraying the encounter between Susanna and the Elders in a way that highlights the erotic and voyeuristic traits of the story. On the other hand, there are Renaissance renderings of the narrative by such artists as Gentileschi and Rembrandt, and playwrights including Birck, which I will discuss in Chapter 6, who emphasize the message the story endorses. That is, these interpretations privilege the thematic function of the story, and as such provide models for readers to emulate in resisting the purely mimetic level of the story and interpretations, both scholarly and aesthetic, based on that level.

Having commented on the characters, their functions, and the trajectory of my remaining examination, I am now in a better position to comment on the story as a whole, i.e., to say something about the possible purpose of the story. Based on my interpretation of the narrative, the rhetoric in the story seems unambiguous and focused almost totally on the thematic function. The author shows Susanna facing social shame, personal danger, and religious sin with fear tempered by an all-encompassing trust in God and God's judgment. Both audiences are shown the Elders' behavior toward God, Susanna, and their own people. Finally, we see Daniel enter the narrative as a result of Susanna's faith, and how he saves Susanna and convicts the Elders. The end of the story illustrates whose values and action the story endorses (Susanna and Daniel) and which characters suffer because of the views and exploits the narrative condemns. This all seems clear from my rhetorical reading of the story. Thus, the story is a thematic one that endorses piety and religiosity, while condemning lust and corruption of power.[126] As Steussy notes, "Both versions [of Susanna] suggest that although God's intervention may be subtle and mediated through creatures (Daniel), God does keep tabs on the world and will not allow sinners to destroy the faithful."[127]

However, as Erich S. Gruen notes, there is more to the story than this straightforward message. He writes,

> To read this yarn simply as a religious fable displaying God's protection of the innocent and punishment of the wicked misses much. The tale directs its mockery at a range of community failings: hypocrisy, false religiosity, inverted values, and unprincipled vacillation... The exposure of pomposity in the leadership and gullibility in the rank and file supplied a pointed reminder to the nation: Jews need to look to their own shortcomings. That such a message could be inserted into the text of Daniel is quite striking. It attests to a notable self-assurance on the part of Hellenistic Jews who exposed the foibles of fellow Jews to public scrutiny. It recalled to mind the basic principles of justice and morality that needed to be observed, especially in Jewish communities that governed their own activities. And it provided a subtle reminder that lapses in adherence to those principles could divide Jews internally, thus setting them up for victimization by greater powers.[128]

Thus, Susanna's story carries in it not only a sense of religious triumphalism, but also a tone of self-criticalness. It may have served as a reminder to form more moral communities or risk being fragmented and possibly dispersed again. In her work, Steussy concludes with a similar note:

> At various times throughout history—in Israel's expansion to an empire under Solomon, in Judea's misadventures under Hellenistic and Roman overlords, in rural America's observations of cosmopolitan New York and San Francisco—devout religious people trained in the "good old traditions" have suspected their leaders of personal and public perversion, private licentiousness and corruption in office. They have asserted, against those fears, that God will not long tolerate such lawlessness. The Susanna story plays well to such an audience. But such disaffection is generally not revolutionary. Whether through fear of anarchy or because a basic identification with the rulers remains, suspicion expresses itself in calls for pious government and private restraint, rather than in attempts to overturn the order. So too with our versions of Susanna.[129]

Thus, the story of Susanna is not a radical call to arms, but more of a hearkening back to some of the basic emphases of Judaism: religiosity and faith in God. Similarly, it is not a mimetic story focused on the physical aspects and actions of characters portrayed "realistically." Rather, Susanna is a narrative whose thematic function is overriding, a story that emphasizes a certain message, viz., those who have faith in God will be rewarded.

126. For a similar reading, see MacKenzie, "The Meaning of the Susanna Story," 211–18.
127. Steussy, *Gardens in Babylon*, 141.
128. Gruen, *Heritage and Hellenism*, 176–77.
129. Steussy, *Gardens in Babylon*, 142–43.

Part II

Susanna in Literature, Art, Music, History, and Society During the Renaissance

Chapter 4

THE RENAISSANCE AND WOMEN

4.1. *Introduction*

The Renaissance period is often referred to as the long sixteenth century, implying that it begins prior to the 1500s and ends after the beginning of the 1600s. More specifically, in this project I will begin my examination at 1450 and end generously at 1650. Most historians agree that the birth pangs of the Renaissance were felt in the late thirteenth–early fourteenth centuries with the work of such writers as Dante (1265–1321), Boccaccio (b. 1313), and Petrarch (1304–1374), and artists like Nicola Pisano (ca. 1220–1284), Giotto (ca. 1266–1337), Lorenzo Ghiberti (1378–1455), Donatello (1386–1466), and Masaccio (1401–1428). However, it was in the middle of the fifteenth century that the intellectual and cultural tide began to change in Europe. There were, of course, innumerous events and causes leading up to this change, but I will only mention two.

The most important result of the new economic and technological conditions of the late Middle Ages was printing. The main figure responsible for this revolution was a German goldsmith named Johannes Gutenberg. In 1446–1448, along with his partner Johann Fust, Gutenberg began printing texts with movable type, which allowed more rapidity in printing as well as some sort of uniformity in terms of type. In 1450, Gutenberg began work on the first complete book printed with movable type, and five years later had completed what is now generally acknowledged as the world's first printed book: the Gutenberg Bible.

Printing with movable type soon became the rage in Europe, and new presses were established all across the continent. One effect of the printing revolution was the incredibly increased availability of knowledge. Of course, not everyone was literate, but everyone who had ears to hear could be read to, which was the most popular method of disseminating knowledge during this period. This new access to literary works, as well as other types of printed media, enlarged the intellectual and psychological horizons of European citizens, and made them aware, some perhaps for the first time, that a large world existed beyond the borders of their village. Another effect of printing was the emphasis it placed on communication in the vernacular. At this time, Latin was still the language of the elite, and was used in liturgical, economic, and political arenas. However, with the advent of printing, persons could now address each other locally in their own dialect. This stress on the vernacular was yet another nail in the coffin of the medieval mind, in that "the dream of a unified Christendom, with a single Latin tongue, was doomed."[1] Thus, printing served not only to distribute knowledge, but also to transform the very culture of Europe as well.

The second main event that sets my lower parameter at 1450 is the fall of Constantinople in 1453. In the fourteenth century, a Turkish Muslim warrior named Osman ('Uthman) began to solidify military strength in the eastern Mediterranean region, and his followers would later be known collectively as the Ottoman Empire. In ca. 1357, the Ottomans first invaded Europe at Gallipoli and subsequently conquered many of the Balkan states. However, their most important conquest was that of Constantinople, renamed Istanbul, in 1453. With this victory, the geographically diverse Ottoman Empire was united, and it went on to achieve its zenith in the sixteenth–seventeenth centuries. The repercussions of the loss of Constantinople were twofold. First, the mere fact that a force of "infidels" could take one of Christianity's most important strongholds was unsettling. Second, and more importantly, the taking of the city sent many refugees to other parts of Europe, seeking escape from Turkish rule. Many of the refugees were scholars, and they brought with them several Greek manuscripts containing works that would revolutionize the way in which scholars and theologians thought about the world and their place in it.[2] William Manchester describes the importance of these texts:

> The implications reached far beyond scholarship, leading to the redefinition of knowledge itself. The eventual impact on the Continent's hidebound educational establishment was to be devastating, discrediting medieval culture and replacing it with ancient, resurrected ideals, paideia, and *humanitas*. The best minds in the West began a scrupulous reappraisal of Scholasticism, which, for two centuries, had been degenerating into an artificial sort of dialectics. In the ancient texts Renaissance scholars found an unexpected reverence for humanity which, without actually dismissing the Bible, certainly overshadowed it. And in the wisdom of antiquity they discovered respect for man in the free expansion of his natural impulses, unfreighted by the corrupting burden of original sin... The Christian faith was not repudiated, but the new concept of the cultivated man was the Renaissance *homo universale*, the universal man: creator, artist, scholar, and encyclopedic genius in the spirit of the ancient paideia.[3]

Manchester's implication is that the rediscovery of ancient Greek texts and the ideas therein leads to the development of Humanism, a major factor contributing to the founding of universities in Europe as well as the Reformation. These ideas represent another important break with the all-encompassing nature of medieval Christianity, and therefore signal the beginning of a new cultural era.

These two events define the lower parameter of my investigation at 1450. In terms of the higher limit, there is less precision. There is no widespread agreement on the end point of the Renaissance. Some scholars date the end of that

1. William Manchester, *A World Lit Only by Fire: The Medieval Mind and the Renaissance, Portrait of an Age* (Boston: Little, Brown & Company, 1992), 97.

2. As Paul Johnson, *The Renaissance: A Short History* (Modern Library Chronicles Series; New York: Random House, 2000), 36–37, notes, this was the third "great transmission of classical Greek literature" in the fifteenth century.

3. Manchester, *A World Lit Only by Fire*, 104–5.

period at ca. 1600, and some extend it to 1620.[4] In this study, I extend my coverage of aesthetic works to 1650.

Many important events occurred after the turn of the seventeenth century, such as the publication of Kepler's work on elliptical planetary orbits in 1609, the death of Shakespeare in 1616, the sailing of the Mayflower in 1620, the founding of New Amsterdam (later New York) in 1625, William Harvey's pioneering work on blood circulation published in 1628, and Galileo appearing before the Roman Inquisition in 1633. However, one of the most influential events to occur after the end of the sixteenth century was the Thirty Years' War (1618–1648) and the subsequent Peace of Westphalia. The War resulted from the inadequacy of the 1555 Peace of Augsburg to regulate religious tolerance as well as religious unrest between Catholics and Protestants in Bohemia. The war was extremely bloody and destructive, and it was only with the help of the young Swedish king Gustavus Adolphus that the Protestants were able to push the Catholics into negotiations. In 1648 the Peace of Westphalia was signed, with France and Sweden receiving the lion's share of land, and all peoples involved in the treaty, royalty as well as subjects, would be free to choose their own religion, as long as it was Catholic, Protestant, or Reformed. The historical impact of the War, however, goes beyond these considerations. As Justo L. González notes,

> The principles of tolerance of the Peace of Westphalia were not born out of a deeper understanding of Christian love, but rather out of a growing indifference to religious matters. The war had amply shown the atrocities that resulted from attempting to settle religious matters by force of arms. In the end, nothing had been resolved. Perhaps rulers should not allow their decisions to be guided by religious or confessional considerations, but rather by their own self-interest, or by the interest of their subjects. *Thus the modern secular state began to develop*. And with it there appeared a multitude of doubt regarding matters that previous generations had taken for granted. On what grounds did theologians dare to affirm they were correct, and that others were mistaken? Could any doctrine be true that produced the atrocities of the Thirty Years' War? Was there not a more tolerant, more profound, and even more Christian way to serve God, than simply following the dictates of Orthodoxy, be it Catholic or Protestant?[5]

Thus, the Thirty Years' War and the Peace of Westphalia led to the development of nation-states, as well as sowed the seeds for the major intellectual movements one finds in the later seventeenth and eighteenth centuries, such as Orthodoxy, Rationalism, and Empiricism, all of which ultimately leads to what historians refer to as the modern age. As such, 1650 serves as an adequate, albeit generous, *terminus ad quem* for my investigation.

In terms of the geographic boundaries of my examination, I will allow the sources at my disposal to dictate my focus. Put another way, there is no need for me to examine how the story of Susanna functioned in a particular geographic

4. For the former date, see the comprehensive work of Thomas A. Brady, Jr. et al., eds., *Handbook of European History, 1400–1600: Late Middle Ages, Renaissance, and Reformation* (2 vols.; Grand Rapids: Eerdmans, 1994–96); for the latter date, see John Hale, *The Civilization of Europe in the Renaissance* (New York: Simon & Schuster, 1993).

5. Justo L. González, *The Story of Christianity*. Vol. 2, *The Reformation to the Present Day* (San Francisco: HarperSanFrancisco, 1985), 140–41 (italics mine).

environment if I can locate no representations of Susanna from that area. Having said that, the majority of Susannas during this period stem from important cultural centers, such as Germany, England, Italy, and the more northern countries including the Netherlands.

4.2. *Sex and Gender in the Renaissance*

In 1389, the Veronese Humanist Antonio Loschi delivered a eulogy for the earliest known female humanist, Maddalena Scrovegni.[6] The latter, a widow, had sealed herself inside a study (*sacellum*) in her father's house and contented herself with academic study. Loschi was evidently so moved by this image that in her eulogy, he morphed Scrovegni into that which she had spent her entire life cultivating; she became the embodiment of Chastity, seated in her Temple. Margaret L. King describes the scene that Loschi paints with his poetry:

> This temple is located in Scythia, the inaccessible homeland of the pure and warlike Amazons, where a lofty and wooded mountain rises from the center of an immense plain encircled by the sea. At its summit, white marble walls enclose a courtyard planted with laurel and resonant with the cries of turtle doves. Within that courtyard stands the Temple of Chastity; within it burns the sacred flame of Vesta, and on its walls are incised images of men and women famed for the virtue it memorializes in stone: Hippolytus, Penelope, Arethusa, Dido, Lucretia, and others. Inside, Chastity presides as queen, enthroned on glass, surrounded by the attendant figures of Continence, Penitence, and Virginity, while her gatekeeper, Frugality, successfully repulses the attacks of the warlike Cupid.[7]

This image of Chastity as a queen, along with the surrounding personified virtues men, even educated, elite humanists like Loschi, want women to embody provides us with a taste of what is to come in the following study of women during the Renaissance. Generally speaking, women were only slightly better off in terms of choices, options, and self-definition than they were in the first century B.C.E.

One of the great benefits of examining idea(l)s of women during this period is that we have an abundance of prescriptive literature penned by men concerning women.[8] All across the continent, humanist scholars were quick to advise women on proper conduct, often using classical and biblical figures as examples.[9] In what follows, I will utilize selected works from this genre, but we should always bear in mind that the ideals described in these texts are products of the male imagination, and do not necessarily reflect social reality. Put another way, we

6. For this incident, see Margaret L. King, "Goddess and Captive: Antonio Loschi's Epistolary Tribute to Maddalena Scrovegni (1389)," *Medievalia et humanistica* 9 (1980): 103–27; and eadem, *Women of the Renaissance* (Women in Culture and Society; Chicago: University of Chicago Press, 1991), 192–93.

7. King, *Women of the Renaissance*, 193.

8. For a good survey of this genre in English literature, see Suzanne W. Hull, *Chaste, Silent, and Obedient: English Books for Women, 1475–1640* (San Marino, Calif.: The Huntington Library, 1982).

9. The best example of this use of classical and biblical antecedents is G. Boccaccio, *Concerning Famous Women* (trans. Guido A. Guarino; New Brunswick, N.J.: Rutgers University Press, 1963).

may never know if Maddalena Scrovegni actually considered herself or desired to imagine herself as the embodiment of Chastity. We should take care not to confine women in the roles and images men have constructed for them. As King notes, "Rigid on her throne, surrounded by her virtuous keepers, within a temple within a courtyard within tall walls on a mountaintop ringed by an icy plain enclosed by the sea, Chastity-Scrovegni is as much prisoner as sovereign."[10] As we shall see, she is not alone.

4.2.1. *Daughters*

The situation of daughters during the Renaissance period is remarkably similar to the situation in first-century Jerusalem. Families still had a preference for male children, and the reasoning behind this partiality was still economic. King writes,

> Sons were preferred to daughters because the former could increase, while the latter threatened, the patrimony… Children offered the possibilities of survival on the one hand, and of ruin on the other. Sons could continue to till the land or manage the business, but too many could divide the patrimony… Daughters posed a persistent problem. Not only could they not take responsibility for the primary economic challenge—to conserve family wealth—but they threatened to consume it and alienate it.[11]

The main economic threat posed by the daughter was the necessity of gathering a proper dowry for her marriage. Olwen Hufton elaborates on the concept of dowry during this period,

> In the case of daughters, a considerable financial outflow would have to be taken into account, a planned surrender of assets in whole or in part to occur on marriage. The dowry became increasingly formalized in the sixteenth and seventeenth centuries and continued to be so as the mark of a more stable and a more commercially evolved society. Women became the bearers of liquid wealth, clothes, jewels, furnishings and above all money, wealth regarded as the guarantee of suitable status for the bride over her entire life.[12]

During the Renaissance both the dowry and marriage for a daughter became almost required. King notes, "Social life did not include a category for the unmarried woman outside of the religious life; the woman who chose that route inhabited an uncomfortable limbo."[13] Parents either provided dowries, or else a young girl would have to try and provide one for herself by leaving the home and seeking work.

In upper-class families, daughters expected their families to provide a suitable dowry for them, and as such the training they received would have been mostly domestic, i.e., skills such as sewing and food preparation. However, as Hufton makes abundantly clear, girls that needed to aid their parents' accumulation of material goods or provide their own dowry had to seek paying work outside the

10. King, *Women of the Renaissance*, 193.
11. King, *Women of the Renaissance*, 25–26.
12. Olwen Hufton, *The Prospect Before Her: A History of Women in Western Europe*. Vol. 1, *1500–1800* (New York: Alfred A. Knopf, 1996), 67.
13. King, *Women of the Renaissance*, 28.

home.[14] Thus, daughters of the lower classes were often forced to work in order to gather capital that would be added to her dowry funds to ensure a marriage that would be advantageous to her family. Most of these working women, aside from those marrying into a family whose source of income was agriculturally based, would concentrate their efforts in the domestic sphere once the marriage was completed. Hufton notes that daughters were "defined by the status of her family, by the limited job potential for women in the workplace, and by a concept of female labor predicated on a notion of woman as future wife," and, as such, "a woman's working life was thus designed to equip her for a single future, marriage."[15] Daughters worked, then, in order to be married, for as King notes, outside of the religious life, unmarried women had little, if any, status during this period. However, the phenomenon of daughters, or more generally unmarried women, working in public constituted a threat to the ideal of women in the Renaissance.

As in the first century B.C.E., the honor of daughters was a great concern for their families. In this regard, it is instructive to hear the testimony of Juan Luis Vives, author of one of the most widely read manuals of instruction for women in the sixteenth century. For Vives, honor is intimately related to the preservation of chastity, even going as far as noting, "The inseparable companions of chastity are a sense of propriety and modest behavior. Chastity (*pudicitia*) seems to be derived from shame (*pudor*), so that one who has no sense of shame cannot be chaste."[16] Chastity emerges in Vives' work as the cipher for all proper womanly behavior and attitudes: "In a woman, chastity is the equivalent of all virtues."[17] Because of the importance placed upon chastity, Vives can, like Sirach, advise men to makes sure that young women remain almost totally secluded: "An unmarried young woman should rarely appear in public, since she has no business there and her most precious possession, chastity, is placed in jeopardy."[18] King correlates this view with the aforementioned necessity of marriage:

> Since women's roles were defined by sexual and economic relationships to men, society made little place for the woman who was unattached to man or God. Moreover, unattached women were especially vulnerable to improper sexual advances, a matter of extraordinary gravity because of the value accorded to chastity in the economic and social system of the Renaissance. Chastity ensured future husbands of the purity of their line, the legitimacy of their heirs, and the reputation of their family. *Thus, the guarding of chastity was the primary business of the daughters of the Renaissance.* Their honor consisted in the maintenance of their chastity; their fathers' honor consisted in their supervision of the chastity of their daughters and wives... Accordingly, the daughter was kept at home and under close supervision.[19]

14. Hufton, *The Prospect Before Her*, 69–101, details the variety of tasks and jobs a young woman could perform.

15. Hufton, *The Prospect Before Her*, 98.

16. Juan Luis Vives, *The Education of a Christian Woman: A Sixteenth-Century Manual* (ed. and trans. Charles Fantazzi; The Other Voice in Early Modern Europe Series; Chicago: University of Chicago, 2000), 116 (1.10.83).

17. Vives, *The Education of a Christian Woman*, 85 (1.6.44).

18. Vives, *The Education of a Christian Woman*, 110 (1.9.74).

19. King, *Women of the Renaissance*, 29–30 (italics mine).

Thus, chastity was a primary concern, at least ideally, for daughters and fathers in the Renaissance, perhaps even more so for the latter, for, as King notes, "marriage was most efficiently and profitably negotiated for a woman whose chastity was intact: for chastity had a cash value in a marriage transaction."[20]

In sum, then, daughters were a source of social and economic stress for their families due to the necessity of a dowry and the requirement of chastity in order to reduce male anxiety over female sexuality. In this regard, the situation is analogous to that in the first century B.C.E. However, daughters did hold some worth for their families aside from whatever love and affection they might have had for them. Daughters could provide offspring that would further the family line. Furthermore, if a daughter's marriage was properly arranged, families could be allied advantageously with other families. As King notes, "Through their daughters, fathers could become connected laterally to useful friends and vertically to future generations."[21] Even taking into account the social worth of daughters to their families in terms of valuable alliances, we should not lose sight of the fact that these alliances were often, if not always, made without the consent of the daughter. King observes, "Daughters, locked at the midpoint between danger and hope, were pressured to conform to strategies for familial economic and social survival, at enormous cost to their autonomy and status."[22] Perhaps many women consoled themselves that they would have more autonomy and increased status once their marriage was complete. It is to that issue that we now turn.

4.2.2. *Wives and Women in Public*

The nature of marriage changed quite a bit during the Renaissance period, as we shall see, but one constant remained: the young woman had little, if any, say in matters of choosing a groom. Members of the upper class had the least input with regards to potential mates due to the wide-reaching importance of securing a beneficial alliance with another powerful family. Daughters of the lower classes, particularly those with no property, might possibly have wielded some influence, but that influence was often tempered by geographic and economic concerns that were the privy of the father. Generally speaking, marriage in the late fifteenth century and very early sixteenth century had little to do with emotions or faithfulness, but was rather a contract involving the exchange of goods and money.

With the advent of the Protestant Reformation, usually dated to 1517, marriage changed. One of the targets of Luther's attacks was the Church's prescription of clerical celibacy. As Merry E. Wiesner-Hanks writes,

> Luther was faithful to Augustine's idea of the link between original sin and sexual desire, but saw desire as so powerful that the truly chaste life was impossible for all but a handful of individuals. Thus the best Christian life was not one which fruitlessly attempted ascetic celibacy, but one in which sexual activity was channeled into marriage. Marriage was not a sacrament—Luther was adamant that it conferred no special

20. King, *Women of the Renaissance*, 31.
21. King, *Women of the Renaissance*, 31.
22. King, *Women of the Renaissance*, 32.

> grace—but it was the ideal state for almost everyone. Thus the restrictions on marriage which had developed in the Middle Ages should be done away with, and everyone should marry, the earlier after puberty the better.[23]

This emphasis on marriage by Luther led to a higher valuation of the familial unit as well as increased the status of married persons, especially in comparison with celibate Catholic priests. It also had positive and negative effects on women. On the one hand, women were now being celebrated for fulfilling roles within marriage, such as mother and homemaker. On the other hand, as Cheri A. Brown notes,

> Defining the role and function of women purely in terms of marriage, along with the concomitant abolishing of convents and cloisters and even bordelles, in effect closed off the main avenues by which widowed and unmarried women prior to the Reformation era had attained social legitimacy and/or, at the very least, economic independence.[24]

In addition to the double-edged impact of Luther's view of marriage on women, it also affected the very process of marriage. Since marriage was so important, new measures were enacted to ensure that marriages were "proper," such as requiring the consent of parents and a public ceremony presided over by a pastor. Marriage, according to Luther and other early Protestants, was a serious business, and solemnity should be the prevailing mood at a ceremony, not the wild celebrations that characterized weddings prior to the sixteenth century. To ensure that these prescriptions were being enacted, "reformers advocated the establishment of courts which would regulate marriage and morals, wrote ordinances regulating marriage and other matters of sexual conduct, and worked closely with the secular rulers in their area, whether city councils or princes."[25] These courts, which would later transform into consistories, were an important mechanism by which reformers ordered sexual behavior and moral conduct. The sermon or homily was also an important prescriptive device used by Protestants, especially since more people were likely to listen to a sermon than read a printed text.[26]

In response to the work of Luther and other early reformers, the Catholic Church launched its own internal reform movement, often termed the Counter-Reformation. The highlight of this movement was the Council of Trent, convened by Paul III, which met intermittently from 1545–1563. This Council defined what it means to be Catholic for hundreds of years, and that definition included sexual activity. As Wiesner-Hanks notes,

23. Merry E. Wiesner-Hanks, *Christianity and Sexuality in the Early Modern World: Regulating Desire, Reforming Practice* (Christianity and Society in the Modern World; London: Routledge, 2000), 63.

24. Cheri A. Brown, "The *Susanna* Drama and the German Reformation," in *Everyman and Company: Essays on the Theme and Structure of the European Moral Play* (ed. Donald Gilman; New York: AMS Press, 1989), 129–53 (139).

25. Wiesner-Hanks, *Christianity and Sexuality*, 67.

26. For an example of homilies and their use in Renaissance England, see Carole Levin, "Advice on Women's Behavior in Three Tudor Homilies," *International Journal of Women's Studies* 6 (1983): 176–85.

> Regulating the sexual lives of both clergy and lay people was a key part of Catholic (and to a lesser degree, Orthodox) reform moves which began in the sixteenth century. Both clergy and laity had to be taught correct doctrine on matters of sexual and marital conduct, so that sexual issues became a central part of Catholic as well as Protestant confessionalization. Education and training alone were not sufficient to encourage godly behavior, however, and Catholics along with Protestants used church and secular courts and other institutions in a process of social disciplining.[27]

Thus it seems that Catholic practices revolving around sexual issues during this time were reactions to, and adaptations of, Protestant views and practices.

In 1563, just before it disbanded, the Council of Trent issued the decree *Tametsi*, in which its views on marriage were stated.[28] Specifically, this decree

> affirmed that the basis of marriage was still the free exchange of vows by spouses, but stipulated that to be valid this exchange had to take place before witnesses, including the priests of the parish where the parties had originally agreed to wed; priests were ordered to keep records of all marriages in their parish. Secret marriages were not binding, and though parental consent was not explicitly required, it became much more difficult for individuals to contract a marriage without the knowledge of their families.[29]

Thus, Catholic views on marriage seem to echo many Protestant ideas, but the main difference is that for Catholics, marriage was still viewed as an inferior alternative to celibacy, which the Council upheld as binding for priests and nuns.[30] In the case of the latter, however, the Council reinforced earlier policies that mandated enclosure or strict separation for all nuns living in female religious establishments. This policy, as Wiesner-Hanks notes, gave rise to a sexual hierarchy of sorts, with celibate priests at the top, non-sexual women such as virgins and nuns in the middle, and married persons at the bottom.[31] The irony of this hierarchy was that the women that inhabited the bottom rung in the Catholic scheme were exalted in Protestant circles as embodying the ideal state of womanhood.

The question now becomes what was expected of married women in either of these situations. King begins her assessment of wives during the Renaissance by noting that a wife constantly had to work out a marital relationship with two incongruous presuppositions as givens: "On the one hand, she was expected to be a companion to her husband, but on the other, she was his subordinate and the object of restrictive regulations imposed by him and other male authorities."[32] The prescriptive literature written during the Renaissance buttresses the importance of wifely submission to her husband. Proceeding from the proposition that marriage is divinely ordained, the making of two humans into one, Vives writes,

27. Wiesner-Hanks, *Christianity and Sexuality*, 104.

28. See H. J. Schroeder, *Canons and Decrees of the Council of Trent* (St. Louis, Mo.: Herder, 1941), 180–90.

29. Wiesner-Hanks, *Christianity and Sexuality*, 106–7.

30. This view is spelled out in the Canons on the Sacrament of Matrimony. See especially Canon 10: "If anyone says that the married state excels the state of virginity or celibacy, and that it is better and happier to be united in matrimony than to remain in virginity or celibacy, let him be anathema" (Schroeder, *Canons and Decrees*, 182).

31. See Wiesner-Hanks, *Christianity and Sexuality*, 107.

32. King, *Women of the Renaissance*, 35.

> A husband is not to be loved as we love a friend or a twin brother, where only love is required. A great amount of respect and veneration, obedience and compliance must be included. Not only the traditions of our ancestors, but all laws, human and divine, and nature itself, proclaim that a woman must be subject to a man and obey him.[33]

Vives also claims that when wives attempt to exercise more power than their husbands, it is analogous to "a soldier demanding the right to give orders to a general, as if the moon were superior to the sun or the arm to the head." This inversion is to be detested, because "In marriage as in human nature, the man stands for the mind, the woman for the body. He must command, and she must serve, if man is to live."[34] Similarly, in his 1415 treatise *De re uxorial*, the humanist Francesco Barbaro laid a heavy emphasis on what he termed "the faculty of obedience, which is her [the wife's] master and companion, because nothing is more important, nothing greater can be demanded of a wife than this."[35]

Along with obedience, wives were also admonished to remain in the house, or private sphere of activity, as much as possible. Vives writes at length on this topic, and his views stem from a distinction between married and unmarried women: "Married women should be seen more rarely in public than unmarried women. For what the latter seem to be seeking, the former have already obtained."[36] New wives should remain completely secluded in their homes, according to Vives, because of the shame they should feel at having lost their virginity.

It seems that for Vives, as well as for Barbaro, one of the main concerns in terms of wives appearing in public is the effect it could have on her husband. Vives expounds on this problems:

> It is not proof of chastity for a woman to be too well known, celebrated, and sung of and to be on people's lips under some name they have given her, as to be called beautiful, or squint-eyed, or red-haired, or lame, or obese, or pale, or skinny. These are characteristics that should not be publicly known in the case of a good woman... There are some women, however, whose manner of life requires that they have public dealings, such as those who buy and sell. I should prefer, if possible, that women did not engage in those affairs, but it depends on the country in which they live and their state of life. If it cannot be avoided, then let old women be employed or married women past middle age. But if it is absolutely necessary that young women be occupied in these activities, let them be courteous without flattery and modest without arrogance and sooner suffer a loss in their sales than in their chastity.[37]

Thus, even though Vives allows some room for women to work outside the home, he is still concerned with the effect(s) it may have on her chastity, i.e., her honor and reputation, which has direct repercussions on her husband. Barbaro takes a more conservative approach to the issue, and writes that wives

33. Vives, *The Education of a Christian Woman*, 193 (2.3.24).
34. Vives, *The Education of a Christian Woman*, 194 (2.3.25).
35. Francesco Barbaro, "On Wifely Duties," in *The Earthly Republic: Italian Humanists on Government and Society* (ed. Benjamin G. Kohl and Ronald G. Witt; Philadelphia: University of Pennsylvania Press, 1978), 179–228 (193).
36. Vives, *The Education of a Christian Woman*, 243 (2.8.93).
37. Vives, *The Education of a Christian Woman*, 248 (2.8.99).

> should not be shut up in their bedrooms as a prison but should be permitted to go out, and this privilege should be taken as evidence of their virtue and propriety. Still, wives should not act with their husbands as the moon does with the sun; for when the moon is near the sun it is never visible, but when it is distant it stands resplendent by itself. Therefore, I would have wives be seen in public with their husbands, but when their husbands are away wives should stay at home.[38]

Both writers also admonish that wives should not be ornately adorned in public, they should be silent as much as possible, and they should take care and responsibility in their domestic duties.[39]

Even though the prescriptive literature of the time advised women to remain at home, Hufton points out that many married women did, in fact, work both inside and outside the home.[40] Merchants' wives generally tended to domestic matters, as well as kept financial books and records. At the lower end of the economic scale, farmers' wives were often needed to work in the fields, and perhaps even accept seasonal migratory labor to help with the family financial situation. Also present in the market were women involved in textile production or wives of workshop masters present to sell goods. Thus, the ideological dilemma of women in public posed by the prescriptive literature of the period mainly applied to those families with the economic means to embrace it. For lower-class families, survival often depended on having as many family members working and bringing in goods and capital as possible, including women.

In sum, while Vives admonished wives to think of their husbands as "father, master, greater, more powerful and better than herself," the social reality of marriage was often more complementary than hierarchical, at least in the lower classes.[41] In the upper classes, however, wives in families of economic means could be expected to fulfill or embody some of the requirements in prescriptive literature. Even though marriage was highly prized in Protestant practice and accepted in Catholic thought, wives did not have much more freedom and/or autonomy than they did prior to marriage. King spells out the situation of married women:

> A couple might love, but the husband was in charge. The family drew together, but the wife was excluded from the economic group that did not entirely coincide with the biological unit of mother, father, and children. The churches supported the domestic unit, but also undermined or invaded it and enhanced the role of its male guardian. The assertion and reassertion of male control over females in marriage during the Renaissance is an inescapable fact, however hard it is to reconcile that fact with other impressions of an age that rediscovered the meaning of liberty. The very age which elevated matrimony as a holy state—by the edicts of Trent within Catholicism, by the cultivation of family sentiment within Protestantism—strengthened, paradoxically, the authority of husband over wife and required her deeper submission.[42]

38. Barbaro, "On Wifely Duties," 204.

39. See, e.g., Vives, *The Education of a Christian Woman*, 236–42 (2.7.84–92); 254–64 (2.9.107–123); and Barbaro, "On Wifely Duties," 204–12, 215–20.

40. See Hufton, *The Prospect Before Her*, 137–76.

41. Vives, *The Education of a Christian Woman*, 215 (2.4.55).

42. King, *Women of the Renaissance*, 38.

In fact, King claims that wives only had one sure and certain power independent of her husband or family's influence: "she could make a will, and thereby dispose of her dowry."[43] However, as we will see, women during the Renaissance could choose an alternative path to that of marriage, and thereby have access to a modicum of autonomy and education; they could choose the religious life.

4.2.3. *Women and Religion*

Women enjoyed a varied involvement in religion and religious practices during the Renaissance. The most visible avenue of spiritual expression in the early Renaissance era was the convent. After the advent of Protestantism, however, the landscape changed for women interested in religion. Catholicism and Protestantism imagined very different roles for women in religion, but underlying these differences was an important similarity, as Hufton notes:

> In some respects the goals of the two dominant orthodoxies, Catholic and Protestant, are remarkable for their similarity. Both stood for a clearly defined moral order based on chastity, fortitude and obedience to God's teaching as expressed in Scripture. If the Protestants posited a holy household, the Catholics worked to promote the model of the holy family. Both enjoined women to accept their subservient role but deplored passivity in the face of sin. Women had souls and were capable of sin and error. The Catholic faith urged upon women the courage to confess and so to speak out their faith. The Protestant confessions put the holy word, in the form of the Bible, into their hands. For both camps, the religious comportment of women was interpreted as a kind of marker. Women epitomized the ignorant and the superstitious, the sexually lax and the profane. The behaviour of women could then serve as a condemnation of, or as a recommendation for, a particular confession... Religious reform involved both sexes, but it focused particularly on chastity and obedience—and who should be more chaste or more obedient than the female? They were, in short, to be brought into line.[44]

Women were, then, not only participants in religion during the Renaissance; they were also one of its main concerns and the targets for its moral vision.

The convent was the most evident and, at the beginning of the Renaissance, the most important outlet for women's religious devotion. However, not all women in nunneries were there by choice. Often families would forcefully commit daughters to convents out of economic concerns. King notes,

> While daughters well placed in marriage to peers or superiors could enhance a man's social standing, too many daughters endangered patrimony. Prudent fathers had few options in their quest to secure wealth: infanticide was forbidden, abandonment discouraged, adoption (as a legal mechanism) unknown. But supernumerary daughters could be prevented from alienating their fathers' resources if they were contained in a place reserved especially for the pursuit of celibacy: the nunnery.[45]

The vast majority of committed nuns were of the elite classes, where fathers had the most to lose from an excess of daughters. The fact that many nuns were forced to inhabit convents perhaps explains why many nunneries faced problems

43. King, *Women of the Renaissance*, 55.
44. Hufton, *The Prospect Before Her*, 369–70.
45. King, *Women of the Renaissance*, 81.

of "loose" morality among their charges, including sexual encounters as well as covert births. King partially explains these realities by noting that forced nuns had not entered convents out of religious concerns. Instead, "they had been placed there because they could not or would not marry and they could not be left free. The history of female monachation is at least in part the history of female imprisonment."[46] This mention of female imprisonment is not hyperbolic. Wiesner-Hanks points out that

> Women's celibacy and chastity was also a great concern of the Council of Trent, particularly because accounts of lustful nuns were a staple of Protestant criticism, both learned and popular. Trent's solution was a new emphasis on Pope Boniface VIII's [1294–1303] policy of strict enclosure for all female religious houses, enforced by a threat of excommunication or secular punishment.[47]

Thus, nuns were prescribed to live cloistered, with no familial visits and no social life. They were expected to dwell in isolation from society and meditate on God and their relation to him. Of course, the reality of claustration differed widely depending on geography and one's lineage.[48]

Even though many nuns were forced to join convents, there were those that renounced the secular world of their own volition. The reasons why a woman would choose to live a life of religious seclusion were many. One of the most important and tangible was the education a woman would receive in a convent, as opposed to any opportunities outside the walls of the nunnery. Many works written by nuns still survive, and they bear witness to the variety and depth of concern held by women during this period. A recurring theme in these works is the lot of women in convents. For example, the morality play entitled *Amor di virtu* (*Love of Virtue*) written by Beatrice del Sara (1515–1586), protests the imprisonment of women in convents.[49] Similarly, Arcangela Tarabotti (1604–1652) wrote a treatise titled *La semplicità ingannata* (*Simplicity Betrayed*) in which she criticizes fathers for committing their daughters to convents simply to horde their wealth.[50] In this work, Tarabotti notes that only women that join nunneries of their own will are able to achieve the religious perfection that is the goal

46. King, *Women of the Renaissance*, 86.

47. Wiesner-Hanks, *Christianity and Sexuality*, 106.

48. See Hufton, *The Prospect Before Her*, 371. As an example of the variety of experiences of cloistered women, see Dava Sobel, *Galileo's Daughter: A Historical Memoir of Science, Faith, and Love* (New York: Walker, 1999). Sobel discusses the relationship between the famous scientist and his daughter Virginia, whom he placed in a convent around her thirteenth birthday. Sobel reproduces many of the 124 surviving letters from Maria Celeste, Virginia's adopted name, to Galileo, and the result is a vivid portrait of a highly intelligent woman who was very much interested in her father's work and its reception by the Church.

49. See Elissa Weaver, "Spiritual Fun: A Study of Sixteenth-Century Tuscan Convent Theater," in *Women in the Middle Ages and the Renaissance: Literary and Historical Perspectives* (ed. Mary Beth Rose; Syracuse: Syracuse University Press, 1986), 173–206.

50. Arcangela Tarabotti, *La semplicità ingannata: Tirannia paterna*, in *Donne e società nel Seicento: Lucrezia Marinelli e Arcangela Tarabotti* (ed. Ginevra Conti Odorisio; Biblioteca di cultura 167; Rome: Bulzoni, 1979), 199–214.

of convents. Another of Tarabotti's works, published posthumously, is entitled *Inferno monacale* (*The Convent as Hell*).[51]

Obviously, these writers were concerned about the uses to which the convent was being put. They were able to rally against what they saw as the illegitimate purpose of the convent due to their status as learned nuns by choice. However, education was not the only benefit of freely joining a nunnery. We have already seen the enormous value placed on female chastity during the Renaissance, and perhaps this emphasis was also a contributing factor in women joining convents. King dwells at length on this issue, and she is worth quoting in detail:

> By the observance of chastity, a woman was removed from the cycles of sexuality and birth and freed from the negative image of seductress. The whole weight of male authority posed her alternatives and beckoned her to choose: Aristotle, the philosopher, described her wandering womb, her instability, her lesser role in the generation of a child, her subordinate standing in the social order; Jerome, the saint, offered her authority, dignity, transcendent power. The ideal of chastity was uniquely prized in Roman Catholic theology and eloquently championed from pulpits. It appealed to women to whom other socially valued goals were unavailable. They could not normally achieve great wealth or great power in their own right, or develop the most esteemed craft or artistic or intellectual skills; but chastity, achieved by negation alone, was a summit for which they could strive. The crown of virginity would become at the end of time the crown of joy, as the 144,000 virgins gathered around the risen Christ. Accordingly, women denied their bodies in order to gain consummation of union with the divine. Self-denial became the path by which many women hoped to gain an eminence that the secular world would not permit them. In chastity, a triumph of denial, women could find a fulfillment parallel to or greater than that of the esteemed wife and mother in secular society.[52]

Thus, women who consciously chose chastity and claustration in a convent were foregoing their socially prescribed role of mother in exchange for the possibility of increased status and the potential of ecstatic religious experience.[53] In addition to these considerations, we should also point out that women undertook this quest in the presence of, and supported by, other women, thus enabling them to commingle in a female environment not likely to be duplicated in the secular world. As King notes, "Female monasticism was the institution that offered the greatest scope for autonomy and dignity to the women of Christian Europe."[54] As we shall see, the convent was not the only avenue for female religious expression in the Renaissance, and it would soon be challenged as the most proper role for religious women to inhabit in society.

The challenge to the many convents in Europe, as well as the underlying assumptions on which they were founded, was provided by Protestantism. These new reformers were deeply distrustful of the Catholic rule of clerical celibacy,

51. Tarabotti, *Inferno monacale*, in *Donne e società nel Seicento*, 231–38.

52. King, *Women of the Renaissance*, 93–94.

53. For an analogous situation in early Christianity, see Elizabeth A. Castelli, "Virginity and Its Meaning for Women's Sexuality in Early Christianity," *Journal of Feminist Studies in Religion* 2 (1986): 61–88.

54. King, *Women of the Renaissance*, 95.

which they saw as an unattainable goal. The best context for religious devotion and sentiment was now considered to be the family, a microcosm of society. This new emphasis on the family meant that convents were not only viewed with suspicion, they were eventually outlawed and the nuns were sent home. As King notes,

> Catholicism had posed two goods for women: the greater one of fruitful virginity, the lesser one of procreative marriage. Protestantism posed only one: the latter. For women en masse, the Reformation above all else was a revolution in the nature of her responsibility to the family. Women who wished to pursue the spiritual life would do so, ideally, amid household hubbub, the homely clank of pots and pans.[55]

Thus, women were relegated to the domestic sphere in their search for religious expression in Protestantism. The question then becomes: What are the differences between and characteristics of Protestantism and Catholicism in regards to women's religious lives?

One of the most immediate differences between the two is Protestantism's removal of the confessor as a key figure in women's devotion. The main figure in a woman's religious life was now her husband or father. He was the "patriarch" of the family, and as such, was entitled to make economic and social judgments. More importantly, though, the father or husband now had the responsibility to ensure his female charges were living a correctly religious life, and since he alone had access to the written Scripture (unless his daughter or wife was literate), his judgments were often the only voice heard.

After the Council of Trent, Catholicism acted to reinforce the position of the confessor. New handbooks were drawn up to instruct priests as to how an effective confession should take place, e.g., what questions should and should not be asked. Women in particular were encouraged to confess regularly and in detail, given their nature. Through confession, women who were not in convents were allowed to come closer to God, and feel as if they were making a vital contribution to their own salvation. Over time, confessors, and the Jesuits in particular, learned that women could be a valued asset in their endeavors, and so began targeting women as objects of confessionals in order to gain as much knowledge about them as possible, including which widow might have money she wished to donate.

In addition to the emphasis on confession, Catholicism also stressed specific cults in order to appeal to those not able to participate in monastic endeavors, the most influential being the cult of the Rosary. Visual imagery, in conjunction with sermons and printed materials, allowed illiterate worshipers to commune with the sacred in a more immediate fashion. For those women in monastic settings, complete enclosure was reasserted. Catholicism still believed in female monasticism, but distrusted the way in which it had been carried out previously. As Hufton notes, though, the extent of enforcement of these, and other, prescriptions often depended on the socio-economic background of the nuns in question.[56] However,

55. King, *Women of the Renaissance*, 136.
56. Hufton, *The Prospect Before Her*, 375.

the convents stayed open, thus allowing women to maintain at least some of the autonomy and freedoms they possessed prior to the Reformation.

Protestantism allowed women to read Scripture (if they were literate) and to discuss theology, since, according to Luther, everyone had the possibility of being their own priest. Women were also allowed to sing with men in liturgical settings. However, Protestantism always viewed women suspiciously unless they were properly "contained," i.e., under the care of a man. If they were not, if they were single, divorced, or widowed, then they could be a danger to themselves and others because of their adulterous instincts. On the other hand, women within the family were admired and some even found a measure of independence in their prescribed role of mother.

In sum, there is no easy answer to the question of whether Catholicism or Protestantism provided more freedoms for women. Both provided positive and negative alternatives, and both can be interpreted as holding out encouraging roles for women. As we shall see, the roles open to women wishing to express religious devotion were not simply limited to nun or *Hausfrau*. Women were able to perform many tasks and embody many roles, though not all of them were officially sanctioned or recognized by ecclesiastical hierarchies.

Women often found an outlet for religious sentiment in informal devotional movements in which they were bound by a common concern to perform charitable acts outside the confines of the monastery. Some of these groups became quite popular, including the Beguines, which originated in Germany and Belgium.[57] Also notable were the *béates* in Spain, and the Sisters of Charity in France.[58] These groups took "unofficial" vows of chastity and poverty, and allowed lower class women who could not enter convents to perform religious services. Many of these organizations educated women and children, and the *béates* even engaged in lace production to help poor girls contribute to their dowries. Over time, however, these "grass-roots" movements were institutionalized and absorbed by the Church, often with negative repercussions for the women involved, as King notes:

> In due course, the informal communities in which these women lived, which inhabited the spaces between the limbs of the gigantic armature of the late medieval and early modern Church, came under the scrutiny of the male clerical establishment. The founders and bearers of a culture of lay female piety were commended for their good intentions and told to step aside. They were to be organized according to one of the rules available for nuns. They were to wear a habit. Their voluntary chastity was to be enforced with bars and vows. They were to cease the production of marketable goods. They were to educate only children, within the confines of the walls. They were to evacuate the streets filled with need and to look only inward. Their convents were walled islands amid the urban maelstrom of the new age, and their experience was to have nothing to do with it. Women could not be trusted with the present moment, nor with the imitation of Christ.[59]

57. See King, *Women of the Renaissance*, 104–5. Also see Elise Boulding, *The Underside of History: A View of Women through Time* (2 vols.; rev. ed.; Newbury Park, Calif.: Sage, 1992), 2:34–42.

58. See Hufton, *The Prospect Before Her*, 386–91.

59. King, *Women of the Renaissance*, 113.

These female communities were, one by one, soaked up by the Church, so that they could be manipulated into the image of "proper" women held within Catholicism and placed under the authority of the male leadership.

Women also found avenues of religious expression in movements the Church considered "heretical," and in the sects of Radical Protestantism. Notable among the former category were the Lollards in England, who were characterized by their interest in reading and teaching from the New Testament. One of the most interesting heretical movements during this period was the Guglielmites, a group that originated in Italy. This group worshipped a prophetess named Guglielma (d. 1279) as the "female incarnation of the Holy Spirit, their organization was headed by a female pope, and their female priests alone could perform the new sacraments of an *ecclesia spiritualis* that had, at last, arrived."[60] After the movement bearing her name ran afoul of the Church, Guglielma's body was exhumed and publicly burned.[61]

Women also found new spiritual opportunities in some of the more liberal branches of Protestantism. Anabaptists were one of the earliest sects in which women participated as near equals with men. Anne Hutchinson, a Puritan in the Massachusetts Bay Colony, felt confident enough in her religious beliefs to teach them to others, and was banished from the Colony for her beliefs. Under the guidance of Margaret Fell, especially her 1667 work, *Women's Speaking Justified, Proved and Allowed of by the Scriptures*, the Society of Friends, or the Quakers, moved towards a position of equivalence between men and women. Later Protestant movements, such as The United Society of Believers in Christ's Second Appearing, or, The Millennial Church, also known as the Shakers, that also emphasize women's roles and participation in ceremony and thought owe much to these earlier movements.[62]

Another interesting development during the Renaissance period that illustrates women's search for a more religious existence is the prevalence of holy women, i.e., women who sought communion with the divine through mystical or ascetic practices. In the fourteenth century, Julian of Norwich, Saint Catherine of Siena, and Margaret Kempe provide three outstanding examples of women (re)visualizing the sacred based on their own experiences as women. The most important female mystic of the Renaissance period, though, was the Spanish saint Teresa of Avila (1515–1582), whose mystical visions and participation in the Carmelite Reform have been enormously influential. Other women during this period, though, sought God not through mysticism, but through penitence and asceticism. One of the most common ascetic practices of this time was excessive fasting, and King points out the importance of this issue: "Food purchase, preparation, and

60. King, *Women of the Renaissance*, 115. For more information on the Guglielmites, see Stephen E. Wessley, "The Thirteenth-Century Guglielmites: Salvation through Women," in *Medieval Women: Dedicated and Presented to Professor Rosalind M. T. Hill on the Occasion of Her Seventieth Birthday* (ed. Derek Baker; Oxford: Blackwell, 1978), 289–303.

61. Boulding, *The Underside of History*, 2:41.

62. For a succinct overview of women in early Protestantism, see Rosemary Radford Ruether, "Christianity," in *Women in World Religions* (ed. Arvind Sharma; Albany, N.Y.: State University of New York Press, 1987), 207–34 (221–28).

consumption was the central business of the familial environment from which consecrated women had come: to reject food was to affirm the vocation of holiness."[63] Women who engaged in mystical and/or ascetic practices often achieved a certain level of influence and even notoriety in the public sphere, as is evidenced by the extant sacred biographies written about them by male admirers.[64] In her work, King holds out great admiration for these more individualistic practitioners: "Female worshippers of God aroused awe for their heroic asceticism, their unstinting service, their otherworldly visions, their inner power. These are surely the heroines of the Renaissance."[65]

Thus, women had several avenues open to them in expressing their religiosity, but many of these were fraught with danger, both ideological and physical. Many women chose to embrace the options available in the Church as well as in the newer forms of Protestantism. Others, though, relished the independence, if not the security, available in heretical movements or sects of Protestantism. Finally, some women reveled in the more mystical or ascetic practices through which they sought to achieve a higher union with the divine. In sum, as King notes, through religious expression, in all of its various guises, women sought

> not only the freedom to pursue their goals in dignity, but also the freedom from those forces that rendered their condition "dismal": the risks and burdens of family existence, whose very basis was the sexual relations from which virginity, if it offered nothing else, meant release.[66]

4.2.4. *Women as Suspected Adulteresses*

Given the importance of chastity and patrilineality during the Renaissance period, it comes as no surprise that adultery was considered a capital offense in almost every country in Europe. The emphasis on addressing and curbing adulterous behavior was linked with men's view(s) of women's sexuality. King notes,

> While proper sexual conduct was required of both men and women, compliance to its unyielding structures was disproportionately women's responsibility. Perhaps women bore that greater burden because they were seen as possessing a greater sexual appetite, one quite gross and uncontrollable: a construct of the philosophers, theologians, physicians, and writers of books. Their violent sexual passions disrupted the social order and were seen as an attack on the social order itself.[67]

In terms of adultery, this bias regarding women's sexuality led to harmful assumptions as well as disastrous outcomes:

> In cases of adultery, they [women] were seen to bear greater guilt than men (while a man's adultery with an unmarried female was a crime that faded into nonexistence), and everywhere suffered the economic and legal consequences of conviction for that offense more than men.[68]

63. King, *Women of the Renaissance*, 125.
64. See King, *Women of the Renaissance*, 127–28.
65. King, *Women of the Renaissance*, 128.
66. King, *Women of the Renaissance*, 135.
67. King, *Women of the Renaissance*, 41.
68. King, *Women of the Renaissance*, 42.

How, then, were women convicted of adultery, and what were the punishments for such a verdict?

After the Reformation began, various ecclesiastical courts or consistories began to emerge to address moral and religious offenses. These marriage courts operated with the cooperation of secular authorities and even engaged in joint investigations when circumstances warranted. Ulrich Zwingli in Zurich established the first of these courts in 1525, and it dealt mainly with marital issues but also with other matters such as gambling, blasphemy, and fornication. The most (in)famous consistory was created by Calvin in 1541. This court, even more than Zwingli's, used its power to punish and excommunicate to observe and regulate the practices of its members, especially in sexual matters. Thus, women who were accused of adultery were likely to be brought before such courts to address the spiritual defect(s) in their character prior to being handed over to secular authorities for more corporal punishments.

As Wiesner-Hanks notes, "Accusations of adultery were taken far more seriously than those of domestic violence or slander, because adultery directly challenged the central link between marriage and procreation as well as impugning male honor."[69] Punishments for the crime of adultery varied according to the nature of the offense: "adulterers were generally punished with fines, prison sentences, corporal punishment or banishment; only when their cases involved multiple partners, public scandal, or incest were they executed."[70] The most common method of execution for female adulterers was drowning. However, social status often determined the extent of one's punishment; the greater one's status and/or wealth, the less one will have to suffer if convicted.

Even though women bore more responsibility for sexually based offenses than men in the popular and educated imagination of the time, the law was less biased. In contrast to the first century B.C.E., the legal definition of adultery included sexual relations between a married man and an unmarried woman. Indeed, men were often tried and convicted of adultery. Even so, it was the act of adultery committed by a married woman that was singled out for the most emphatic condemnation, as Wiesner-Hanks notes, "adultery by a married man with a single woman did not threaten the family and lineage in the way that adultery by a married woman did, for it could not bring the child of another man into a family."[71] Indeed, men were shielded by law against legal actions from their wives, and often profited economically by accusations of adultery being leveled against their wives. As Keith Thomas notes, only women of financial means had legal remedies against adulterous husbands or were able to obtain separations:

> Adultery by either partner was good grounds for a separation and here it might seem as if the double standard went into abeyance. But such an impression would be misleading, for in practice it usually only the husband who was in a position to take advantage of this. The wife was seldom able to claim a separation from her husband. The reasons for this were economic; she would probably be unable to support herself during such a

69. Wiesner-Hanks, *Christianity and Sexuality*, 77.
70. Wiesner-Hanks, *Christianity and Sexuality*, 77.
71. Wiesner-Hanks, *Christianity and Sexuality*, 77.

> separation because, although separated, she was still subject to all the legal disabilities of a married woman. In other words, she was now in a state of virtual outlawry, for her husband retained all his rights over her property, including even the wages she might earn after her separation; she was incapable of conducting a legal action by herself, and she could not even claim access to her children. All she had was a small allowance in the shape of alimony and the payment of this was often difficult to enforce. As a result it was only those wives of higher social status with independent property rights secured to them by equity who were in a position to take advantage of their theoretical right to gain a separation from a husband on the grounds of his adultery.[72]

Even though Thomas focuses on the situation of women in England, the same legal discrimination was found in Europe. In France, a husband could kill his adulterous wife legally, and appropriate her dowry; a woman separated from her husband for adultery in Venice lost control of her dowry.[73] As King notes, "adultery was the most effective solvent, prejudicial to the wife, of the marriage tie."[74]

In sum, adulterous relationships represented a threat to both female chastity and paternal inheritance, and as such were condemned by both secular and religious authorities. Women stood to lose more, socially, economically, and physically, from accusations of adultery than men did owing to the economic and social security held by men that the law did not afford to women. In fact, this legal disproportion was taken to an extreme by Louis XIV when, in 1658, he ordered all women found guilty of adultery, prostitution, or fornication to be imprisoned in the women's prison at Salpêtrière until the priests and nuns in charge were convinced of their remorse.[75] This action, effectively creating the concept of a "reformatory," can be seen as a result of the overemphasis on chastity and "correct" behavior (dis)placed onto women by men with social, economic, and religious power during and before the Renaissance period. In effect, these men—and the women who cooperated with them in establishing patriarchal systems across Europe—created and named the very behavior and offenses they would come to regard as abnormal and criminal.

4.3. *Conclusion*

It would seem that the common denominator among the above categories of women is the emphasis on chastity, coupled with the stability it brings to society. As I note above, King goes so far as to claim "the guarding of chastity was the primary business of the daughters of the Renaissance."[76] Of course, chastity before and in marriage, as well as virginity for nuns and religious women was not a new phenomenon; the emphasis on the "proper" sexual state for women is an ancient occurrence, as we saw in Chapter 2. Chastity, or proper continence, is a major theme in the *Apocryphal Acts of the Apostles*, as Kate Cooper and Virginia

72. Keith Thomas, "The Double Standard," *Journal of the History of Ideas* 20 (1959): 195–216 (200–201).

73. See King, *Women of the Renaissance*, 42.

74. King, *Women of the Renaissance*, 42.

75. See Wiesner-Hanks, *Christianity and Sexuality*, 125–26.

76. King, *Women of the Renaissance*, 29.

Burrus note.[77] Gillian Cloke, in her study of women during the Patristic period (350–450 C.E.) notes that committed virgins during this period were viewed highly by Patristic writers, even claiming "virgins should properly be the first rank in heaven, the vanguard of the church."[78] Finally, during the Middle Ages, chastity and virginity were increasingly "tested" in order to maintain a standard for physical and spiritual purity, as Kathleen Coyne Kelly notes.[79]

During the Renaissance period, though, an explosion of prescriptive literature aimed at men and extolling certain virtues of women increased the emphasis on "proper" behavior, including the importance of chastity. Alongside the many examples quoted above, two illustrations will suffice. Vives, in his highly influential handbook, writes,

> Many things are required of a man: wisdom, eloquence, knowledge of political affairs, talent, memory, some trade to live by, justice, liberality, magnanimity, and other qualities it would take a long time to rehearse. If some of these are lacking, he seems to have less blame as long as some are present. But in a woman, no one requires eloquence or talent or wisdom or professional skills or administration of the republic or justice or generosity; no one asks anything of her but chastity. If that one thing is missing, it is as if all were lacking to a man.[80]

Ideally, then, women were expected to perform only one task, to fulfill only one role, to present only one appearance: that of chastity.

A century earlier than Vives, the great Florentine architect, musician, and theorist Leon Battista Alberti (ca. 1402–1472) wrote a treatise entitled *Della Famiglia* (*On the Family*), in which he addresses the topic of women and chastity while discussing good household management. In his dialogue, he recounts an address made to his wife on the subject of chaste behavior, and his view is worth quoting at length:

> Know that nothing will be so dear to God, pleasing to me, and useful to our children as your chastity. Chastity in a wife has always been the ornament of a family; a mother's chastity has always been part of a daughter's dowry; chastity has always been worth more to anyone than beauty. A beautiful face is to be praised, but wayward eyes cover it with disgrace, make it blush from shame or turn pale from grief or anger. A graceful body is charming, but one immodest gesture, one unchaste act will soon defile it. Immodesty displeases God, and you see that God never punishes women so severely as when they are unchaste, making them infamous and dissatisfied for the rest of their lives. Immodesty is hateful to one who really and truly loves. An unchaste woman sees that her dishonesty pleases only her enemies. Only those who wish you harm can be pleased by seeing dishonesty in you. Therefore, my dear wife, you must avoid all dishonesty and must appear chaste to all, otherwise you will offend God, me, our children, and yourself. Only in this way will you gain everyone's love and praise, and can hope

77. See Kate Cooper, *The Virgin and the Bride: Idealized Womanhood in Late Antiquity* (Cambridge, Mass.: Harvard University Press, 1995); and Virginia Burrus, *Chastity as Autonomy: Women in the Stories of Apocryphal Acts* (Lewiston, N.Y.: Edwin Mellen, 1987).

78. Gillian Cloke, *This Female Man of God: Women and Spiritual Power in the Patristic Age, AD 350–450* (London: Routledge, 1995), 58.

79. Kathleen Coyne Kelly, *Performing Virginity and Testing Chastity in the Middle Ages* (Routledge Research in Medieval Studies; London: Routledge, 2000).

80. Vives, *The Education of a Christian Woman*, 85 (1.6.44).

> that God will answer your prayers. If you wished to be praised for your chastity, then, you will avoid any dishonest act, any immodest word, any sign of a fickle and incontinent nature. First of all, you must abhor the frivolities through which some foolish women try to please men. They think men like them better when they are all painted and dressed in immodest, indecent clothes than when they show themselves adorned with pure simplicity and true honesty. There are many very foolish, vain women who show themselves painted and immodest and think that those who look at them praise them, without realizing that they are being condemned. They do not see, poor fools, that with those signs of immodesty they attract crowds of libertines who go after them boldly, assiduously, or deceitfully, until the wretched, unfortunate girls fall, not to rise again without the stains of eternal infamy.[81]

For Alberti, like Vives, chastity serves as a cipher for all that men deem proper in women and their behavior. Immodesty, here the opposite of chastity, leads to a breakdown of socially accepted sexual relationships and results in "eternal infamy." Unchaste behavior has repercussions for everyone associated with the women who perform it; Alberti posits a hierarchy of offended parties, beginning with God, then the husband and family, and finally, the woman herself. By placing the woman at the lowest end of those affected by "immodest" behavior, Alberti implies that the effect her behavior has on everyone else is of more consequence than the effect it has on her. Indeed, Alberti is specifically concerned with his wife appearing chaste to others, and thereby eliciting their love and praise, which would inevitably lead to an increase in his own status.

In fact, one could argue that the concern seen in the work of Vives and Alberti over chastity reflects nothing more than a sense of self-preservation, a desire to increase their—and other men's—status and honor by properly "controlling" their women's sexuality. As Thomas notes,

> Fundamentally, female chastity has been seen as a matter of property; not, however, the property of legitimate heirs, but the property of men in women. The language in which virginity is most often described should tell us this, for it is that of the commercial market... In other words, girls who have lost their "honor" have also lost their saleability in the marriage market. The double standard, therefore, is the reflection of that view that men have property in women and that the value of this property is immeasurably diminished if the woman at any time has sexual relations with anyone other than her husband.[82]

This emphasis on women as property recalls the importance confirmed chastity plays in the marriage transaction. As I note above, in the eyes of many men, daughters had but one pragmatic use, and that was marriage, hopefully a beneficial one that would allow the father to increase his social status and/or wealth. Thomas comments on this use of women by men, and speaks of a

> whole code of social conduct for women which was in turn based entirely upon their place in society in relation to men. The value set on female chastity varied directly according to the extent to which it was considered that women's function was a purely

81. Leon Battista Alberti, *Della Famiglia*, in *The Albertis of Florence: Leon Battista Alberti's* Della Famiglia (trans. Guido A. Guarino; Bucknell Renaissance Texts in Translation Series; Lewisburg: Bucknell University Press, 1971), 27–326 (221–22).

82. Thomas, "The Double Standard," 209–10.

> sexual one. Until modern times women were, broadly speaking, thought of as incomplete in themselves and as existing primarily for the sake of men... The virtue of women was relative to their function and their function was to cater to the needs of men. For this task the first qualification was chastity; hence, chastity was the essence of female virtue.[83]

Thus, in anthropological terms, women were viewed by many men as commodities, as pawns in developing relationships, or kinship systems, with other men in order to increase and solidify social status and ensure the continuation of their vision of social organization. In an influential study of this phenomenon, Gayle Rubin makes clear what is involved in this "exchange of women."

> Kinship systems do not merely exchange women. They exchange sexual access, genealogical statuses, lineage names and ancestors, rights and *people*—men, women, and children—in concrete systems of social relationships. These relationships always include certain rights for men, others for women. "Exchange of women" is a shorthand for expressing that the social relations of a kinship system specify that men have certain rights in their female kin, and that women do not have the same rights either to themselves or to their male kin. In this sense, the exchange of women is a profound perception of a system in which women do not have full rights to themselves.[84]

Thus, the patriarchal and androcentric system of viewing women as commodities and the concomitant value placed on chastity during the Renaissance deprived women of full rights to themselves, allowing them only few options for living, and even fewer, if any, for autonomy.

Even so, there were those—men and women—during the Renaissance who argued that women should be viewed as at least equals, and at most superior to men. In his work on this topic, Conor Fahy lists forty-one extant works of this nature.[85] One of the most interesting pieces of this genre is a pamphlet entitled "The Women's Sharpe Revenge." This pamphlet, published in 1640, was evidently written by a man named John Taylor as a facetious satire of earlier pamphlets that denigrated women and advocated male superiority. This rather dubious origin does not mean the work contains nothing of interest; obviously it was popular enough among both men and women to be preserved, and some of its arguments are very intriguing. One in particular illuminates the situation of women during the Renaissance period in a wonderful fashion:

> When we [women], whom they [men] style by the name of "weaker vessels", though of a more delicate, fine, soft and more pliant flesh, and therefore of a temper most capable of the best impression, have not that generous and liberal education lest we should be made able to vindicate our own injuries: we are set only to the needle, to prick our fingers; or else to the wheel to spin a fair thread for our own undoings; or perchance to some more dirty and debased drudgery. If we be taught to read, then they confine us within the compass of our mother's tongue, and that limit we are not suffered to pass; or

83. Thomas, "The Double Standard," 213–14.

84. Gayle Rubin, "The Traffic in Women: Notes on the 'Political Economy' of Sex," in *Toward an Anthropology of Women* (ed. Rayna R. Reiter; New York: Monthly Review Press, 1975), 157–210 (177).

85. See Conor Fahy, "Three Early Renaissance Treatises on Women," *Italian Studies* 11 (1956): 30–55.

> if (which sometimes happeneth) we are brought up to music, to singing and dancing, it is not for any benefit that thereby we can engross unto ourselves, but for their own particular ends—the better to please and content their licentious appetites when we come to our maturity and ripeness. *And thus, if we be weak by nature, they strive to make us more weak by our nurture; and, if in degree of place low, they strive by their policy to keep us more under.*[86]

Even though this was written by a man who bore little sympathy for the emotions and situation it describes, this description of a woman's place in the Renaissance is, on the whole, accurate. This pamphlet, and the many more like it, also provides evidence that even though the social system of the time viewed women mainly as commodities, there were those who challenged that view, and, as we saw above in our discussion of holy women, those who exorcised themselves from the system altogether.

Thus, the place of women in the Renaissance was precarious due to the economic, social, and sexual anxieties they caused for men. However, as we have seen, this was also a time of great beginnings for women, not only in human rights, but also in educational opportunities and religious expression. In my next two chapters, I will examine how these disparate views of women, along with the social and historical circumstances that occasioned them, influence and were influenced by the story of Susanna in artistic, musical, and literary interpretations.

86. Taken from "The Women's Sharpe Revenge," in *The Women's Sharp Revenge: Five Women's Pamphlets from the Renaissance* (ed. Simon Shepherd; New York: St. Martin's Press, 1985), 159–93 (170) (italics mine).

Chapter 5

THE STANDARD DEPICTION OF SUSANNA DURING THE RENAISSANCE

5.1. *Introduction*

The customary artistic interpretation of Susanna during the Renaissance was a sexual, eroticizing one. This trend resulted from patrons and artists focusing on the mimetic level of the narrative, which contains the sexual, voyeuristic aspects of the plot. In her work, Mary D. Garrard describes this tendency, writing, "In art, a sexually exploitative and morally meaningless interpretation of the [Susanna] theme has prevailed, most simply, because most artists and patrons have been men, drawn by instinct to identify more with the villains than with the heroine."[1] In addition to this focus on the sexual qualities of the story, issues of sex and gender also contributed to this tendency to highlight the erotic attributes of the apocryphal narrative. This, in turn, de-emphasizes the thematic purpose of the story. That is, these portrayals of Susanna focus on the sexually charged and abusive encounter between Susanna and the Elders in lieu of highlighting the thematic emphasis on faith in God found in the story. I will argue that representations of this sort seek to coerce the viewer into complicity with the Elders in terms of their desire for Susanna and thus render their sexually aggressive actions less reprehensible. Because of this tendency, these interpretations are harmful ideologically in that they portray the desire to possess Susanna via rape as a natural result of viewing female beauty.

5.2. *Renaissance Interpretations of Susanna*

I have chosen three painters who produced some of the most influential eroticizing recyclings of Susanna during the Renaissance to examine chronologically. In my discussion of specific interpretations, I will mention other works for the purpose of comparing or contrasting, and I will list all aesthetic interpretations I cite in this chapter and the next in Appendix 2. Additionally, for reasons of space as well as clarity, I will introduce biographical information in a selective fashion, i.e., either when a producer of a specific interpretation is not well known, or when these data will prove useful in illuminating a rendering's production. The examples I discuss in the next two chapters have been chosen for various reasons.

1. Mary D. Garrard, "Artemesia and Susanna," in *Feminism and Art History: Questioning the Litany* (ed. Norma Broude and Mary D. Garrard; New York: Harper & Row, 1982), 146–71 (153).

In some cases, the choice was obvious, e.g., the works of Tintoretto, Gentileschi, and Rembrandt are so recognized that their notoriety warranted their inclusion. In other cases, e.g., the drama of Birck, as well as the poem of Guéroult, my considerations were geographical as well. Put another way, I grouped several examples based on their geographic origin, so that we could chart how Susanna's story was used in different contexts.

5.2.1. *Tintoretto (Jacopo Robusti)*
Tintoretto's career is intimately bound up with the city in which he spent his entire life: Venice. Born Jacopo Robusti, he was the son of a cloth dyer, thus his nickname Tintoretto, meaning "the little dyer." Little is known about his training, but early sources report that he worked briefly in Titian's workshop, before being expelled prior to 1539.[2] The Mannerist movement influenced much of his early work, and there is still debate over whether or not his mature work represents a break with that style or an embracing of it.[3] Either way, it was his 1547/8 painting of *St. Mark Rescuing the Slave* that brought him widespread recognition in Venice.[4] Because of this painting, he began to receive more prestigious commissions. Even though his family did not enjoy higher citizen status (*cittadino originario*), by 1553 Tintoretto had married the daughter of an important member of the Scuola Grande di S. Marco, and thus was initiated into the "pious, civic-minded and essentially conservative world of the non-noble confraternities."[5] The *scuole* in Renaissance Venice were upper class, yet not noble, devotional groups that were active in terms of both charitable causes and the arts.[6] These confraternities would figure prominently in Tintoretto's life. He was admitted to the Scuola Grande di S. Rocco in ca. 1565, and would spend the remainder of his life decorating their meeting house. The last two decades of his life were the most prolific. He not only did extensive work at the Scuole Grande di S. Rocco, he was also involved in redecorating the Doge's palace after two fires caused considerable damage in 1574 and 1577. After Titian's death in 1576, Tintoretto received court commissions from abroad, including Prague. He also completed Paolo Veronese's commission for the Doge's palace between 1588 and 1590 after

2. See, e.g., the testimony of Carlo Ridolfi from 1642, now available in *The Life of Tintoretto* (trans. Catherine and Robert Enggass; University Park: The Pennsylvania State University Press, 1984), 15.

3. For a definition of Mannerism, see Linda Murray, *The Late Renaissance and Mannerism* (Praeger World of Art; New York: Frederick A. Praeger, 1967), 30–31. In that work, she treats Tintoretto as a Mannerist (see pp. 99–112), while Tomas Nichols, "Jacopo Tintoretto," *The Grove Dictionary of Art Online*, n.p. [1998]. Online: http://www.groveart.com/index.html, argues that "the essentially communicative and moral intention of Tintoretto's formal manipulations distance his work from contemporary Mannerism." Also see Peter Humfrey, *Painting in Renaissance Venice* (New Haven: Yale University Press, 1995), 193: "Few art historians now accept the earlier twentieth-century view of Tintoretto as one of the most typical representatives of Italian Mannerism."

4. For a discussion of this work, see David Rosand, *Painting in Sixteenth-Century Venice: Titian, Veronese, Tintoretto* (rev. ed.; Cambridge: Cambridge University Press, 1997), 134–39.

5. Nichols, "Jacopo Tintoretto."

6. For a brief discussion of *scuole*, see Humfrey, *Painting in Renaissance Venice*, 28.

Veronese's death in 1588, and did several large, important works for the church of S. Giorgio Maggiore between 1591 and his death in 1594, among them his last rendition of *The Last Supper*.

Over the course of his career, Tintoretto produced four different renditions of the Susanna story. His most famous version is the 1555/6 *Susanna and the Elders* (Fig. 1), which I will discuss below. In the early to mid-1550s, Tintoretto engaged in what Terisio Pignatti terms "an undisguised ideological and stylistic confrontation" with his major contemporaries, Titian and Veronese.[7] Basically, Tintoretto took up either techniques or subjects utilized by the older, more established artists in order both to challenge himself and present his talent comparatively.

Figure 1. Tintoretto, *Susanna and the Elders*, ca. 1555/6.
Vienna, Kunsthistorisches Museum

One of the fruits of this confrontation was his first known *Susanna and the Elders* (Fig. 2 [next page]). In this work, Tintoretto shows Susanna being attended to by her servants, a scene not present in the apocryphal narrative. In the story, Susanna sends her maids to retrieve olive oil and ointment so that she may bathe. The servants only return later when one of the Elders shouts out after Susanna refuses their advances. Also, the Elders are rather inconspicuously rendered in the far upper right corner of the piece, so they have not confronted Susanna yet. Since most interpretations of Susanna during the Renaissance choose to depict the encounter between Susanna and the Elders, this choice seems odd. Finally, Susanna herself is looking directly at the viewer, again an uncommon icono-

7. See Pignatti, "Life and Works," in Francesco Valcanover and Terisio Pignatti, *Tintoretto* (The Library of Great Painters Series; trans. Robert Erich Wolf; New York: Abrams, 1985), 9–56 (27).

graphical choice during this time period. Based on these brief observations, we may ask what Tintoretto's intention(s) may have been in rendering Susanna in this fashion. Gail A. Bonjione offers the following answer to the question:

> In this work, two servants attend to her grooming needs, either combing her long tresses or manicuring her toes. Because of this attention to her body, which displays the muscular style of Michelangelo, Susanna appears somewhat vain. The mirror beneath her extended leg reinforces this *vanitas* element... Tintoretto obviously intended to focus on the figure of Susanna and her vanity and not on the actions of the Elders. The notion of Susanna as a victim is diminished because she is actively enticing the spectator with her direct gaze. She does not seem vulnerable at all.[8]

In this work, then, Tintoretto is rendering Susanna in such a way that would allow the viewer to take part, both visually and psychologically, in the Elders' lust for Susanna.

Figure 2. Tintoretto, *Susanna and the Elders*, 1550–1555.
Paris, the Louvre

In his second painting of Susanna, commonly known as the Viennese *Susanna* (Fig. 1), Tintoretto portrays the heroine in much the same fashion.[9] In this work, the figure of Susanna dominates the frame. She is sitting comfortably behind a

8. Gail A. Bonjione, "Shifting Images: Susanna through the Ages" (Ph. D. diss., Florida State University, 1997), 91. However, in her examination, Marie-Louise Fabre does not view the gaze of Susanna as an enticement. Rather, "Suzanne regarde le spectateur avec une indifférence absente, sans sourire." See Fabre's *Suzanne ou les avatars d'un motif biblique* (Sémantiques; Paris: L'Harmattan, 2000), 227. I do not agree with Fabre's position, as I will state below.

9. For a more technical description of this piece, see Michaela Herrmann, *Vom Schauen als Metapher des Begehrens: Die venezianischen Darstellungen der "Susanna im Bade" im Cinquecento* (Dissertationes 4; Marburg: Hitzeroth, 1990), 48–53.

wall in her garden with one foot dangling carelessly in her bath, gazing at herself in a mirror. She seems totally at ease, not knowing that the two Elders are spying on her while she, in turn, looks at herself. One Elder is in the foreground, lying on the ground in an attempt to watch unnoticed, while the other maneuvers around the far edge of the wall. As one gazes at the Elders gazing at Susanna who is gazing at herself, a problem arises. If Susanna is so involved with her beauty—and the placement of oil and other items implies the *vanitas* element already present in the Louvre *Susanna* (Fig. 2)—then one might wonder how *this* Susanna would respond to the Elders' advances. That is, because of the way in which Susanna exhibits her sexuality and her self-admiration, the viewer is led to the conclusion that she is open to a sexual encounter with the Elders.

The key to this line of investigation is the gaze of Susanna into her mirror. John Berger, in an oft-quoted analysis, comments on the function of the mirror:

> Susannah is looking at herself in a mirror. Thus she joins the spectators of herself. The mirror was often used as a symbol of the vanity of woman. The moralizing, however, was mostly hypocritical. You painted a naked woman because you enjoyed looking at her, you put a mirror in her hand and you called the painting *Vanity*, thus morally condemning the woman whose nakedness you had depicted for your own pleasure. The real function of the mirror was otherwise. It was to make the woman connive in treating herself as, first and foremost, a sight.[10]

As I have shown in Chapter 2, this auto-voyeurism is not present in the apocryphal narrative. Why then would Tintoretto have incorporated it into his work and heightened the erotic presence in the picture as a result? Garrard provides a possible answer:

> Renaissance and Baroque artists, however, like the early church fathers, ignored the fundamental moral point concerning the discovery of truth and the execution of justice, to focus instead upon the secondary plot devices of temptation, seduction, and the erotic escapades of the Elders... Both the patristic and the artistic conceptions of Susanna, whether as an Eve triumphant over her own impulses or as a voluptuous sex object who may not bother to resist, are linked by the same erroneous assumption: that Susanna's dilemma was whether or not to give in to her sexual instincts.[11]

Along with this factor, one of the main reasons for this heightened sense of the erotic in sixteenth-century interpretations of Susanna was that many artists used Venus and Lucretia as models for rendering Susanna.[12] As Garrard notes,

10. John Berger, *Ways of Seeing* (London: BBC/Penguin, 1972), 50–51.

11. Garrard, "Artemesia and Susanna," 152–53. One of the most important works that depicts Susanna as an Eve-like figure is Jacopo Bassano's 1566/7 *Susanna and the Elders* (Ottawa, the National Gallery of Canada). See W. R. Rearick, "Jacopo Bassano and Changing Religious Imagery in the Mid-Cinquecento," in *Essays Presented to Myron P. Gilmore*. Vol. 2, *History of Art, History of Music* (ed. Sergio Bertelli and Gloria Ramakus; Villa I Tatti 2; Florence: La Nuova Italia Editrice, 1978), 331–43 (339–41); Bernard Aikema, *Jacopo Bassano and His Public: Moralizing Pictures in an Age of Reform, ca. 1535–1600* (trans. Andrew P. McCormick; Princeton, N.J.: Princeton University Press, 1996), 126–31; and Herrmann, *Vom Schauen als Metapher des Begehrens*, 55–61.

12. For a survey of portrayals of Venus, see Kenneth Clark, *The Nude: A Study in Ideal Form* (Garden City, N.Y.: Doubleday, 1956), 109–232. See also the critique of Clark's work by Lynda Nead in her *The Female Nude: Art, Obscenity and Sexuality* (London: Routledge, 1992).

> The frequent echo of these antique prototypes in paintings of the Susanna theme underlies their use as a device to evoke erotic recollections, in the classic formulation of having it both ways: adhering superficially to the requirement that Susanna be chaste, while appealing subliminally to the memory of the Venus archetype, whose gestures of modesty call attention to what she conceals.[13]

In her examination of nakedness in the West, Margaret R. Miles agrees with Garrard's analysis. She writes that Tintoretto's work attempts

> to reproduce, in the eyes of an assumed male viewer, the Elders' intense erotic attraction, projected and displayed on Susanna's flesh. The Elders, placed in crepuscular shadows, do not bear the weight of communicating the urgency of their active desire; rather, her body represents that desire. Viewers are directed—trained—by the management of light and shadow and by the central position of Susanna's body to see Susanna as object, even as cause, of male desire. In the painting, Susanna's innocence becomes guilt as her body communicates and explains the Elders' lust. As this visual narration indicates, female nakedness has received its symbolic representation, in the societies of the Christian West, from "the Elders." Female nakedness has a range of meanings assigned by voyeurs for whom female bodies represented simultaneously threat, danger, and delight.[14]

Thus, because of the use of antique models for the depiction of Susanna, the gendered material conditions of production of artistic works based on Susanna during the Renaissance, and the gendered position of viewers, Susanna is somehow forced to identify with a position that results in harmful views and actions against herself. That is, due to the interests and needs of those producing and financing interpretations of the story of Susanna, the figure of Susanna as presented in the story is twisted into a figure that not only causes male desire, but who is open to it as well.

Not long after he painted the Viennese *Susanna*, perhaps even in the same year, Tintoretto produced a series of ceiling paintings in which he again mimicked the style of Veronese. The seven works in this cycle include *Joseph and Potiphar's Wife*, *Judith and Holofernes*, and *Esther and Ahasuerus*. The cycle also includes a small *Susanna and the Elders* (Fig. 3) in which Tintoretto seems to reference his previous Viennese work. Specifically, the two Elders seem to be almost identical in both works, and the garden wall in both is remarkably similar. However, the placement of the subjects has been altered considerably. In accordance with the standard rendering of the theme during the Renaissance, the Elders are confronting Susanna. One stands to the right of her and assumes a gesture of

13. Garrard, "Artemesia and Susanna," 154. Interestingly, Bonjione ("Shifting Images," 92–93) notes that some critics have interpreted the Viennese *Susanna* as containing Marian imagery. She writes, "Like the Virgin Mary, Susanna is unattainable. The rose hedge, symbolic of Mary, protects her from harm. Also, the fact that Tintoretto places one of her legs in the clear water could refer to a kind of baptism or renewal" (p. 93). I do not find her argument convincing, in part because she does not cite the critics to whom she refers, but her point is interesting given Albrecht Altdorfer's portrayal of Susanna (Fig. 6), which I will discuss in the next chapter. More interestingly, Fabre (*Suzanne ou les avatars d'un motif biblique*, 231–33), explores the possible connection between the work and the myths of Diana and Artemis.

14. Margaret R. Miles, *Carnal Knowing: Female Nakedness and Religious Meaning in the Christian West* (Boston: Beacon, 1989), 123–24.

speaking softly to her, while the Elder on her left is clutching her breast. Certainly we are never told of any physical contact between the Elders and Susanna in the apocryphal story, but this did not stop artists from embellishing the story to heighten the erotic overtones. In fact, Marie-Louise Fabre notes other examples of Tintoretto's work that portray "scenes of seduction and aggression where the woman's posture is rather laviscious," and writes that this "makes one think that he wanted to show that he was as capable as anyone else at representing a naked female temptress."[15] Thus, by adding a sexually explicit scene not found in the apocryphal narrative, Tintoretto, like other artists throughout the ages, is calling into question Susanna's willingness to refute the advances of the Elders.

Figure 3. Tintoretto, *Susanna and the Elders*, ca. 1555.
Madrid, Museo del Prado

There is one final painting of *Susanna and the Elders* by Tintoretto to consider: the ca. 1575 print in the National Gallery in Washington D.C.[16] Even more than the Viennese *Susanna*, the figure of Susanna dominates this work. She is shown in the very center of the foreground with one foot in the water, like in the Viennese piece, receiving what presumably is oil for her bath from a servant. Unlike his first two efforts, here Susanna's partial nakedness is on direct display to the viewer. However, like his Louvre print, Tintoretto places the Elders off in the far distance; indeed they appear to be almost in a fog. Even so, they can easily see Susanna, for the foliage close to them is shaped like an arch, thus allowing them to see Susanna, and the viewer to see them. One possible reason for the difference in presentation here could be biographical. By ca. 1575, Tintoretto was beginning his intensive work on the Scuole Grande di S. Rocco, as well as starting work on the Doge's palace. As such, he might have relied on his workshop apprentices, including his son Domenico and daughter Marietta, to help him complete many works around this time. Tintoretto had always used a workshop like other artists of the period, but his swiftness in completing paintings had

15. Fabre, *Suzanne ou les avatars d'un motif biblique*, 227.

16. Online: http://www.nga.gov/cgi-bin/pinfo?Object=375+0+none.

always necessitated a heightened reliance. Humfrey acknowledges this increased dependence on his apprentices toward the end of his life and comments that "The inevitable result was a decline in quality in most of Tintoretto's late works."[17] In fact, Nichols writes, "After 1580 relatively few paintings can be attributed to Tintoretto alone."[18] Was this growing reliance on his apprentices behind the different view of the theme in this work? Perhaps, but the important point to make is that here, again, we see the theme of *vanitas* and the presentation of Susanna as a sumptuous nude. Ellen Spolsky writes concerning these issues:

> At the same time the painting itself is an *objet d'art*, the painted woman is also an object, available to the viewer's gaze. His stare might be illicit, but the painter helps him over his guilt, as it were, by picturing her nudity as vanity; her preening legitimates his gaze, and she is thus made accessible to the viewer.[19]

Given the presence of these elements, the concerns I raise above with regard to the three earlier works also apply here.

Tintoretto's interpretations of Susanna have, by and large, been praised for their technique and atmosphere, but also critiqued for their assumptions and presentation of Susanna as perhaps more involved in the advances of the Elders than the apocryphal story implies. However, none of the analyses of the Susanna paintings tries to understand them in light of the religious nature of Tintoretto's work. He was, after all, a native of Venice and a member of one of the religiously conservative *scuole*, and as such would have brought a sense of devotion, perhaps even piety, to his work. Certainly the sheer number of religious paintings in his vast output testifies to his preoccupation with religious themes, e.g., he painted works based on the Last Supper at least eight different times. In his analysis of Tintoretto's religious works, David Rosand reaches the following conclusion regarding Tintoretto's expression(s) of piety:

> Tintoretto's piety can be considered Counter-Reformatory only in the most general way, if at all, and to discuss it with specific references to the decrees of the Council of Trent may be somewhat misleading. It belongs, rather, in the larger context of pre-Tridentine Catholic reform, with its emphasis on the basic tenets of spiritual responsibility. It would seem more appropriate to talk about the fundamentalism of Tintoretto's Christian faith—or at least the faith that is figured in his paintings... Tintoretto's own religious vision is neither mystical nor exclusively personal; rather, it is open and popular, common in the sense of shared conviction.[20]

17. Humfrey, *Painting in Renaissance Venice*, 236.

18. Nichols, "Jacopo Tintoretto." A case in point is a *Susanna and the Elders* in the Frick Art Museum in Pittsburgh, Pa. Many scholars have attributed this piece to Tintoretto, as do Dorothée Sölle et al., *Great Women of the Bible in Art and Literature* (Grand Rapids: Eerdmans, 1993), 240 and 294. In their survey of Tintoretto's work, Carlo Bernari and Pierluigi de Vecchi date the piece to 1589, and deny any attribution to him. See *L'Opera Completa del Tintoretto* (Milan: Rizzoli Editore, 1970), 131. Walter Read Hovey, in *Treasures of the Frick Art Museum* (Pittsburgh, Pa.: The Frick Art Museum, 1975), 58, hypothesizes that Tintoretto's daughter Marietta may have painted the piece. Although such a theory certainly fits with what we know of Tintoretto's later working habits, in the absence of any hard evidence, it must remain a theory.

19. Ellen Spolsky, "Law or the Garden: The Betrayal of Susanna in Pastoral Painting," in Spolsky, ed., *The Judgment of Susanna*, 101–18 (102–3).

20. Rosand, *Painting in Sixteenth-Century Venice*, 159.

In a similar vein, Humfrey even goes so far as to analyze Tintoretto's religious works theologically:

> By setting his biblical stories in humble, mundane and shadowy surroundings, and then illuminating them with sudden pools and shafts of light, Tintoretto triumphantly succeeds in conveying a sense that the world of ordinary sinful humanity is subject to workings of divine providence.[21]

However, one finds no trace of an emphasis on divine providence in his interpretations of Susanna—a remarkable fact, given the intervention of God via Daniel in the story. Based on his religious paintings, one could argue, as Rosand does, that Tintoretto's religiosity is so generic that he had no proverbial axe to grind, in contrast to other interpreters, as I will show in Chapter 6. It is possible, of course, that Tintoretto held strong religious beliefs and that these beliefs influenced his work, but nothing in his Susannas attests to that theory. Instead, I find it more likely that in the case of his Susanna paintings, Tintoretto was following standard artistic conventions established by masters such as Titian and Veronese and decided to depict Susanna as a sexually aware, attractive nude figure, perhaps in the hopes of receiving further commissions. As such, his Susanna *oeuvre* in no way constitutes a statement on his religious proclivities, but rather a more common desire to paint an inviting nude. As Garrard notes,

> Few artistic themes have offered so satisfying an opportunity for legitimized voyeurism as Susanna and the Elders. The subject was taken up with relish by artists from the sixteenth through eighteenth centuries as an opportunity to display the female nude, in much the same spirit that such themes as Danae or Lucretia were approached, but with the added advantage that the nude's erotic appeal could be heightened by the presence of two lecherous old men, whose inclusion was both iconographically justified and pornographically effective. It is a remarkable testament to the indomitable male ego that a biblical theme holding forth an exemplum of female chastity should have become in painting a celebration of sexual opportunity, or, as Max Rooses enthusiastically described Rubens's version, a "gallant enterprise mounted by two bold adventurers."[22]

Thus, Tintoretto's depictions of Susanna have no religious significance or theological message. Rather, the theme is simply a vehicle for the pornographic display of the female nude, and an increased opportunity for biblically sanctioned voyeurism.

5.2.2. *Guido Reni*

Guido Reni, who was born in 1575 in Bologna, was one of the most important painters in Italy during the Renaissance. His talent was recognized early, and in 1584 was sent to study with Denys Calvaert, a Flemish painter.[23] Another of Calvaert's pupils at this time was Domenico Zampieri, better known as Domenichino (1581–1641), who also rose to prominence during the seventeenth

21. Humfrey, *Painting in Renaissance Venice*, 234.
22. Garrard, "Artemesia and Susanna," 149–50.
23. The biographical information for Reni is based on Richard E. Spear, "Reni, Guido," *The Grove Dictionary of Art Online*, n.p.

century.[24] Later, both Domenichino and Reni left Calvaert to study in the famous Academy of the Carracci family. Reni left Calvaert in the mid-1590s, and was instructed mainly by Agostino and Ludovico Carracci, because the arguably more famous Annibale had gone to Rome in 1595. However, Reni only stayed in the Carracci Academy until 1598, when he had a rather nasty quarrel with Ludovico.

By 1601, Reni had moved to Rome, and was patronized by the wealthy Borghese family. In fact, one of the Borgheses became Pope Paul V (1605–1621), and Reni became one of his favorite painters. During this time, he completed many important pieces despite occasional run-ins with the papacy over the timeliness and cost of his work. Reni eventually had enough of working for wealthy patrons, and in 1614 moved back to Bologna, where he stayed for the rest of his life. Not long after this move, he began to paint some of his most important religious works. Among these are his *Baptism of Christ* (1622/3) and the altarpiece for the Santa Trinitá dei Pellegrini in Rome (1625/6). Shortly after this productive period, Reni began to spend more and more time indulging himself in a long-standing habit: gambling. By the mid- to late 1630s, Reni had evidently lost more money than he could ever hope of repaying. In order to appease his creditors, he started to rely on assistants more to produce works for sale more quickly. At the time of his death in 1642 in Bologna, he had numerous debts, as well as many unfinished works, but his artistic reputation was secured.

Reni's *Susanna and the Elders* (Fig. 4) was produced during his most prolific decade, and stands firmly in the tradition of Tintoretto's mimetic, sexualizing portrayals of Susanna. Here Susanna is depicted as a very young woman, hardly the way the apocryphal narrative portrays her. In fact, Th mentions Susanna's children, and in the OG version of the apocryphal narrative the narrator tells us that she has four children. The two Elders are painted not as caricatures, as in other depictions, but as normal looking, love-struck men. The left Elder clutches Susanna's garment with his right hand while he adjures her to be silent with his left. The other Elder places his left hand on Susanna's shoulder and makes a pacifying gesture with his right hand, all the while looking with mute adoration at Susanna. For her part, Susanna looks shocked and/or frightened by their presence and actions. With one hand, she is grabbing her garment and the other hand is reaching to stay the hand of the Elder attempting to remove it. Overall, the picture portrays the confrontation between the Elders and Susanna as one of misunderstood courtship rather than attempted rape. Due to the depiction of the Elders as ordinary men who are in awe of Susanna, as well as the frontal revelation of Susanna's breasts, Reni is interpreting the story in such a way that male viewers would enjoy Susanna's beauty, and perhaps even sympathize with the Elders in their admiration.

24. In 1603, Domenichino would paint his own *Susanna and the Elders* (Rome, Galleria Doria Pamphili), in which he displays his indebtedness to the Carraccis.

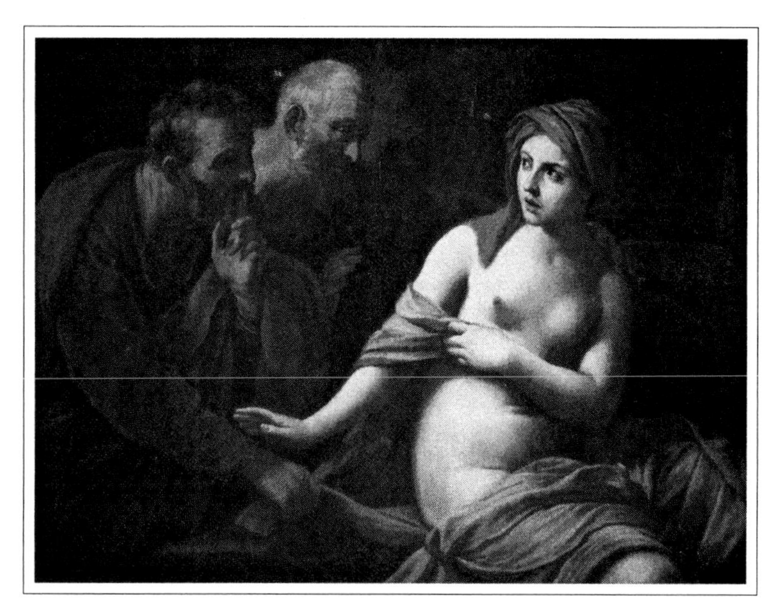

Figure 4. Guido Reni, *Susanna and the Elders*, ca. 1622/3.
Florence, Galleria degli Uffizi

Reni's portrayal of Susanna was influenced by two main factors. First, as a pupil in the Carracci Academy, he would have undoubtedly been exposed to the works of these famous painters and engravers. All three Carraccis created Susannas, and they are all disparate and important works. In 1590/1, Annibale Carracci produced his etching and engraving of Susanna (*Susanna and the Elders*, Washington, D.C., National Gallery of Art).[25] In this work, Susanna is seated and her head is turned to face the Elders, who are entreating her from behind a gate. Susanna seems calm and at ease; one finds no trace of a woman who is shocked or even anxious about the Elders' actions. In this regard, Babette Bohn comments that Annibale's Susanna "looks calmly at the Elders as if considering a reasonable proposition."[26] About the time Reni came to the Academy, Agostino Carracci completed his engraving of Susanna (*Susanna and the Elders*, ca. 1595). This, along with the engraving of Pencz I mentioned in Chapter 1 represents one of the most sexually aggressive representations of Susanna I have encountered during the Renaissance. In this piece, Susanna is shown as a full frontal nude, and is being attacked by one Elder who has grabbed her posterior. The other Elder is clutching his crotch while looking at his partner attack Susanna, and even though the architecture in the work obscures exactly what he is doing with himself, there is no doubt that it is out of his excitement at watching a fully nude Susanna be sexually attacked.

25. Online: http://www.nga.gov/cgi-bin/pinfo?Object=55577+0+none.

26. Babette Bohn, "Rape and the Gendered Gaze: *Susanna and the Elders* in Early Modern Bologna," *BibInt* 9 (2001): 259–86 (276).

The work of Ludovico Carracci represents an attempt to break away from the tradition of his cousins. That is, his depictions of Susanna are more in keeping with the thematic points of the apocryphal narrative, and focus less on the mimetic encounter between Susanna and the Elders, which his cousins chose to portray in an erotic fashion.[27] However, two factors militate against Ludovico influencing Reni. First, Ludovico's first painting of Susanna (Modena, Banca popolare dell' Emilia) was not produced until 1598, which was the year that Reni left the Academy, coincidentally after having a disagreement with Ludovico. Second, Reni's painting does not show any of the stylistic features that characterize Ludovico's work. Even though Ludovico's second depiction of Susanna (*Susanna and the Elders*, 1616; London, National Gallery)[28] resembles the composition of Reni's work, the overall impression of the London *Susanna* is not one of eroticism. In this regard, Bohn is correct in arguing that Reni's work was mostly influenced by Annibale's more serene portrayal of seduction, rather than Ludovico's impression of violent struggle.[29]

The second reason behind Reni's portrayal of Susanna is his own attitude toward women. His earliest biographer, Carlo Cesare Malvasia, notes that he became like marble when he drew a female model, and would not be alone with a female model.[30] It also seems that Reni was something of a "mama's boy" in that he adored and idolized his mother. When she died in 1630, he would no longer allow any woman to enter his house, his gambling problems increased, and the quality of his output decreased. Furthermore, it was generally acknowledged that Reni, being unmarried, was a virgin. In fact, many scholars have argued that Reni was gay.[31] In his examination of Reni's attitudes toward women, Richard E. Spear notes that he was especially afraid of older women, due to the prevalent fear of witchcraft during this period.[32] As a staunch Catholic, Reni would have been exposed to both the Church's teachings on women as well as stories about witches.

In addition to his almost paranoid distrust of women, Reni was a faithful devotee of the Virgin Mary. After the Council of Trent, various cults were allowed to multiply by the Church, and several of these focused on Mary. One of Reni's main patron's during his Roman period, Paul V, was himself a loyal follower of Mary. As Marina Warner notes, Paul V allowed the Servites, a very popular group devoted to the Virgin, to establish new confraternities to spread their particular message.[33] While there is no evidence that Reni was a member of this group, he was attached to the Capuchins, for whom he painted several

27. For this position, see Bohn, "Rape and the Gendered Gaze," 267–75.

28. Online: http://www.nationalgallery.org.uk/cgi-bin/WebObjects.dll/CollectionPublisher.woa/wa/work?workNumber=ng28.

29. See Bohn, "Rape and the Gendered Gaze," 277–78.

30. Quoted in Spear, *The "Divine" Guido: Religion, Sex, Money and Art in the World of Guido Reni* (New Haven: Yale University Press, 1997), 44.

31. For a judicious examination of this issue, see Spear, *The "Divine" Guido*, 51–76.

32. Spear, *The "Divine" Guido*, 45–50. See also King, *Women of the Renaissance*, 144–56.

33. Marina Warner, *Alone of All Her Sex: The Myth and the Cult of the Virgin Mary* (New York: Alfred A. Knopf, 1976), 218.

works.[34] In his exhaustive examination of Reni and his world, Spear discusses controversies current during Reni's life and how these may have affected the painter.[35] The portrait that emerges is of a man deeply devoted to Mary, but with little regard for other women. In fact, his idealization of Mary may have led him to possess unrealistic expectations for women, which may have fed his dislike for and fear of women during his life.[36] For Reni, the simultaneity of Marian devotion and misogyny does not seem to have been incongruous.

Reni's intense dislike and disregard for women, combined with the influence of Annibale and Agostino Carracci's works and lessons, more than accounts for the eroticizing nature of his *Susanna and the Elders*. That is, due to his misogyny and the sexually charged, mimetically focused works of his teachers, Reni continued in their line and imposed an erotic meaning on the story of Susanna. In so doing, he followed in Tintoretto's footsteps and made Susanna both the cause and object of the Elders' lust, and his painting invites viewers to partake of that lust.

5.2.3. *Guercino (Giovanni Francesco Barbieri)*

Giovanni Francesco Barbieri, known to posterity as Guercino ("Squinter"), was born in 1591 in the town of Cento.[37] Like Reni, his talent was recognized early and in 1607 he was apprenticed to Bendetto Gennari the Elder (d. 1610). Another early point of contact between Reni and Guercino is their mutual admiration for the Carraccis. Both painters were heavily influenced by their work, and even though Reni's reliance on the Carraccis tended to favor Annibale and Agostino, Guercino exhibits a more complete dependence on all the Carraccis, including Ludovico.

In 1613, Guercino received his first major commission in Cento, for an altarpiece in the church of Santo Spirito. Three years later, he was successful enough to open a drawing academy. In fact, his success and the number of commissions he received during this time forced him to close the academy after only two years. One of the most important events in his life occurred in 1621, when his early patron Cardinal Ludovisi was elected as Pope Gregory XV. Guercino was called to Rome to decorate part of St. Peter's, but left Rome in 1623 when Gregory died unexpectedly. Short as it was, his period in Rome affected his style greatly, as he became more influenced by the classicism of artists like Reni. After leaving Rome, he returned to Cento where he remained until 1642. Reni died in that year, and Guercino immediately moved to Reni's hometown of Bologna

34. Spear, *The "Divine" Guido*, 140.

35. See especially Spear, *The "Divine" Guido*, 128–62. Evidently there was much debate at the time over the status of Mary; so much so that in 1616 Pope Paul V banned any discussion of these issues from the pulpit. See Warner, *Alone of All Her Sex*, 249.

36. Interestingly, one of the interpreters I will examine in Chapter 6, Albrecht Altdorfer, was a member of the *Schöne Maria* cult in Regensburg. His portrayal of Susanna (Fig. 6) is something of an homage to Mary, as I will show.

37. The biographical information for Guercino is based on Nicholas Turner, "Guercino [Barbieri, Giovanni Francesco]," *The Grove Dictionary of Art Online*, n.p.

where he quickly established himself as that city's most important painter. From about 1650 until his death in 1666, he was in ill health and painted much more seldom.

Figure 5. Guercino, *Susanna and the Elders*, 1617.
Madrid, Museo del Prado

Guercino took up the subject of Susanna three times in his long career, and these three disparate works provide an interesting test case for the distinction(s) between the mimetic depictions of Susanna I addressed above, and the more thematic renderings I will discuss in Chapter 6. Specifically, Guercino alters between the two poles of presentation amid his Susannas. His first rendering, dated to 1617 (Fig. 5), is interesting for several reasons. First, the shading in the work highlights Susanna as she sits, casually bathing herself. She is not cast in the classic Venus pose, yet her drapery and right arm serve to conceal while revealing, a hallmark of the Venus pose. Second, the two Elders, concealed in the darkness, betray both their excitement and shame. The former is personified by the Elder crouching on the right, with his eyes as wide as can be and his right hand suspended in a gesture of amazement. Their shame is found in the standing Elder on the left, who is gazing out of the frame at the viewer with one finger aloft, asking for our silence. Spolsky elaborates on this work:

> In the Guercino, the Elder is grasping a stick, visually analogous to his male member. As we can see from his upright position, he is indeed holding or restraining himself from moving toward Susanna. He seems to be immobilized by her loveliness, painted as a halo of light around her. The Elder standing above him faces out of the picture and

> raises a pointed finger—conventionally in these pictures to silence Susanna but here extended toward the viewer, as if to say "Don't disturb her"—and at the same time, "Don't be so quick to judge us—wouldn't you also be enchanted by her?"[38]

It is the voyeuristic quality that is emphasized here; the Elder on the left is in effect asking the viewer to participate in their preliminary peeping prior to the attempted rape.

There are also two other Susannas by Guercino, though they should be treated together. We have a chalk sketch, made in 1649 (*Susanna and the Elders*), that most likely represents a study for an oil painting produced in 1649/50 (*Susanna and the Elders*, Parma, Galleria Nazionale).[39] In the chalk piece, Susanna is very much the center of attention. She is almost completely naked, yet her right arm still crosses over her torso like the Venus pose. Her expression is curiously calm, considering the two Elders to the left of her, who seem almost an afterthought to the composition of the work. In fact, this near serenity has caused some critics to compare this drawing with the aforementioned earlier etching made by Annibale Carracci.[40]

The oil of 1649/50 reflects some of this tranquility, yet Guercino altered the figure of Susanna. She is still at the center of the work and is still mostly naked. However, she now holds her left hand aloft in either a gesture of supplication or restraint while she gazes up to heaven. This gaze and its object reflect the apocryphal story's emphasis on Susanna's reliance on God as well as her looking up to heaven in v. 35. Regarding this issue, Bohn writes,

> Susanna's piety, expressed by her heavenward gaze and by the divine light that illuminates her exclusively, is belied by the provocative exposure of her almost-naked body. As the object of the elder's gaze, she is implicitly guilty for the elder's temptation.[41]

Bohn's analysis is focused too much on the sexual aspects of the piece, and not enough on the thematic connotations it produces. In fact, Bohn points out in her article that Artemisia Gentileschi's 1610 *Susanna and the Elders*, which I will discuss in the next chapter, represents an exception to the eroticizing tendency of Renaissance portrayals of Susanna.[42] I agree with her in this respect, but am puzzled as to why she then critiques Guercino's last Susanna, given the obvious affinities between the two works. In sum, while Bohn feels Guercino's piece emphasizes the sexual aspects of the theme, I hold that the opposite is true. That is, Susanna's piety overshadows her nakedness. This is due to the thematic associations I mention above, as well as the presentation of the Elders. Here, as opposed to his early piece, Guercino allows the Elders neither excitement nor action. Instead, they appear to be in the midst of making what they consider a routine business arrangement. In portraying Susanna and the Elders in this fashion, then, Guercino has effectively removed almost all of the eroticizing attributes one finds so readily in Tintoretto and Reni.

38. Spolsky, "Law or the Garden," 102.
39. Online: http://www.galleriaestense.it/sovrane/images/Image18b.jpg.
40. Bohn, "Rape and the Gendered Gaze," 279.
41. Bohn, "Rape and the Gendered Gaze," 279.
42. Bohn, "Rape and the Gendered Gaze," 266–67.

In spite of Bohn's argument, in my opinion Guercino's 1649/50 oil of Susanna was directly influenced by Ludovico Carracci's 1616 work. It also shares an affinity with a 1610 painting by Sisto Badalocchio (*Susanna and the Elders*, Sarasota, Fla., Ringling Museum of Art).[43] Badalocchio worked in the Carracci workshop, and was Agostino's apprentice for a time, so the mutual connection between him and Guercino certainly can account for the parallels between their works. Based on my above comments, the influence of Ludovico should come as no surprise; after all, Guercino showed a heavy debt to the Carraccis. The surprise comes from Guercino's use of Ludovico's interpretation of Susanna, as opposed to Annibale or Agostino's renderings. As Bohn has shown, Ludovico's paintings of Susanna represent a "significant departure" from the standard, sexually charged and morally vacuous representations characteristic of his cousins, as well as Tintoretto, Reni, and others.[44] Even though Bohn argues to the contrary, i.e., that Guercino resists that standard style of representation, I maintain that in his second *Susanna*, Guercino opts for a more thematic rendering.[45]

Thus, within the span of one man's artistic development, one sees both interpretive tendencies explored. In his 1617 painting, there is an overt attempt to sexualize the encounter between Susanna and the Elders, as well as to charm, even seduce, viewers into accepting the Elders' perspective of the encounter. As Spolsky notes, "Beauty, as enchantment, has power over the viewer; Susanna's beauty seduces the elders, and the painting's beauty enchants its viewers."[46] However, in his 1649/50 oil, Guercino rejects this line of interpretation and embraces a more thematic assessment of the theme, one that highlights Susanna's religiosity in accordance with the apocryphal narrative.

5.3. *Conclusion*

As one can see from even these selective examples, the standard Renaissance artistic rendering of the apocryphal story was an erotic one, focused on the interaction between Susanna and the Elders, most often while she is bathing. Again, the focus of artistic works is most likely related to genre, if not patronage. That is, Renaissance paintings do not usually tell a narrative; rather they concentrate on one particular moment for illumination.[47] In addition, the artist's patron

43. Online: http://www.wga.hu/art/b/badalocc/susanna.jpg.

44. Bohn, "Rape and the Gendered Gaze," 269.

45. Other *Susannas* that exhibit similarities to Guercino's 1649/50 *Susanna* include those of Domenichino, mentioned above; Cornelius van Haarlem (Ottawa, the National Gallery of Canada, ca. 1599); Jan Saenredam (*Susanna and the Elders*; online: http://www.spaightwoodgalleries.com/Pages/Saenredam.html, sixteenth century); and Joachim Wtewael (The National Museum of Art of Romania, ca. 1613).

46. Spolsky, "Law or the Garden," 109.

47. See Don Harrán, "Stories from the Hebrew Bible in the Music of the Renaissance," *Musica Disciplina* 37 (1983): 235–88 (283): "painting, in the sixteenth century, usually covers less ground textually than does music: the painting is likely to derive from a single verse whereas the music may be set to two or more verses...the painters can, and often do, represent moments of action whereas the composers seem to concentrate on moments of reflection."

usually chose the particular moment, and would decide on the intended audience for the work. In her work, Spolsky comments on the interplay between painter, subject, and viewer:

> The *raison d'etre* of all the paintings, of course, is the representation of Susanna's beauty. By their choice of subject matter alone, then, the painters are caught committing the Elders' own sin. They picture her naked beauty on canvas as the Elders pictured it in their minds' eye... Most of the painters acknowledge the dilemma of entrapment and guilt, while finding ways to make it easier for a viewer to enjoy the beautiful woman and condemn the men in the picture instead of himself.[48]

This eroticizing and voyeuristic rendering of Susanna is obvious in Tintoretto's work, as well as other artistic examples I did not discuss, e.g., the work of George Pencz; Guiseppe Cesari (ca. 1610); Allesandro Allori (late sixteenth century; Lyon, Musée Magnin[49]); Johann König (ca. 1620; Nürnberg, German National Museum); and Peter Paul Rubens (ca. 1606; Madrid, Real Academia de Bellas Artes de San Fernando), to name a few.

Miles is skeptical regarding artistic representations of Susanna accurately relating the message of chastity in the apocryphal story. She writes,

> In the societies of the Christian West, the story of Susanna and the Elders apparently could not be translated into a visual image that accurately preserved the story's emphasis on Susanna's innocence. In the visual mode, Susanna's nakedness inevitably contradicted her virtue.[50]

Miles is correct in that the paintings in which Susanna is clothed the emphasis is automatically deferred away from the erotic, and more toward the message of the story itself. However, many of these works are not interested in staying true to the story, perhaps due to its marginal canonical status. For example, as Cristelle L. Baskins has shown, *cassoni*, or painted wedding chests meant to be publicly displayed along with the bride that depict Susanna's story are not descriptive but prescriptive. That is, they participate "in a counterfactual construction of exemplary behaviours and virtues, whose potentiality is both made plausible and yet contained by pictorial narrative."[51] By extension, then, perhaps the more erotic works depicting Susanna are not failing to preserve qualities in the story because those qualities are not meant to be emphasized at all in the works.

However, at least one scholar has argued that lascivious depictions of Susanna serve a prescriptive function that reinforces the themes I detailed in Chapter 3. As Susan Dackerman notes, there was a heated debate during the Reformation and the subsequent Counter-Reformation as to the efficacy of religious images in worship.[52] The Reformers, most notably Zwingli and Andreas Karlstadt

48. Spolsky, "Law or the Garden," 102 and 106.

49. *Susanna and the Elders*; online: http://www.wga.hu/art/a/allori/alessand/susanna.jpg.

50. Miles, *Carnal Knowing*, 124.

51. C. L. Baskins, "La Festa di Susanna: Virtue on Trial in Renaissance Sacred Drama and Painted Wedding Chests," *Art History* 14.3 (1991): 329–44 (340).

52. See Dackerman, "The Danger of Visual Seduction: Netherlandish Prints of Susanna and the Elders" (Ph.D. diss., Bryn Mawr College, 1995).

(ca. 1480–1541) challenged the use of images and art out of fear of idolatry. However, there were many, both Protestant and Catholic, who defended the use of religious images. In a conciliatory attempt, though, many of these defenders began to object to images "that exhibited seductive characteristics and could thus potentially incite lascivious thoughts and behaviors."[53] In 1563, the Council of Trent published a statement on images in which it reminded the faithful not to mistake the representation for reality, and to avoid erotic imagery altogether.[54] This pronouncement occasioned a number of responses from those who defended religious images, and in these exchanges Susanna is used as an example.

As Dackerman notes, after the Council's admonition on images, and specifically lascivious images, prints and depictions of Susanna began to flourish in the Netherlands. At first, this occurrence seems incongruous; after all, why would dozens of prints of a nude Susanna and the Elders waiting to try and rape her be produced in the wake of such a pronouncement? Dackerman argues that

> although the images in question actually demonstrate the anxieties expressed in the Counter-Reformation texts, they functioned as visual admonitions of the dangers of viewing lascivious images. They were visual analogues of the printed texts, and were read as such… In viewing prints of Susanna and the Elders, the dangers of sight were "presented to the eyes" of the Christian public so that they could "see" them enacted, and believe them for themselves… Prints of Susanna and the Elders visually demonstrate the effect on the Elders of seeing an alluring female nude, and provide an admonitory lesson because the Elders were ultimately punished for their response.[55]

Thus, Dackerman claims, these images were actually preserving the thematic function of the story, viz., the behavior of the Elders is to be condemned in favor of the actions and disposition of Susanna. In this case, then, our complicit looking with the Elders is beneficial because we know what happens to them as a result of their actions. It is Dackerman's argument that placing ourselves in the position of the Elders actually causes us to resist their behavior due to our knowledge of the outcome of the story.

Dackerman's thesis is interesting, and there is much to commend it. However, there is no primary evidence to support her claim. She even notes that other scholars have argued for a position exactly opposite of hers, i.e., lascivious prints of Susanna appeared as a form of resistance to the moralizing discussion over the ethics of erotic images.[56] Furthermore, the prints Dackerman discusses are exceptions to the general portrayal of Susanna in art during the Renaissance. Most artistic renderings are content to titillate, not remonstrate, their viewers, and most are not concerned with adherence to the narrative's thematic emphases. As Bal notes, "The Biblical story becomes a pre-text, and a pretext, for its radical reversal; the exemplum of chastity becomes the celebration of sexual opportunity;

53. Dackerman, "The Danger of Visual Seduction," 77.

54. See Schroeder, *Canons and Decrees of the Council of Trent*, 216–17.

55. Dackerman, "The Danger of Visual Seduction," 93 and 96.

56. Dackerman specifically notes the work of Eric J. Sluijter, "Venus, Visus en Pictura," *Nederlands Kunsthistorisch Jaarboek* 42–43 (1991–92): 337–96, in this regard.

and, of course, the justification of rape is not far away."[57] Thus, artistic interpretations that highlight the erotic, mimetic level of the story are using Susanna's story as an excuse to satisfy other agendas, usually commissions from wealthy patrons who were invested in the patriarchal status quo and who therefore might not be as interested in Susanna as a feminine symbol of piety.

57. Mieke Bal, "Between Focalization and Voyeurism: The Representation of Vision," in *Reading "Rembrandt": Beyond the Word–Image Opposition* (Cambridge New Art History and Criticism; Cambridge: Cambridge University Press, 1991), 138–76 (140).

Chapter 6

COUNTER-READINGS OF SUSANNA DURING THE RENAISSANCE

6.1. *Introduction*

In this chapter, I will examine counter-readings to the standard rendering(s) of Susanna during the Renaissance. These interpretations seek to challenge or alter the customary presentation of the Susanna theme by altering conventional arrangements of figures or by investing Susanna with more of the thematic qualities found in the apocryphal narrative. By their imaginative challenge to the more sexualizing trend of interpretation, these renderings can provide a model for modern readers to emulate in order to resist a mimetic, erotically focused reading of the story or similarly shaped aesthetic renderings.

6.2. *Renaissance Interpretations of Susanna*

I have chosen select renderings to analyze based on popularity as well as significance and geographical concerns. In my discussion of individual works, I will mention biographical data only when it illuminates a specific rendering or if a particular interpreter is not well known. In the case of Sixt Birck's play, I have provided a lengthy summary of the work so that readers are aware of the nature of his interpretation. Finally, all the works I mention here will be listed in Appendix 2, and the text of Guillaume Guéroult's poem, as well as others like it, will appear in Appendix 3.

6.2.1. *Albrecht Altdorfer*

The career of Albrecht Altdorfer (ca. 1480–1538) spans the late medieval period to the flowering of the Renaissance. His training began as a book illustrator and a miniaturist, but he later turned to engravings due to the influence of Albrecht Dürer (1471–1528). However, his importance as an artist is due primarily to his connection with the so-called "Danube School" of art in early sixteenth-century Bavaria.[1] There are certain characteristics that allow us to group contemporary

1. There is no consensus in modern scholarship as to the coherence of the group usually termed the "Danube School," so we must be cautious in our use of the term. Murray, in her *The Late Renaissance and Mannerism*, 149, notes, "The term Danube School is a complete misnomer, in that it never was a 'school' in the sense of a group of artists working together with a common aim. The members of it were contemporary, but there was little or no contact between them, and only two of them were in any way connected with the Danube." For a discussion of this "school" and Altdorfer's central

artists together with Altdorfer in terms of style and subject matter. Artists such as Altdorfer, Wolf Huber (ca. 1490–1553), and Lucas Cranach the Elder (1472–1553), to name a few, all share "a feeling for landscape, not just a background, but as a subject in itself," and to a lesser degree "a predilection for large, shaggy fir trees, which make an expressive—even romantic—effect."[2] This feeling for the countryside, his "expressive use of nature," make Altdorfer the pioneer of landscape paintings.[3]

His life is intimately tied to the city where he spent the majority of his life: Regensburg. City records show that he became a citizen in 1505, and between 1515 and 1532 was prosperous enough to buy three houses and several vineyards. His interest in the city led him to serve on numerous councils from 1517 onwards, and in 1526 he was appointed the city's architect. In 1529/30, he also assumed a military role, as he was charged with reinforcing the city's fortifications in response to a Turkish attack.

Altdorfer also contributed to the religious life of Regensburg, a staunchly Catholic city, by lending his art to the cult of the *Schöne Maria*. After the Reformation began, the Church began to endorse various popular cults at the local level to increase devotion and loyalty to the Church and its policies. In Regensburg, though, this cult also was very influential in political matters due to the fact that almost all members of the city council, including Altdorfer, were members of the cult. This influence is most clearly seen in a 1519 order for all Jews to be expelled from the town, and the synagogue to be raided.[4] It is no accident that the order for expulsion was given on February 22, 1519, only a few months after the death of Emperor Maximilian, who had been fairly protective of Jewish populations in the area. As the Guillauds note, owing to the "economic decline of the once wealthy city of Regensburg and the rising indebtedness of the Christians to the Jews, the good relationship which had existed for centuries between the two groups turned into a hatred for the Jewish community."[5] Altdorfer was not only among the delegation that informed the Jews of the edict, but he did make two etchings of the Regensburg synagogue prior to its destruction, the second of which bears an inscription that reads in part, *iusto dei iudicio*, "according to God's just judgment."[6]

position in it, see Fedja Anzelewski, "Albrecht Altdorfer and the Question of 'the Danube School,'" in *Altdorfer and Fantastic Realism in German Art* (ed. Jacqueline and Maurice Guillaud; Paris: Guillaud Editions; New York: Rizzoli, 1985), 10–47.

2. Murray, *The Late Renaissance and Mannerism*, 150.

3. See Charles Talbot, "Altdorfer," *The Grove Dictionary of Art Online*, n.p., and Murray, *The Late Renaissance and Mannerism*, 156.

4. For primary documentation of this event, see Klaus Matzel and Jörg Riecke, "Das Pfandregister der Regensburger Juden vom Jahre 1519," *Zeitschrift für Bayerische Landesgeschichte* 51 (1988): 767–806. For a history of the Jewish community in Regensburg, see Raphael Straus, *Regensburg and Augsburg* (trans. Felix N. Gerson; Jewish Communities Series; Philadelphia: Jewish Publication Society, 1939), 87–170.

5. Guillaud and Guillaud, eds., *Altdorfer and Fantastic Realism in German Art*, 275.

6. For these etchings, see Guillaud and Guillaud, eds., *Altdorfer and Fantastic Realism in German Art*, 112–13.

The *Schöne Maria* cult benefited from this act due to a widespread rumor that one of the workmen had suffered an injury in the razing of the synagogue, and that the Virgin Mary had subsequently cured him. Following the destruction of the synagogue, a makeshift shrine was erected to Mary on the same site, and once the rumor of the miraculous healing became known, it became one of the most important pilgrimage sites of the period. In fact, Michael Ostendorfer (ca. 1490/95–1559) made an engraving of the shrine being visited by spiritual pilgrims in ca. 1520, and it seems obvious that the members of the cult had economic as well as spiritual interests in the shrine.[7] About a year later, Altdorfer himself designed an altarpiece for the new church, complete with a portrait of the Virgin Mary.[8]

After this period, Altdorfer's work began to receive wider acclaim, and he began to receive more prestigious commissions. Two of his most important works were the result of his association with Duke William IV, the Wittelsbach Duke of Bavaria (1493–1550; ruled from 1508). In 1526, Altdorfer painted his *Susanna and the Elders* (Fig. 6) for the Duke. After declining the position of burgomaster of Regensburg in 1528, Altdorfer painted his masterpiece, *The Battle of Alexander at Issus* (1529; Munich, Alte Pinakothek),[9] for a series of paintings commissioned by the Duke and his wife, Jacobäa von Baden (1507–1580) for their residence in Munich.[10] His last known work, *Lot and His Daughters* (1537; Vienna, Kunsthistorisches Museum)[11] displays his adaptation to the newer emphasis on portraying nudes and figures.

In Altdorfer's *Susanna and the Elders*, one is immediately struck by the immense architectural focus of the work, and the almost negligible attention paid to Susanna and her story. In fact, the figure of Susanna seems almost incidental to the main focus of the painting, which seems to be the large building in the middle and right of the frame. However, upon closer inspection the picture exhibits what Cordula Bischoff, in her excellent study of the work, terms "compositional simultaneity," an effect common in medieval art wherein several points of a given story are all displayed at the same time.[12] Thus, the Elders are hiding in the foliage to the left of Susanna. The young Daniel addresses the crowd in front of the clock tower on the far right of the frame, and the Elders are being stoned in the foreground of the courtyard.[13] The only scenes that are

7. For this engraving, see Guillaud and Guillaud, *Altdorfer and Fantastic Realism in German Art*, 448–49.

8. See Christopher S. Wood, *Albrecht Altdorfer and the Origins of Landscape* (Chicago: University of Chicago Press, 1993), 174.

9. Online: http://www.wga.hu/art/a/altdorfe/1/5battle.jpg.

10. For reproductions and a discussion of this work, see Gisela Goldberg, "Albrecht Altdorfer: The Battle of Alexander the Great against the Great Persian King Darius III at Issus in 333 B.C. (The Battle of Alexander)," in Guillaud and Guillaud, eds., *Altdorfer and Fantastic Realism in German Art*, 245–68.

11. Online: http://www.wga.hu/art/a/altdorfe/1/7lot_dau.jpg.

12. See Cordula Bischoff, "Albrecht Altdorfer's *Susanna and the Elders*: Female Virtues, Male Politics," *Racar* 23, nos. 1–2 (1996): 22–35 (24).

13. This technique, as well as the emphasis on architecture, is also found in Hans Schöpfer's *History of Susanna* (1537; Munich, Alte Pinakothek). Coincidentally, as Bischoff notes, this work

omitted are the actual encounter between the Elders and Susanna, and the trial of Susanna. The reasons for these omissions, as we shall see, lie in the specific and innovative way in which Altdorfer presents Susanna.

Figure 6. Albrecht Altdorfer, *Susanna in the Bath and the Stoning of the Elders*, 1526. Munich, Alte Pinakothek

Given that the huge building dominates so much of the frame, the question arises: What did Altdorfer mean to imply by its inclusion? One answer seems self-evident: the picture was painted in the same year in which Altdorfer was appointed chief architect of Regensburg, so obviously the subject would be much

was painted for William IV as well. See "Albrecht Altdorfer's *Susanna and the Elders*," 34 n. 21. See also Kurt Löcher, "Hans Schöpfers *Geschichte der Susanna* in der Alte Pinakothek in München," *Pantheon* 28 (1970): 279–83.

on his mind. After examining the representation of the building, Bischoff makes a different conclusion: the "combination of different architectural elements results in a synthesis of church, town hall and palace."[14] This synthesis, moreover, means that "functions that are distributed amongst several powers are thus symbolically united and demonstrated: canonical and secular jurisdiction under courtly, that is, sovereign control."[15] This synthesis and uniting of diverse powers under sovereign control most likely represents an attempt on Altdorfer's part to appease his patron, Duke William IV, who was responsible for judicial matters in Bavaria. In fact, as Bischoff notes, during the reign of William IV new law codes were enacted that attempted to increase the power of the ducal court by standardizing legal proceedings and tenets in Bavaria.[16] Emphasis on courtly justice was not the only way in which Altdorfer sought to please his patron; he also did so by his particular presentation of Susanna.

Most Renaissance portrayals of Susanna are modeled on depictions of either Venus or Lucretia. However, Altdorfer's representation of Susanna resembles neither. Bischoff argues persuasively that Altdorfer portrays Susanna as a type of the Virgin Mary. She writes:

> In this picture Altdorfer assimilated Susanna into the figure of the Virgin Mary by the adoption of characteristic iconography: Susanna is wearing a blue and red garment similar to that of Mary, slightly old-fashioned to indicate timelessness; her loose hair emphasized by brushing symbolizes innocence and virginity; the little pet dog, a sign of marital faithfulness, is held like the infant Jesus; and the orange in Susanna's left hand as a symbol of purity derives from the fruit in Madonna paintings. More evident still is the Marian symbolism in the arrangement of the garden... Altdorfer takes up a motif from fifteenth-century art, the so-called *hortus conclusus*, depicting Mary sitting in a rose arbour or in a garden symbolizing her virginity or, more particularly, the immaculate conception. Like the rose bush, a spring or well is a symbolic representation of her virtues: purity, love and virginity.[17]

Bischoff even argues that the woman climbing the stairs to the right of Susanna resembles Mary in that a similar pose is found in many depictions of the *Presentation of the Virgin*, a common theme in the early Renaissance.[18] Why, then, would Altdorfer have taken pains to depart from the customary representation of Susanna and have instead depicted her in this fashion?

The answer seems obvious: Altdorfer, as we already have seen, was by all accounts a devoted member of the cult of the *Schöne Maria*, so his interest in Mary and Marian imagery would have been keen. Second, since this work was intended for William IV, and can be seen as reinforcing the importance of courtly laws, perhaps Altdorfer was trying to emphasize the justice one finds at court by depicting Susanna as the patron saint of Bavaria and the figure that would

14. Bischoff, "Albrecht Altdorfer's *Susanna and the Elders*," 24.
15. Bischoff, "Albrecht Altdorfer's *Susanna and the Elders*," 25.
16. Bischoff, "Albrecht Altdorfer's *Susanna and the Elders*," 29.
17. Bischoff, "Albrecht Altdorfer's *Susanna and the Elders*," 26–27. For another reading of the Altdorfer painting that does not discuss the Marian imagery, see Bonjione, "Shifting Images: Susanna through the Ages," 73–76.
18. Bischoff, "Albrecht Altdorfer's *Susanna and the Elders*," 27.

embody the Counter-Reformation for William IV: the Virgin Mary.[19] In her examination of the painting, Bischoff notes the importance of Mary for the duke, and concludes by writing, "To provide a clear reference to the court of the Bavarian duke, it was most important that Susanna should have the attributes of the Virgin Mary."[20]

The Reformation ideal for/of women emphasized marriage, procreation, and submission in the domestic sphere to a male patriarch responsible for scriptural interpretation. In turn, the Counter-Reformation re-emphasized total seclusion for nuns and harsher rules for cloistered women. Both ideologies included passivity, submission, and above all chastity as the most prized traits for women, and many works were disseminated attempting to persuade men and women of the worth of those traits. In this work, Altdorfer provides an endorsement of those basic values by displaying a model for women to emulate. As Bischoff notes,

> Women can and shall triumph over their innate weakness, if they follow the examples of Susanna and Mary—being chaste, virtuous and passive… Within the picture an ideal is exhibited, proclaiming the socially desirable virtues of beauty, faithfulness and seclusion as the "proper destiny of woman."[21]

In fact, Bischoff argues that the painting's emphases are even more specific than these generic values. She claims that by emphasizing the aspects of Mary, Altdorfer is holding up virginity, and therefore nunneries, as the "proper" status for women over and against the Lutheran emphasis on marriage.[22]

In sum, the portrayal of Susanna by Altdorfer breaks with the standard iconographic *topos* that I discuss in Chapter 5 in that Susanna has no contact with the Elders at all; she cannot be said to entice them in any way. More importantly, though, Altdorfer sought to depict her as possessing traits commonly associated with the Virgin Mary. This depiction was most likely intended to demonstrate a particular set of theses, viz., that virginity is the proper condition for women, and, by extension, nunneries are not only acceptable but also necessary. The painting's emphasis on Mary is especially interesting, given that in Chapter 5 we saw that another devotee of Mary, Reni, did not feel it necessary to express his Marian devotion in his rendering of Susanna. Furthermore, in the context of the painting itself, Daniel presides in, and the Elders receive their (just) punishment in the courtyard of the building, which, as I noted above, serves as a cipher for courtly, i.e., ducal, authority. Thus, not only would the political position and judicial influence of Altdorfer's patron, Duke William IV, be reinforced, but the already nascent emphases of the Counter-Reformation would also be underscored by the characterization of Susanna. Altdorfer's work, in essence, has transformed Susanna's story into a vehicle for the propagation of certain ideological and religious sentiments and stances, and, as we shall see, he is not alone in this use of her story.

19. See Bischoff, "Albrecht Altdorfer's *Susanna and the Elders*," 29–30.
20. Bischoff, "Albrecht Altdorfer's *Susanna and the Elders*," 30.
21. Bischoff, "Albrecht Altdorfer's *Susanna and the Elders*," 30.
22. Bischoff, "Albrecht Altdorfer's *Susanna and the Elders*," 32.

6.2.2. *Sixt Birck*

The German playwright Sixt Birck (1501–1554) produced two treatments of the Susanna story around the mid-sixteenth century. In fact, Paul F. Casey claims that Birck's first Susanna play, written in 1531/2, was the "first version of the Susanna theme during the Reformation period."[23] Birck, the son of a weaver, was born in Augsburg, but spent the majority of his young life in Basel, from 1523 to 1536. The first version of *Susanna* was written in German while Birck was teaching at the St. Theodor School in Basel.[24] However, as Casey notes, the play was not just for Birck's students. Rather, "the drama was intended for public performance with the aim of bringing to the people the newly revised classical form of the drama in the vernacular," which, as I noted in Chapter 4, was entirely in keeping with the new Humanist emphases.[25] Almost all of the secondary literature concerned with Birck's work on Susanna focuses on this first German version.[26] For this reason, I will examine Birck's second treatment of Susanna, composed after Birck moved back to his hometown of Augsburg in 1536.[27] The town council offered Birck the position of headmaster at the Gymnasium of St. Anna, the new Latin grammar school, a position that he held for almost twenty years.[28] He translated and slightly revised his earlier play into Latin in 1537/8 explicitly for his students to perform.

The Latin version of Birck's drama begins with a prefatory letter to the Augsburg Senate in which Birck makes a point of discussing the importance of state sponsored schooling for boys in "a Christian state," as opposed to the situation of the "Papists." Luther himself initiated this emphasis on didactic drama in schools among Reformers. As Brown notes, Luther not only gave his permission to stage dramas in school, but he also emphasized "the Apocryphal stories are useful ('nützlich') as a means of inculcating piety in both performers and spectators."[29] Furthermore, Luther wrote to Johannes Callerius that,

23. Casey, *The Susanna Theme in German Literature*, 44.

24. Outside of "Susanna," published in ca. 1532, all of Birck's other dramas composed in German while living in Basel were published after he returned to Augsburg. For an analysis of Birck's Basel dramas, see Mark Anthony Sims, "The Basel Dramas of Sixt Birck" (M.A. thesis, Vanderbilt University, 1991).

25. Casey, *The Susanna Theme in German Literature*, 44.

26. Aside from the work of Casey, see the pioneering work of Robert Pilger, "Die Dramatisierungen der Susanna im 16. Jahrhundert," *Zeitschrift für deutsche Philologie* 11 (1879–80): 129–217 (142–85); and Brown, "The *Susanna* Drama and the German Reformation," 129–53.

27. Birck's German drama is found in Jacob Bächtold, *Scweizerische Schauspiele des 16. Jahrhunderts*, vol. 2 (Frauenfeld, 1891), 3–97, and in Sixt Birck, "Die history von der fromen Gottsförchtigen frouwen Susanna [1532]," in *Sämtliche Werke* (ed. Manfred Brauneck; 2 vols.; New York: de Gruyter, 1976), 2:1–53. The Latin version of Birck's work is also found in his *Sämtliche Werke* ("Susanna, Comoedia tragica [1538]," in *Sämtliche Werke*, 2:167–72), and the English translation of this drama is "Susanna, a Tragi-Comedy [1538]", translated by C. C. Love, n.p. Online: http://www.chass. utoronto.ca/epc/rnlp/susanna.html. All subsequent citations from Birck's Latin version are taken from this translation.

28. See Derek van Abbé, *Drama in Renaissance Germany and Switzerland* (Melbourne: Melbourne University Press, 1961), 11.

29. Brown, "The *Susanna* Drama and the German Reformation," 136.

> The youth in the schools should not be restrained from performing comedies, but rather this is to be approved and encouraged, first so that they can practice the Latin language, and secondly, since in comedies which are well composed, such figures are created and presented that the people may learn from them, and each individual is reminded of his responsibility and station, and what conduct is appropriate to a servant, a master, to the young and the old...as a mirror.[30]

Thus, as Brown comments, "this statement makes clear that the educational function of drama is of prime importance, and further, that the drama is an instrument of exemplifying and solidifying the social order of Luther's Worldly Kingdom, the 'weltliches Regiment.'"[31] We shall see how Birck adapted the Susanna story to fit the emphases of the Reformation, specifically with regards to women and expectations of female behavior.

Act 1, Scenes 1–2 are concerned specifically with the Elders, here named Achab and Sedechias. They explain their lust to the audience and to each other, using terms like "madness," and "burning desire." Susanna is introduced in the following Scene. From the beginning, she is characterized as a religious woman who is concerned with her modesty. She explains her request that the gate of the garden be locked by noting that if it is locked, "No schemer...may build up deceit or evil machinations against my modesty."

The confrontation between Susanna and the Elders takes place in Act 1, Scene 4. When Achab and Sedechias approach her, her first thought is the danger to her honor, an emphasis that parallels the initial characterization of Susanna I discussed in Chapter 3. In this regard, it is interesting to note that Sedechias tells Achab not to falter in their plan, because "for us, shame is too late." This admission on Sedechias' part makes explicit what remains implicit in the apocryphal narrative: the Elders have forgone their social status and honor due to their lust for Susanna. In this Scene, both Elders try to persuade Susanna to acquiesce using various arguments, e.g., "Since our sin shall be secret, what witness will there be?," and Sedechias' claim that they need Susanna to "cure our very holy lust." If she does, he claims, she "will be doing a holy work." These statements reflect the misunderstanding of God and their role as judges that I adumbrated in my earlier reading of the narrative.

Susanna remains steadfastly concerned with her religious and, more importantly, her familial identity: "My honour and my fidelity will remain always, as long as God shall will and I shall always preserve them for my most chaste husband... Keep your filthy hands far from my chaste body." Following these statements, Birck's Elders go much further than the apocryphal story in their responses. Achab assures Susanna that "You will receive a gift you won't be sorry to have," while Sedechias makes an overt threat of rape, saying, "You will feel our force, unless of your own free will you comply with our wishes." Sedechias elaborates on this threat with a typically masculine rationalization: "Many may complain of force, but force is pleasing to girls, and the more violent sexual love is, the more pleasing it is." These statements parallel the OG account

30. Quoted in Brown, "The *Susanna* Drama and the German Reformation," 137.

31. Brown, "The *Susanna* Drama and the German Reformation," 137.

of the story in which the Elders try to force Susanna to have sex with them, while the explicit violence is toned down somewhat in Th. Susanna responds to these comments by bemoaning her situation, much in the same way she does in the apocryphal narrative. However, here Susanna specifically notes that when judges go bad, justice and chastity are in danger. Achab satirizes this emphasis on chastity when he opens the doors to the garden to call to the servants: "One who was a pattern of chastity to all now will be an example of lust."

In Act 1, Scene 5 Achab and Sedechias tell Susanna's servants their stories, but unlike the apocryphal account, the servants do not believe them. One servant in particular, Herophilus, calls Sedechias a "slanderer," and accuses him of "making up these charges." Another servant, Spudoecius, defends Susanna by noting that the Elders are "accomplices in a wicked trick," and then appeals to Susanna's upbringing: "She has been so instructed in the law from her cradle; she fears God; she is modest and has a chaste character." Act 1 ends with a chorus based on Ps 30, the first of five such choruses in Birck's work.[32]

Act 2 contains five scenes in which we find preparatory information related to the trial of Susanna, and ends with a second chorus, based on Prov 8. In this act, there is little character development, and not much action. In fact, one of the most significant critiques of Birck's drama has been this emphasis on portraying legal proceedings at such length. As Casey notes, "Late nineteenth and early twentieth-century critics are largely of the opinion that this segment of the drama [i.e. the 'Gerichtsverhandlung']—which comprises approximately half the work—is to be wholeheartedly condemned as dramatically ineffective."[33] However, as Casey argues, the scenes were not intended for entertainment, but rather for "nurturing an appreciation for justice among younger citizens and students."[34] In his discussion of this issue, Derek Van Abbé concurs and writes, "Birck's hidden moral in *Susanna* was his interest in municipal government."[35] The lengthy trial scene, therefore, is part of the message of the play and rather superfluous to the action of the plot, because in it, Birck is attempting to show the audience the way in which "proper" court procedures should be carried out. This would have been important in Switzerland and Germany at the time, due to the legal worries brought about by the Reformation. It might also serve to reinforce faith in the workings of various ecclesiastical courts or consistories formed after the beginning of the Reformation to deal with moral and religious offenses. That is, if Susanna is brought before a court for a moral and religious offense and is justly found innocent, people might be led to believe that real consistories offered justice as well.

It is not until Act 3, Scene 2 that Achab publicly accuses Susanna in open court. This Scene is also when Joachim finds out that the Elders have targeted his wife. His response is telling; he fervently denies Achab's accusations and even

32. For a brief discussion of the choruses in Birck's work, see Casey, *The Susanna Theme in German Literature*, 49–50.

33. Casey, *The Susanna Theme in German Literature*, 56.

34. Casey, *The Susanna Theme in German Literature*, 57.

35. Van Abbé, *Drama in Renaissance Germany and Switzerland*, 66.

resigns his position as judge. This reaction, containing his belief that his wife is innocent, is a far cry from his total lack of involvement in the apocryphal narrative, as well as earlier dramatic treatments of the theme, specifically the so-called "Viennese" Susanna. In the former, Joachim never appears on Susanna's behalf at her trial. In the latter, Joachim is present, but seems to be more concerned about the ramifications her situation may have on his social position and honor than the punishment she may have to endure.[36] In fact, Casey writes, "In no other Susanna drama is the husband quite so ready to accept his wife's guilt and quite so concerned with the reflection of her deed on himself."[37] However, in Birck's drama, Joachim rises to his wife's defense and supports her throughout the trial. This portrayal of family devotion is also connected to Birck's underlying Reformist ideology.

The remainder of Act 3 is concerned with the Examiner expressing his views on the accusations made by Achab and Sedechias. In Scene 3, the Examiner details the duties of a good judge, presumably to allow the audience to draw a parallel between the description and the behavior of the Elders. Also, in Scene 4, the Examiner orders the case against Susanna to progress, and for Susanna to defend herself against the charges. However, it is obvious that the Examiner has a high opinion of Susanna. In this scene, his order reads as follows: "Order the chaste wife of our best man Joachim and the glory of innocence to defend her innocence by public order." Obviously, the Examiner is echoing what the audience, and the Elders, already knows: that Susanna is innocent. Act 3 then ends with a third chorus based on Ps 118.

One of the innovations of Birck's Susanna drama is found in Act 4, Scene 2, in which we are introduced to Susanna's children, who respond to the charges against their mother. Her son, Benjamin, and her daughter, also named Susanna, express disbelief at the accusations made against Susanna. Susanna's mother Rachel and father Chelkias also appear in this scene, and likewise encourage Susanna not to despair. Joachim once again reassures his wife that all will be well, telling her that since "you have always hitherto preserved your most chaste honour by your chaste character," the present tribulation will also be overcome.

36. This play (Anonymous, "The Wiener Susanna") is found in *Fastnachtspiele aus dem fünfzehnten Jahrhundert: Nachlese* (ed. Adelbert von Keller; Stuttgart: Schriften des litterarischen Vereins, 1858), 231–45. For a discussion of this play, see Casey, *The Susanna Theme in German Literature*, 33–44; and Brown, "The *Susanna* Drama and the German Reformation," 131–39.

37. Casey, *The Susanna Theme in German Literature*, 37. In Heinrich Julius' ca. 1593 drama, Joachim behaves much the same; see Casey, *The Susanna Theme in German Literature*, 127. As Marvin T. Herrick notes, in Tibortio Sacco's 1537 play, *Tragedia nova, initiolata Sosanna, raccolta da Daniello Profeta*, Joachim believes Susanna is guilty, and even asks her "Faithless wife, why have you treated me as a base-born peasant?" Susanna's father also believes his daughter is guilty, although her mother waits to judge her until after the trial. See Herrick, "Susanna and the Elders in Sixteenth-Century Drama," in *Studies in Honor of T. W. Baldwin* (ed. Don Cameron Allen; Urbana: University of Illinois Press, 1958), 125–35 (130). Another example of Joachim's quick acceptance of Susanna's guilt can be found in the anonymous Dutch play, *Tspeel van Susanna*, produced in 1607. Here, Joachim tells Susanna, "O, I thought you loyal, pure cherry tree / But you have changed from gold to lead." See Peter Happé, "Two *Susannas*: Dutch and English Plays Compared," *Dutch Crossing* 20 (1996): 108–27 (114).

Again, this scene of family unity and concern underscores one of Birck's main emphases in this work.

In the next scene, both the Examiner and Rachel express uncanny insight into the nature of the Elders' guilt and passion for Susanna. First, the Examiner notes, "Let the legitimate process of the law be used against her [Susanna], and let evil guile be absent, *lest through shamelessness you seems to gratify evil passions* and to wish to use cunning to make your case" (italics mine). Similarly, Rachel lets loose with a vitriolic attack on Sedechias after he orders Susanna to be unveiled:

> Traitor. Villain. Your raging lust, not our father's custom, is dictating that, you villain. Do you not know that it is fitting for a magistrate not only to have clean hands, nay, it is fitting also for his eyes to be free from all lust? Have you not yet sufficiently satisfied your lusts, you most evil men? A sinister fire is boiling in you and black hatred and the blazing dart of madness.

Sedechias is not intimidated; he orders Rachel to be silent and calls her a "triple poisoner-witch," perhaps an allusion to the prevalence of witch imagery and the trials of witches that took place during this period.[38] She then responds that even though Susanna may give up her life to them, "she gives her honour to no one." Thus, Birck portrays the mother of Susanna as being a strong and unusually knowledgeable character.

Achab and Sedechias testify against Susanna in Act 4, Scene 4. Achab's testimony is longer, and in it, he attacks Susanna's reputation for chastity and honor. One interesting feature of his testimony is that he highlights the voyeuristic aspect of the fictional encounter between Susanna and the unnamed young man. Achab claims, "Lest our weak sight should be deceiving us, we then came out of the shade and approached nearer them; there they lay in their shame." This emphasis on watching the couple embracing parallels Bal's interpretation I mentioned in Chapter 3 of their testimony in the apocryphal narrative as a sexual fantasy of sorts. In other words, Achab here is repeating a fabricated story of Susanna and an unnamed lover, imagining the two of them together, and possibly reveling in the freedom to invent tantalizing details that would satisfy his lust for Susanna. The inventiveness of his testimony is not endangered by Sedechias, who simply affirms the correctness of Achab's witness. Susanna's response to this testimony is succinct: she flatly denies their claims, and even points out that they cannot prove any of their claims.

In the next scene, the twelve judges deliberate on the testimony. Gender expectations play an important role in their considerations. One of the judges named Arradan argues, "a comparison of sex be made," in which both sides of the story are examined based on assumptions regarding gender roles. He says,

> On the one side are elder men of high authority and leaders in our order who agree in their evidence, men to whom it would be a religious offence to swear falsely the oath which they have offered to make. On the other side it is evident that woman is fragile and that the young could not resist the drive of lust. Why could she not be broken down

38. For this issue, see King, *Women of the Renaissance*, 144–56.

> by fear and by such grave danger? If to do wrong and to defile the honour sacred to her husband was not a religious offence to her, by so much will she be less afraid now to cheat God.

Of course, the audience would recognize the irony apparent in these assumptions. In fact, Arradan has the situation almost totally reversed, and thus his expectations based on gender are shown to be fallacious. Another judge, Dibon, responds that Susanna's "sex does not prevent her making an oath," thus emphasizing the fact that even though Susanna is female, her behavior and honor exceeds that of the Elders. These Elders take the oath mentioned by Arradan in the next scene, which specifies numerous punishments for them if their testimony is false. Of course, they show no hesitation whatsoever. Following this oath, the people order Susanna to be carried away and stoned.

The next two scenes in Act 4 are the clearest indicators as to the importance of chastity as a theme in the drama. In Scene 7, Susanna and her family react to her sentence. Joachim first addresses Susanna as "my chaste wife," indicating his continued support for her innocence, and then notes that only God, "the most uncorrupt judge," can help her now. Susanna acknowledges this fact and bolsters her claim by reinforcing her marital fidelity, saying,

> God alone knows my innocence, my faithfulness to my marriage bed, the secrets of my heart. I call on the King of the Heavens. Then goodbye now, my dearest husband; I will bear witness to my faithfulness to my marriage with the drops of my blood.

This emphasis on marital chastity is also relayed in Susanna's next comment, in which she addresses her daughter and female servants:

> My dear daughter, I now leave you exposed to like evil. Look, death is the undeserved reward for a chaste life. The same evil hangs over you, my Promptula and Spudaea. Chastity will no longer have value in the future.

Thus, Susanna bemoans not her own fate, but the legacy left and repercussions caused by her execution, i.e., other women's chastity will be at risk since the Elders have successfully questioned hers.

Act 4 concludes in Scene 8, in which Susanna gives a last testament of sorts. She again laments the fate of chastity in her community. She proclaims to the court:

> You know by what trickery these elders have beset me since I refused to acquiesce to their lustful requests. You are aware that the case is being sustained by evil guile, and my blood will bear witness to this. People of my nation and citizens of Babylon, listen: take note that this most powerful desire be in you that the chastity of both your wives and daughters may be safe. You to whom it is of importance to see that the state receives no harm and that evils do not assail it, blunt the wicked stratagems of these crafty graybeards. Otherwise this evil pestilence will creep in more cruelly. Chastity will sicken to its death.

Here we see Susanna pleading for the very survival of chastity, which will be in jeopardy if the plans of the Elders, and others like them, are not thwarted. In Susanna's view, it is not just individuals that are in danger, but the state itself is threatened by their evil. Following this comment, Act 4 concludes with another Chorus based on Ps 82.

In the final act of the drama, events move rather quickly compared to the rest of the work. Daniel is introduced in Act 5, Scene 1, and is characterized as a boy. However, this boy has supernatural knowledge and abilities, and is also very critical of the judges, reminding them that age and social standing do not a judge make. In Scenes 3 and 4, Daniel cross-examines Achab and Sedechias, respectively. Of course, their stories conflict over which tree the lovers were supposedly under, Daniel condemns them, and the people respond to his speech with material from Ps 8. The twelve judges declare Susanna innocent in Scene 6, and in Scene 7 Nebuchadnezzar himself enters the action. The Examiner explains the case to him, paying special attention to Susanna's character ("this women of remarkable chastity and of honest and chaste character"), and Nebuchadnezzar gives his royal approval to the sentence of execution for Achab and Sedechias.

The Examiner informs Susanna of her acquittal in Act 5, Scene 8, again using chastity-laden language: "Susanna, exceptional glory of chastity... Your chastity has been revealed to be unviolated, constant and whole." In turn, Susanna praises God for saving her in her time of need. The Examiner then addresses Joachim, saying, "You are now sure of your wife's chastity; you have gold proved by tests and a lily has been born among the harsh thorns." Of course, his statement is quite ironic; Joachim knew all along Susanna was innocent, and her name literally means "lily" in Hebrew. Following this, Joachim speaks to Susanna:

> O companion of my marriage, by your constancy you have preserved your honour for me, from the time when you came into my hands as a bride. Indeed, they say generally that she is chaste whom no man has solicited. But when tested you resisted their entreaties; your mind did not yield to their machinations nor did your chastity submit to their force.

In the end, then, Joachim's character does display a bit of self-interest regarding his own honor and status. However, Susanna's parents are simply overjoyed at the vindication of their child. Susanna's penultimate comment to her parents re-emphasizes that her concern lies not with women, but rather women's chastity: "Hereafter I think that this place will be safe for chaste mothers and for young girls."

The play then concludes with the execution of the Elders in Scene 9. Ironically, some of the most didactic comments stem from the final testimony of Achab and Sedechias. The former adjures the other judges to guard themselves against "depraved lust," and to "learn good sense from our danger." Achab, in turn, reminds those present that "he is not free from crime who does not plan it," thus adding "dimension to the moral of the play: not only the initiators of evil are punished, but those who follow them into injustice as well."[39] After the Elders have been executed, another judge named Abed comments, "Now I think chastity is safe," thus reinforcing Susanna's earlier comments after her acquittal. Act 5 concludes with a fifth chorus, based on Ps 1. Birck adds an Epilogue to his work in which he addresses the Augsburg Senate, and again notes the importance of correct upbringing for young men.

39. Casey, *The Susanna Theme in German Literature*, 56.

Given Birck's German origin, as well as his Reformist leanings, it is not surprising to find his drama reinforcing many of the views and expectations of women I discussed in Chapter 4. Thus we see Susanna as a member of a family in which she plays an important role; we see many characters commenting on the importance of chastity; we hear Joachim praise his wife's fidelity and chaste behavior; and we see Susanna herself repeatedly mention the necessity of chastity and marital commitment. All of these emphases are in keeping with Luther's various admonitions regarding women and the family. As Brown notes, "Sustaining peace in the individual household and in society at large required the proper submissiveness of the wife and mother," and that Birck's drama "not surprisingly idealize[s] this model of feminine behavior."[40] Furthermore, in accordance with Luther's ideas regarding women, "Confining the locus of women's influence to the home and family had as corollary effect an increasing emphasis on wifely fidelity, which is the primary virtue Susanna embodies in the play."[41]

One of the most interesting aspects of Birck's interpretation of Susanna, as well as other renderings I will discuss below, is the freedom with which he treats the apocryphal story. This freedom most likely stems from the fact that the canonically marginal status of the Apocrypha during the Reformation would allow for greater interpretive opportunities than one might take with other biblical stories, e.g., that of the Virgin Mary. Of course, one of the hallmarks of the Reformation is the designation of certain works as apocryphal, i.e., not *really* scriptural. Luther himself argued for the exclusion of certain works from the canon, even though he included many of these works, Susanna among them, in an Appendix to his 1534 translation of the Vulgate into German. Luther even went so far as to note that Susanna and other apocryphal works are "beautiful religious fictions," and "much that is good…is to be found in them."[42] In his *Confession Concerning Christ's Supper* (1528), Luther uses the Elders as a discordant example, and in the illustrations for his *Great Catechism* (1529), he allows a Susanna image to exemplify the breaking of the Eighth Commandment.[43] This ambiguity on Luther's part may be indicative of a more widespread attitude towards apocryphal literature, i.e., it is not canonical but still useful. The vagueness Luther and others showed with regard to the status, canonical or otherwise, of apocryphal literature may have opened the door for various interpreters to produce multiple and variegated renderings of the Susanna story. Interpreters readily took advantage of Susanna's ambiguous literary status to emphasize a range of positions.

40. Brown, "The *Susanna* Drama and the German Reformation," 130.

41. Brown, "The *Susanna* Drama and the German Reformation," 142.

42. See Martin Luther, "Prefaces to the Apocrypha," in *Luther's Works*. Vol. 35, *Word and Sacrament I* (ed. and trans. E. Theodore Bachmann; Philadelphia: Fortress, 1960), 353–54.

43. See Martin Luther "Confession Concerning Christ's Supper," in *Luther's Works*. Vol. 37, *Word and Sacrament III* (ed. and trans. Robert H. Fischer; Philadelphia: Fortress, 1961), 151–372 (322). In her work, Catherine Brown Tkacz mentions that Lucas Cranach the Elder produced an image of Susanna for Luther's *Great Catechism*. See "Susanna as a Type of Christ," 129 and 152 n. 77.

Finally, as Casey notes, it is possible to interpret Birck's work as containing a political message. Casey writes:

> The fact that Susanna was a perennial favorite with German dramatists arises from the inherently dramatic nature of the story, but also from the possibility of using it as a political vehicle. Susanna as embodiment of the Lutheran Church under attack by the older and more experienced exponents of the Catholic faith is perhaps not too far-fetched an interpretation of Birck's play. The elders are unjust in their attack, they are members of the ruling class of their society and they are corrupt. Susanna is young, has only her family about her and is in no position to defend herself adequately. She is condemned without a thorough investigation. These features might be seen as supporting such a political reading of the play.[44]

Mark Anthony Sims agrees with Casey's assessment, noting,

> The popularity of the Susanna theme among the post-Reformation dramatists was partially due to its ease of adaptability into a political vehicle. Birck's version is no exception with the two unjust elders representative of the attacking Catholic Church while the chaste Susanna can be seen as Lutheranism initially on the defensive but ultimately triumphant.[45]

Ironically, early on in the life of the Susanna story, prior to the Reformation, the Church had used the Susanna story in much the same fashion. Specifically, in the third century C.E., Hippolytus read the story of Susanna as an allegory relating to the situation of the Church during his own time.[46] In short, he used the story of Susanna to exhort his readers to "imitate Susannah" so that the Church may not be overtaken by its enemies like the elders tried to rape Susanna.

I find this political reading of Birck's work persuasive. When we note the concern for "proper" behavior for women, especially regarding the issue of chastity, the case becomes even stronger that Birck's Susanna drama was meant to reinforce nascent Lutheran ideas regarding women, as well as advocate basic Lutheran emphases such as properly constituted legal proceedings, male leadership in society and at home, and the importance of family.

The importance of Birck's work lies not just in its literary value; it also served as a model for one of the most celebrated Susanna dramas of the sixteenth century in Germany: Paul Rebhun's *Susanna*.[47] Composed in 1536 and revised in 1544, Rebhun's work parallels many of the innovations initiated by Birck, but also represents a more advanced dramatic structure in that it embraces the classic

44. Casey, *The Susanna Theme in German Literature*, 60–61.

45. Sims, "The Basel Dramas of Sixt Birck," 31.

46. Hippolytus', "Fragments from Commentaries: On Susanna," in *ANF* 5:191–94.

47. For this play, see Paul Rebhun, *Susanna: Eingeleitet und redigiert von Walter Zitzenbacher* (Graz: Stiasny-Verlag, 1961); and more recently Rebhun, *Ein geistlich Spiel, von der Gotfürchtigen vnd keuschen Frawen Susannen, auffs new gemehret vnd gebessert, gantz lustig und fruchtbarlich zu lessen*, in *Deutsche Spiele und Dramen des 15. und 16. Jahrhunderts* (ed. Hellmut Thomke; Frankfurt am Main: Deutscher Klassiker, 1996), 329–444. M. John Hanak has translated the 1544 version into English. See Rebhun, "Susanna: A Miracle Play." For the parallels between Birck and Rebhun's dramas, see Casey, *The Susanna Theme in German Literature*, 71–72; and idem, *Paul Rebhun: A Biographical Study* (Stuttgart: Steiner, 1986), 86–87. Casey discusses the play in detail in *The Susanna Theme in German Literature*, 70–89.

pattern of exposition (Act 1), complication (Acts 2–3), resolution (Act 4), and conclusion (Act 5).[48] Even though Rebhun's drama is technically superior to Birck's, he adapts many of the same themes and motifs as Birck, including an emphasis on womanly honor, the importance of the family, and the centrality of marriage to the proper ordering of society.[49] In fact, Rebhun's work has often been seen as being just as Lutheran as Birck's.[50] One of the main reasons for this claim, however, is the theory that Rebhun actually lived with Luther for a time. However, even though this is disputed, no one disagrees with the fact that Rebhun was ordained by Luther on May 30, 1538, and had a fairly close relationship with Melanchthon, and thus stood in close alliance with Reformist ideology.[51] Whatever the case, it is clear that Rebhun, like Birck, adapted the story of Susanna to demonstrate several aspects of Luther's program with similar results.[52]

Thus, in contrast to Altdorfer's specifically Catholic interpretation of Susanna, here we see two uniquely Lutheran views of the story. These examples already validate one of my central claims: the story of Susanna is remarkably malleable in that various communities adapt and interpret it to fit their own religious, political, and ideological needs. The works of Altdorfer, Birck, and Rebhun also contain interesting messages regarding the status of women in that in all three, women represent the ideal characteristics held by either the producer or the patron of the rendering. These characteristics, moreover, do not advance an eroticizing take on the story of Susanna.

6.2.3. *Guillaume Guéroult and Didier Lupi Second*

A rather obscure composer named Didier Lupi Second made one of the most important contributions to vocal music during the Renaissance period. We know very little about Lupi's life and training, but most scholars agree that he was active mainly in the middle of the sixteenth century, and that his activity took

48. See Brown, "The *Susanna* Drama and the German Reformation," 145–46. Interestingly, the choruses found in Rebhun's work were scored for two voices by Rebhun himself. See Clement A. Miller, "Rebhuhn [Rephuhn], Paul," in *The New Grove Dictionary of Music and Musicians*, n.p. [2d ed. 2001]. Online: http://www.grovemusic.com.

49. See Casey, *Paul Rebhun*, 79–80.

50. For this position, see S. L. Clark and David Duewall, "Give and Take: Good, Evil, and Language in Rebhun's *Susanna*," *Euphorion* 75 (1981): 325–41, especially their conclusion on p. 341. Casey, *Paul Rebhun*, 98–99, argues that even though this claim can be made, "a socio-critical commentary on Reformation Germany was not his primary goal" (p. 99).

51. Even though several scholars assume this, Casey, *Paul Rebhun*, 19–21, argues that there is little evidence to support any intimate relationship between Rebhun and Luther.

52. Even though most work on Rebhun's *Susanna* has been laudatory, David Price, in his "'Schweyg liebe tochter': A Reevaluation of Paul Rebhun's *Susanna* (1536)," in *Studies in German and Scandinavian Literature after 1500: A Festschrift for George C. Schoolfield* (ed. James A. Parente, Jr. and Richard Erich Schade; Columbia: Camden House, 1993), 40–49, adopts a harshly critical tone. He writes that "Susanna's...didacticism not only leaves no room for social criticism, it also articulates a pernicious view of social order by prescribing a political rhetoric of silence for women and the oppressed... When a didactic play is arbitrarily unequivocal on questions of morality and politics, as sometimes happens in Renaissance German literature, can it and its author be worthy of unqualified praise?" (p. 47).

place in the French town of Lyons.[53] Lupi probably hailed from Italy, though, because his first musical publication in Lyons, dated 1548 and published by Godefroy and Marcellin Beringen, contains a dedication to merchants and bankers from Lucca in Italy, who had supported him since his arrival in Lyons. This first publication in 1548 contained almost exclusively secular chansons, and was not especially popular.

It was also in 1548, though, that the Beringen brothers published a second musical book by Lupi, entitled *Premier livre de chansons spirituelles nouvellement composées par Guillaume Gueroult, mises en musique par Didier Lupi Second*. As Frank Dobbins notes, this volume "was a considerable success, going through at least seven more editions."[54] This collection contained twenty-one pieces scored for four voices, and it included five psalms as well as many settings of Guillaume Guéroult's poetry. Guéroult was a Huguenot poet who worked as an editor in Lyons. Most of his literary activity was bound up with his religious beliefs. He was staunchly Protestant, and almost all of his poems were intended to be used as *chansons spirituelles*, i.e., spiritual songs used for edificatory and didactic purposes in the intimate religious gatherings of Protestants in France at the time.[55] Two of the *chansons spirituelles* included in Lupi's 1548 collection have Susanna as their subject, entitled "Dames qui au plaisant son," and "Susanne un jour," and the second of these achieved mass renown.[56]

Lupi's four-voice setting of Guéroult's poem was arguably one of, if not *the*, most popular chanson of the mid-sixteenth century. As Kenneth Jay Levy notes,

> Already by the '70s, Susannes were in the printed collections more often than any other chanson. By the end of the century the *dixain* [i.e. Guéroult's poem] had been set to music four or five times as often as any contemporary rival for public favor. And it was not, finally, till the mid 17th century that this text and the memorable tune supplied by its first musician disappeared from the musical scene.[57]

Much of the success of Guéroult's poem has to do with Lupi's setting. In fact, Levy claims that Lupi's "Tenor supplied the musical model used by almost all the versions that followed."[58] In his analysis of multiple Susanne settings, Levy concludes, "Of thirty seven vocal settings which followed Lupi probably no more than four did not use his melody. And these were only to translations of Guéroult's French text, not the original."[59] Two composers, viz., Claude Le Jeune

53. See, e.g., the miniscule entry on Lupi by Marc Honegger and Frank Dobbins in *The New Grove Dictionary of Music and Musicians*, n.p.

54. See Frank Dobbins, *Music in Renaissance Lyons* (Oxford Monographs on Music; Oxford: Clarendon, 1992), 200.

55. See Georg Becker, *Guillaume Guéroult et ses Chansons Spirituelles* (Paris: Librarie Sandoz & Fischbacher, 1880).

56. Becker includes the text and notation for the former poem, although he titles it "Complainte de Sainte Suzanne." See *Guillaume Guéroult et ses Chansons Spirituelles*, 25–34.

57. Kenneth Jay Levy, "'Susanne un jour': The History of a Sixteenth-Century Chanson," *Annales Musicologiques* 1 (1953): 375–408 (376).

58. Levy, "'Susanne un jour,'" 375–76. Levy reproduces Lupi's setting on 403–4.

59. Levy, "'Susanne un jour,'" 377. Those four include two Flemish settings by Episcopius and Gerard Turnhout, both in 1572, and the two English settings by William Byrd in 1588 and 1589 (see

and Jan Sweelinck, copied Lupi's Tenor line exactly, and out of the thirty-eight settings of "Susanne un jour" Levy discusses, twenty-five are dependent on Lupi's version.

Given the success of Guéroult and Lupi's 1548 "Susanne un jour," one may reasonably ask what the reasons were behind its popularity. I will begin by briefly examining the poem itself.[60] The poem is economical by design, focusing on a brief moment in the story of Susanna. However, the succinctness of the piece is overshadowed by the expressiveness of the language. Here we see the pivotal encounter between Susanna and the Elders, but the emphasis is entirely on Susanna and her reactions to the entreaty of the Elders. One hears her refusal and the reasons behind it, but it is at this point that Guéroult ends the poem, thus indicating his intent. Rather than an attempt to summarize the story of Susanna in verse, Guéroult is highlighting Susanna's character and her faith in God. Put another way, by focusing solely on her refusal, Guéroult imagines Susanna as a paragon of devotional volition, refusing that which is in conflict with her religious beliefs. This intent, of course, is informed by the genre of the piece. As Levy writes, Guéroult "wrote Susanne as a *chanson spirituelle*, as a poem intended for devotional use among protestants," and that "He would have hoped that it might proselytize for his Reformed religion."[61] Dobbins clarifies the meaning of the term *chanson spirituelle*: "At first the term was applied to collections of chanson texts which substitute 'purified' sacred, moral, or polemical words, retaining a familiar opening gambit and an identical prosodic structure from a secular model."[62]

The main reasons for the proliferation of *chanson spirituelles* first by Protestant composers and later by Catholics have to do with the religious and political climate in France at the time. King Francis I (1515–1547) held an ambiguous position regarding the new Reformed sects. On the one hand, "he had no desire to see Protestantism enter his territories and divide them, but he encouraged its spread in Germany, where it was a thorn in the flesh of his rival Charles V."[63] Because of this stance, as well as Lyons' proximity to important Humanist centers like Geneva, Protestantism grew increasingly strong in the southwest region of France. The primary influence on French Protestantism at this point was Calvin, especially after his instillation at Geneva in 1539. It was in this same year that the Church authorized the suppression of heretical behavior by any means necessary. Practitioners of the new Protestant sects began to be publicly executed not long after this order. Even so, those who embraced the Reformed traditions as well as those with Humanist leanings began to dig in their heels, and by 1561

p. 377 n. 5). Of these, the Byrd piece(s) were much more popular. The most influential setting of the piece was that of Orlando Lassus, whose 1560 chanson also served as the basis for his 1577 "Missa Susanne un jour."

60. The text of the poem is found in Levy, "'Susanne un jour,'" 375. The English translation in Appendix 3 is taken from the liner notes to the Toronto Consort, *Orlando di Lasso: Chansons and Madrigals* (Dorian Discovery DIS-80149 1994, 1996).

61. Levy, "'Susanne un jour,'" 376–77.

62. Dobbins, *Music in Renaissance Lyons*, 264.

63. González, *The Story of Christianity*, 2:102.

were meeting publicly to worship. At these meetings, psalms and *chanson spirituelles* were often sung as a means of professing religious piety, but also to protest the Church's persecution of their fledgling sects.[64] Evidently the Church finally realized the usefulness of music for didactic and pietistic purposes, because the Council of Trent was specific in its requirements for composition.[65]

In his article, Levy, too, tries to account for what he calls Susanna's "vogue." He dismisses the possibility that it was simply a "fad," and similarly finds a solely musical explanation lacking. His insights are worth quoting at length:

> Susanne's popularity may be explained by reasons beyond the purely musical. A *chanson spirituelle* would naturally attract the protestant musicians. And three possibilities might explain the large number of settings by non-protestants during the '50s and '60s: either Catholic composers chose to ignore the partisan origin of the text; or their settings reflected a general feeling voiced in the articles of Reformation proposed by the French delegation at Trent in 1562: "That in parish Masses...or in other hours, spiritual hymns or Psalms of David, approved by the Bishop, may be sung in the [vernacular] language"; or (the most tempting hypothesis), they made a special point of pillaging the Huguenots' musical arsenal by appropriating Susanne as a symbol of their own, royalist party.[66]

Of course, we have already seen the malleability of the Susanna story, and it is this very characteristic that allowed both Protestants and Catholics to use Susanna's story as a metaphoric sign for their own struggles during this period. Levy adds that Guéroult's use of Susanna

> as the symbol of his own persecuted sect, was quite apt; he was not the first protestant to emphasize a parallel between the conditions of primitive Christianity and those of early Protestantism; Luther, among many others, used this. But the intriguing possibility of turning the tables on Guéroult and the protestants by using this same Susanna, particularly since she would represent the same Catholic Church of old (again under attack), and more particularly since her name [i.e. "lily"] emblemized the religious orthodoxy of the house of Valois...this possibility could not have escaped the royalist theologians.[67]

Thus, Guéroult composed his poem as a *chanson spirituelle* to inculcate piety and devotion in Protestants, and Catholic composers used not only his poem but also Lupi's setting to portray their ancient traditions as threatened, yet righteous. It is again one of the great strengths of Susanna, as well as an historical irony, that her story is sufficiently pliable to be used as propaganda of sorts by rival ideologies. Finally, by focusing exclusively on Susanna's faith and her refusal of the Elders, Guéroult recovers the thematic emphases in the apocryphal narrative, rather than dwelling on the sexual or voyeuristic aspects of the story, as do the interpreters I discussed in Chapter 5.

64. See Dobbins, *Music in Renaissance Lyons*, 9–13, for political and religious background information on Lyons.

65. See Michael A. Mullett, "The Catholic Reformation and the Arts," in *The Catholic Reformation* (London: Routledge, 1999), 196–214 (211–13); and Howard M. Brown and Louise K. Stein, "The Music of the Reformation and the Council of Trent," in *Music in the Renaissance* (2d ed.; Prentice Hall History of Music; Upper Saddle River, N.J.: Prentice–Hall, 1999), 273–80.

66. Levy, "'Susanne un jour,'" 380.

67. Levy, "'Susanne un jour,'" 380–81 n. 2.

6.2.4. *Artemisia Gentileschi*

Artemisia Gentileschi, the only talented child of renowned painter Orazio Gentileschi, was born in Rome in July 1593. Orazio took responsibility for teaching his daughter his trade, both for personal and pragmatic reasons. Garrard writes, "Since females were not eligible for normal paths to artistic careers, such as training with more than one established master, travel, or membership in guilds, Artemisia's apprenticeship to her father would have been her only access to the profession."[68] Artemisia learned quickly and learned much from her father's tutelage, but he could not teach her everything. Orazio hired a colleague named Agostino Tassi to teach his daughter perspective. Under their dual guidance, but showing a remarkable innovation, she produced her first masterpiece at the tender age of seventeen: the 1610 *Susanna and the Elders* (Pommerfelden, Germany, Schloss Weissenstein),[69] which I will discuss in detail below.

One year after her first success, Artemisia endured one of the most scandalous events in the history of art. In 1611, she had an encounter with Tassi that he described as seductive, but she claimed was a rape. Early in 1612, Orazio initiated a lawsuit against Tassi, which then became a public trial in which Artemisia claimed Tassi raped her and then promised to marry her.[70] Several witnesses were brought forth both to support and refute Artemisia's claim, and Artemisia even voluntarily submitted to torture and a virginity test to prove she told the truth. Even though the verdict has not been recorded, most scholars assume that Tassi was convicted, but probably not sentenced. A few months after the trial, Artemisia was married to Pietro Stiattesi, a relative of one of Tassi's friends and a key witness at the trial. The couple moved to Florence at the end of 1612 or the beginning of 1613.

Gentileschi's first major effort after moving to Florence was her ca. 1613 *Judith Beheading Holofernes* (Naples, Museo di Capodimonte),[71] which she gave to Cosimo II de' Medici. In this work, she imitates Caravaggio's 1598/9 oil of the same subject (Rome, Galleria Nazionale d'Arte Antica, Palazzo Barberini).[72] It is tempting to interpret Gentileschi's *Judith* based on her encounter with Tassi, and as such claim that it represents some sort of pictorial revenge, the attainment of psychological closure.[73] Ann Sutherland Harris, however, notes:

68. M. D. Garrard, *Artemisia Gentileschi: The Image of the Female Hero in Italian Baroque Art* (Princeton, N.J.: Princeton University Press, 1989), 16–17.

69. Online: http://www.wga.hu/art/g/gentiles/artemisi/susanna.jpg.

70. In her work, Garrard reproduces the trial transcripts in an English translation. See Garrard, *Artemisia Gentileschi*, 403–87. In his work, R. Ward Bissell warns of oversimplifying the relationship between Artemisia and Tassi. He notes that there most likely was some sort of emotional relationship between the two after the rape. See *Artemisia Gentileschi and the Authority of Art: Critical Reading and Catalogue Raisonné* (University Park, Pa.: University of Pennsylvania Press, 1999), 15. Garrard, however, tempers Bissell's claim by noting, "After being raped, Artemisia's best chance for salvaging her honor would have been to go along with the sexual demands of the rapist, since that was her only leverage for getting him to marry her" (p. 206).

71. Online: http://www.wga.hu/art/g/gentiles/artemisi/judit.jpg.

72. Online: http://www.wga.hu/art/c/caravagg/03/17judit.jpg.

73. For an excellent critique of this position, see Griselda Pollock, "The Female Hero and the Making of a Feminist Canon: Artemisia Gentileschi's Representations of Susanna and Judith," in

> It was surely Artemisia's intention to announce her arrival in Florence with a work that could not be overlooked and further that demanded comparison with one of the most celebrated painters of the day whose work was still hardly known outside Rome.[74]

Of course, these two approaches are not mutually exclusive. The painting could be a personal statement of Artemisia's based on her rape by Tassi, and serve as a formidable calling card to Florence. Either way, *Judith* made an impact; in 1616, she became the first woman artist to join the Academia del Disegno. Her connections with the Medici family, and with Michelangelo Buonarroti the Younger, probably helped her overcome this gender barrier as well.[75]

She returned to Rome in ca. 1620, and made several important visits to neighboring cities in 1621, including Genoa and Venice. She most likely met the northern painter Anthony Van Dyck during her stay in Genoa, and Garrard notes that Artemisia's 1610 *Susanna* most likely influenced Van Dyck's ca. 1625 *Susanna and the Elders* (Munich, Alte Pinakothek).[76] By 1630, she was living in Naples. There she began to paint more traditional religious themes from the New Testament for a variety of private patrons, including Empress Maria of Austria. Garrard even raises the possibility of Gentileschi working with Massimo Stanzione and the Spanish painter Diego Velázquez.[77] As early as 1635, though, Gentileschi was looking for new patrons on other areas. She found them, and by 1638 was in London working with her father at the court of Charles I. She and Orazio, who died in 1639, both worked on his commission to decorate the ceiling of the Queen's house in Greenwich. Not long after Orazio's death and the completion of the ceiling panels, Artemisia was on the move once again, this time to familiar terrain. She returned to Naples in ca. 1642, and spent the rest of her life there painting private commissions, most notably for a Sicilian named Don Antonio Ruffo. Her work for Ruffo, as well as her surviving correspondence from this period, shows her to be a shrewd businesswoman and one of the most talented artists operating within Italy during the late Renaissance.[78]

The most influential interpreter of Gentileschi's 1610 *Susanna* has been Garrard, who argues forcefully for the work as representing a type of proto-feminist statement. As I showed in Chapter 4, sentiments now labeled as "feminist" were not common, but present nonetheless during the Renaissance. Garrard's argument begins by examining the piece in comparison with other Susannas of the period, specifically Annibale Carracci's 1590/1 etching and engraving. She writes,

Differencing the Canon: Feminist Desire and the Writing of Art's Histories (London: Routledge, 1999), 97–127 (115–24).

74. Ann Sutherland Harris, "Artemisia Gentileschi," in *The Grove Dictionary of Art Online*, n.p.

75. See Garrard, *Artemisia Gentileschi*, 34–35.

76. Garrard, *Artemisia Gentileschi*, 57. Online: http://www.wga.hu/art/d/dyck_van/3other/susanna.jpg.

77. Garrard, *Artemisia Gentileschi*, 91 and 97. Stanzione painted his own *Susanna and the Elders*, in which he portrays Susanna as resisting the Elders (seventeenth century; Frankfurt: Städelches Kunstinstitut).

78. For all of the extant letters of Gentileschi, see Garrard, *Artemisia Gentileschi*, 373–401.

> While Susanna's legs correspond generally in pose with those in Annibale's print, the position of the arms has been decisively changed, and her image accordingly revised, from that of a sexually available and responsive female to an emotionally distressed young women [*sic*], whose vulnerability is emphasized in the awkward twisting of her body. The artist has also eliminated the sexually allusive garden setting, replacing the lush foliage, spurting fountain and sculpted satyr heads that appear in the Carracci circle works with an austere rectilinear balustrade that subtly reinforces our sense of Susanna's discomfort. The expressive core of this picture is the heroine's plight, not the villains' anticipated pleasure.[79]

Garrard's description is apt; the picture is much more stark than other renderings of Susanna, primarily because the garden is absent. In its place is hard stone. Also, even though Gentileschi portrays the confrontation between the Elders and Susanna, the interaction is not laden with sexual tension. In fact, it seems to depict the consternation of Susanna in the apocryphal story. The Elders are portrayed as conspiratorial; one is either whispering something to Susanna or instructing her to be silent, while the other is giving some secret advice to his comrade. Susanna is shown as troubled, holding her arms up in a gesture of resistance against the Elders, and the overall tone of the picture is one of distress.

Furthermore, almost all of the Susannas produced during the Renaissance period use the Venus or Lucretia model as a basis for the portrayal of Susanna. However, in the 1610 *Susanna*, Gentileschi carefully shuns those classical models. Garrard argues that, instead, Gentileschi's *Susanna* alludes to the figure of Orestes' nurse on a Roman Orestes sarcophagus, who is in a position of anguish.[80] Even more interesting, Garrard suggests that Artemisia turned to Michelangelo's frescoes in the Sistine Chapel for the color scheme and design in this piece, meaning that "in her earliest signed and dated painting, Artemisia sought inspiration for a heroic female character in the heroic males created by a revered High Renaissance master."[81]

Along with these formal observations, Garrard also raises the possibility that Artemisia's first *Susanna* expressed personal anguish on the part of its creator based on her rape by Tassi. Certainly there are many parallels between the story of Susanna and the events and trial surrounding Tassi's rape of Gentileschi, but there is one major problem in this line of interpretation: the rape did not occur until 1611, while the painting is dated one year earlier, in 1610.[82] However, this problem is easily accounted for: Artemisia repeatedly declares in her testimony that Tassi and his friend Cosimo Quorli had been harassing her for some time to have sex with them, and as such the painting could represent the torment undergone by Susanna prior to the attempted rape. As Garrard puts it, "What the painting gives us then is a reflection, not of the rape itself, but rather of how the

79. Garrard, "Artemesia and Susanna," 148–49.

80. Garrard, "Artemesia and Susanna," 154–55. Orestes' nurse is mentioned in "The Libation Bearers," the second play of Aeschylus' *Oresteia Triology*. She is usually portrayed as a distressed old woman because she has cared for Orestes since he was a child, and is saddened by the false report of his death, which she must report to Aegisthus, his stepfather.

81. Garrard, *Artemisia Gentileschi*, 17.

82. See Garrard, *Artemisia Gentileschi*, 204–9, for these parallels.

young woman artist felt about her own sexual vulnerability in the year 1610."[83] Thus, the 1610 *Susanna* portrays the psychological state of its creator, a young girl who felt threatened sexually, and who sought to express those feelings of vulnerability and defenselessness. In sum, according to Garrard, this *Susanna* resembles Artemisia's Judiths

> in her physically active resistance of her oppressors and in her expressive intensity. She conveys through her awkward pose and her nudity the full range of feelings of anxiety, fear and shame felt by a victimized woman faced with a choice between rape and slanderous public denouncement. As a pictorial conception, Susanna presents an image rare in art, of a three-dimensional female character who is heroic in the classical sense. For in her struggle against forces ultimately beyond her control, she exhibits a spectrum of human emotions that move us, as with Oedipus or Achilles, both to pity and to awe.[84]

This reading of Gentileschi's 1610 *Susanna*, her first masterpiece, also holds for the only other rendering of the subject scholars can confidently assign to her, viz., her 1649 oil (*Susanna and the Elders*, Moravská Galerie, Brno, Czech Republic).[85] There are two other extant paintings of Susanna connected to Gentileschi, but scholars are divided over her role in their production.[86]

On the whole, Garrard's interpretation of Gentileschi's first *Susanna* has held sway among art historians. However, there have been critiques of her position, most notably by Harris and Griselda Pollock.[87] Harris critiques Garrard's position on the feminist slant of the work. She writes,

> Artemisia's choice for this subject was not casual, nor can it be simply an inspired bit of personal feminism provoked by the cat calls and crude attempts to solicit her attention that she undoubtedly had to tolerate every time she left the house without her father as an escort. Indeed, her willingness to depict what 20th century feminists have labelled "woman as sex object" would seem, I think, to preclude any feminist awareness on her part of a kind we now regard as elementary.[88]

Instead of anguish over her sexual harassment or some sort of proto-feminist cognizance, Harris posits a more pragmatic reason for Artemisia's choice and portrayal of Susanna:

83. Garrard, "Artemesia and Susanna," 165.

84. Garrard, "Artemesia and Susanna," 158.

85. Online: http://www.moravska-galerie.cz/Photos/large/019.jpg.

86. In a recent work, Garrard argues forcefully that an oil in the Burghley House Collection depicting Susanna should be attributed to Artemisia. See her *Artemesia Gentileschi around 1622: The Shaping and Reshaping of an Artistic Identity* (Discovery; Berkeley: University of California Press, 2001), 77–113. In his work, though, Bissell does not accept this attribution. See *Artemisia Gentileschi and the Authority of Art*, 348–53. Another Susanna proves to be even more of a mystery. In 1995, Sotheby's sold a painting of Susanna to a buyer who has remained anonymous. That *Susanna* may be a collaborative effort between Artemisia and two other painters, viz., Domenico Gargiulo and Bernard Cavallino, but no close inspection of the painting has taken place, even though Bissell concludes that Gentileschi is primarily responsible for the canvas (pp. 266–67).

87. See Pollock, "The Female Hero," 103–15.

88. Ann Sutherland Harris, "Artemisia Gentileschi: The Literate Illiterate or Learning from Example," in *Docere Delectare Movere: Affetti, Devozione e Retorico nel Linguaggio Artistico del Primo Barocco Romano* (Rome: Instituto Olandese a Roma, 1998), 105–20 (113).

> Her choice of this subject and her treatment of it display her acute awareness of the burgeoning popularity of this theme among artists then enjoying particular success in Rome, and an awesome degree of ambition for a woman not yet twenty, who was thus openly inviting comparison with all of them, despite the disadvantages that her sex imposed on her education and artistic formation. Not only would she have to be judged as a history painter, but also for her *giudizio* as she composed her interpretation, and her capacity for *invenzione*, or perhaps *variatio*, as she offered her public yet another image of Susanna surprised bathing by two randy and powerful men.[89]

In her work, Pollock evaluates Garrard's claims and finds them too simplistic, i.e., Garrard's analysis of the work is too "modern" in that it does not take into account the malleability of "Artemisia" as a product of competing social, historical, and artistic forces. Neither does it account for the multiple interpretations possible, given the various locations of various viewers.[90] Finally, Pollock critiques Garrard's reading of *Susanna* as related to Artemisia's rape trial as both failing to address adequately an understanding of the psychic workings of trauma as well as representing an unsophisticated attempt to correlate artistic expression with personal experience.

Harris' analysis of Gentileschi is intriguing, and offers a more concrete alternative to Garrard's more ideological reading of the piece. That is, Harris' work seems to be grounded more in what we can know historically than in the subjective critiques of Pollock. In that regard, Harris' discussion can be seen as complementary to Garrard's. On the other hand, I find Pollock's analysis insightful, yet unconstructive in that she proposes no thoroughgoing alternative to Garrard's reading. In my opinion, then, Garrard's reading, even taking these critiques into account, is still persuasive. In sum, Gentileschi's 1610 representation of Susanna seems to be different in motivation than the other artistic interpretations I have examined thus far. It does not express a religious fervor, nor does it seem to privilege the erotic nature of so many other Susannas during this period. Instead, the painting exhibits a subjective sense of despair and anguish in the figure of Susanna, with her arms raised in a gesture of both defense and pleading. One can almost imagine this Susanna as a real woman, in the sense that she does not seem to be an idealized type of either chastity or acquiescence. Rather, she perhaps more than any other Susanna under discussion resembles the character of Susanna in Patrick Smith's extended poem *Susannah and the Elders*, when she says in a dialogue with Joachim:

> not eve joachim though sinner i am not sin…
>
> i am not an eve unfaithful to god
> oh wife susannah

89. Harris, "Artemisia Gentileschi," 113–14.

90. In this regard, the work of George L. Hershey is interesting. Hershey reads Garrard reading Artemisia as a male viewer. In one particularly intriguing passage, Hershey writes that the male viewer or patron might not find Artemisia's women attractive, but they would still be titillated because of their creator's reputation. See Goerge Hershey, "Female and Male Art: *Postille* to Garrard's *Artemisia Gentileschi*," in *Parthenope's Splendor: Art of the Golden Age in Naples* (ed. Jeanne Chenault Porter and Susan Scott Munshower; University Park, Pa.: University of Pennsylvania Press, 1993), 323–35.

> though death approaches me
> oh wife
>
> i am not eve i am some new thing since found
> susannah
>
> i am susannah
> innocent woman daughter sister lover wife and mother[91]

Artemisia's Susanna seems ultimately and exceptionally human, and unique in the history of the development of the Susanna theme.

6.2.5. *Rembrandt*

The last examples of the Susanna theme in the Renaissance I wish to discuss are also arguably the most famous, viz., the two Susannas of Rembrandt. Owing to the massive biographical literature available on Rembrandt, I will only mention data of that nature to enhance my examination of his interpretations of Susanna. Following this examination, I will offer some concluding remarks to this chapter.

In the early 1630s, Rembrandt moved from Leiden to Amsterdam, and there worked for and lived with an art dealer named Hendrik van Uylenburgh. He married in 1634 and spent most of his time painting commissioned portraits that van Uylenburgh arranged for him. During this time, though, he still managed to work on various historical and biblical subjects, and in ca. 1636 painted his first *Susanna and the Elders* (Fig. 7).

Almost all scholars agree that one of Rembrandt's primary models for this work was Pieter Lastman's 1614 oil on the same subject (*Susanna and the Elders*, Berlin, Gemäldegalerie).[92] This influence should come as no surprise; when Rembrandt was nineteen years old, he began a six-month apprenticeship with Lastman in Amsterdam. When Lastman died in 1633, Rembrandt made several drawings of his former master's paintings, among them a Susanna. In Lastman's *Susanna*, the two Elders are in plain view, surrounded by lush foliage, and in the midst of attempting to persuade Susanna to let them rape her. Susanna appears in the classic *Venus pudica* pose, trying to conceal her genitalia, and looking toward heaven, as if she is already entreating God for help. The tone of the picture is somber, with the landscape predominantly dark and only Susanna shown in full light. In sum, Lastman's interpretation of Susanna is idiosyncratic in that the mood of the painting is solemn; yet by adopting the Venus pose for Susanna and portraying her exposed breasts it stands in the long line of eroticizing and voyeuristic readings of the apocryphal story.

Rembrandt's work based on Lastman's oil exhibits many of the same characteristics. Here, too, we see Susanna in the Venus pose covering not only her genitalia but also her breasts.[93] The landscape of the piece is also similar in that it

91. Patrick Smith, *Susannah and the Elders* (San Francisco: Pancake Press, 1992), 18–19.

92. Online: http://socrates.berkeley.edu/~ah172/history/lastman.htm.

93. *Contra* this statement, see Bal, "Between Focalization and Voyeurism," 170: "In terms of iconographic traditions, the pose of Susanna is less strictly tied to the Medici Venus, and thus there is a less direct evocation of a traditionally erotic meaning."

is dark, even more so than Lastman's work, and Susanna occupies almost all of the visual field. However, there are at least two striking innovations in this painting not found in Lastman's. First, the Elders are almost completely hidden from sight. In fact, only one Elder is detectable, and only after serious study of the dense foliage to the right of Susanna.[94] The effects of this (dis)placement of the Elders, usually considered to be a cipher for the male viewer, will be discussed below. The second innovation is Susanna herself, i.e., her position, sense of movement, and direct gaze out of the frame all represent a new wrinkle in the standard renderings of the theme.[95]

Figure 7. Rembrandt van Rijn, *Susanna and the Elders*, ca. 1636. Mauritshuis, the Hague

94. Bal, "The Elders and Susanna," 2, notes that the visible Elder in this work is "assumed to be a later addition."

95. Tintoretto's *Susanna and the Elders*, in the Louvre (Fig. 2) also portrays Susanna gazing out of the frame, but, as I will note below, the two works differ in their overall portrayal of Susanna.

In an interesting article, "Rembrandt's Early Paintings of the Female Nude: *Andromeda* and *Susanna*," Sluijter argues that Rembrandt knowingly altered the conventional treatment of the Susanna theme, especially those works that might have influenced his interpretations, including the works of Lastman, Cornelius van Haarlem, Peter Paul Rubens (ca. 1606; Rome, Galleria Borghese), Lucas Vorsterman (ca. 1620; after Rubens' ca. 1606 piece), and perhaps even the work of Annibale Carracci.[96] Sluijter notes that Rembrandt tried both to involve the viewer and depict Susanna's state of mind. He did so, as I noted above, by adopting Lastman's use of the *Venus pudica* pose, as well as alluding to another classical model, the *Venus Doidalsas*, or Crouching Venus, thus heightening Susanna's erotic appeal.[97] However, the most important advance according to Sluijter is Rembrandt's choice of which moment to represent. Almost all of the Renaissance interpretations of Susanna depict the moment when the Elders confront Susanna in her garden, and as such are able to represent a naked woman in a sexual situation. In Rembrandt's first *Susanna*, though,

> What the viewer sees is a Susanna who suddenly realizes that she is being watched—one could imagine that she has just heard a twig snap. She starts in fear and begins to rise from a sitting position. Her weight is already on her feet, which emphasizes the agitated suddenness of her reaction and gives a suggestion of wavering unbalance... In the process she steps on her slipper; thus Rembrandt stressed the abrupt clumsiness of her spontaneous movement, which is at the same time brilliantly used as a metaphoric motif referring to her chasteness. Slightly turning away her upper body from the onlooker, trying to hide her secret parts, her large dark eyes look intensely at the viewer. It is the viewer she confronts as the intruder who made her start in fear.[98]

The simulated movement of Susanna suggests clumsy movement in response to a presence, real or imagined, and as viewers we expect that presence to be filled by the Elders. However, their almost total absence from this painting means that presence is filled by another party, viz., the viewer of the work, the recipient of Susanna's pleading and fearful gaze. Both Sluijter and Mieke Bal agree that this gaze, as well as the position of the viewer, serves to heighten the erotic appeal of the work:

> It is the gaze of the viewer to which she reacts so forcefully. Unlike Rubens's *Susanna*, her reaction is not ambiguous: the viewer is recognized as the intruder and primary offender. Susanna is trapped by the beholder's gaze, which becomes explicitly the illicit gaze of the voyeur. At the same time this makes the image more intensely erotic. In this very erotically charged moment, the engaged viewer experiences, as it were, the rush of being caught in an illicit act by the source of his sensual enjoyment. In this way the moral and erotic tension are linked as never before.[99]

96. See Eric J. Sluijter, "Rembrandt's Early Paintings of the Female Nude: *Andromeda* and *Susanna*," in *Rembrandt and His Pupils* (ed. Görel Cavalli-Björkman; Uddevalla, Sweden: Risbergs Tryckeri, 1993), 31–54. To my knowledge, the most extensive work on any of the Susannas of these artists is that of Mark C. Leach on Rubens. See Leach, "Rubens and the Theme of Susanna and the Elders" (M.A. thesis, University of Delaware, 1974).
97. Sluijter, "Rembrandt's Early Paintings," 41.
98. Sluijter, "Rembrandt's Early Paintings," 41–42.
99. Sluijter, "Rembrandt's Early Paintings," 44.

Bal argues that since the gaze of Susanna has no connection to any internal narrative structure, it represents a de-narrativized look directed at the viewer of the work, and as such engages the spectator in an act of uninvited voyeuristic pleasure.[100] This pleasure can even be seen as malicious. Spolsky writes, "It is difficult not to see the painter's choice of this moment as sadistic; the viewer is allowed to enjoy her [Susanna's] shock and fear."[101] Thus, many interpreters argue that even though Rembrandt alters the traditional iconographic topos of the Susanna theme in this work, he does so in a way that heightens the erotic and voyeuristic undertones present in other interpretations of the story.

The 1640s were not as kind to Rembrandt as the previous decade had been. In 1642, his wife Saskia died of tuberculosis, leaving him alone with their young son Titus. Not long after her death, Rembrandt hired a nurse named Geertge Dircx, with whom he became sexually involved. By 1649, though, he wished to dispense her to take up with a twenty-three-year-old named Hendrickje Stoffels. Evidently, Geertge was unhappy with her severance allowance, and a court case began, which she later won. Following the trial, Rembrandt started publicly to defame her, to the point that she was consigned to a reformatory where she remained for five years. Thus, his second *Susanna and the Elders* (Fig. 8), painted in ca. 1647, was created in a stressful period of conflicting personal commitments. Owing to his personal problems, it was actually one of the last pieces he painted in the 1640s.

Figure 8. Rembrandt, *Susanna and the Elders*, 1647.
Staatliche Museen zu Berlin—Preußischer Kulturbesitz, Gemäldegale

100. Bal, "The Elders and Susanna," 14.
101. Spolsky, "Law or the Garden," 104.

The two works are obviously similar in many respects. The landscape and foliage are alike; both are dark and foreboding, as is typical of Rembrandt. The shading of both works highlights the figure of Susanna, which is roughly the same in both paintings. In the Berlin *Susanna* she is more stylized, i.e., there is less sense of movement and almost no awkwardness, and her shoe is missing. Even so, she still is positioned in the Venus pose, and her body and features are almost identical. The most noticeable difference between the two works is the presence of the Elders. Whereas in the 1636 piece they are hidden for the most part, here they are both fully represented on the same visual plane as Susanna. The Elder on the left takes up a familiar position in other representations of the theme: he is trying to disrobe Susanna and could be whispering in her ear.[102] The second Elder is approaching the pair on the far right, grasping what appears to be a staff. The presence of the Elders echoes earlier treatments of the story, and could be seen as an adoption of the more traditional presentation of Susanna in art during this period.

However, in her work Bal disagrees, and argues that the differences introduced in the Berlin *Susanna* actually resist the voyeuristic aspects of the 1636 piece.[103] She focuses her attention first on Susanna's left hand, which alludes to the Venus pose. Bal claims that at the same time this intertextual citation is made, the citation is also undermined by the defensive posture of Susanna's figure.[104] Furthermore, the Elder on the left is attempting to disrobe Susanna, and as such could be taken as a cipher for male desire in and from the painting. Bal, though, notes that

> Syntactically, in combination with Susanna's appeal to the viewer to turn his eyes away if the undressing eventually occurs, it [the Elder's action] can simultaneously be taken to criticize the gesture: It says, the body may be naked in a moment, but please don't look. The vulnerability of this young, helpless female figure is certainly a possible occasion for voyeurism in its sadistic variant. But this *ideologeme* is counterbalanced by the opposite ideologeme, the strongly active look.[105]

Finally, in order to read against the interpretation of this work that sees continuity present with other eroticizing renderings of the theme, Bal focuses on the Elders themselves as potential imitative examples. She argues that the presentation of the Elders in the painting vitiates against any potential wish viewers might have to emulate their gaze, or possibly even their actions, including

102. Interestingly, Ernst van de Wetering notes that a drawing of this work in an early stage by Barent Fabritius shows the Elder on the left reaching around Susanna, trying to clutch her breast. See *Rembrandt: The Painter at Work* (Berkeley: University of California Press, 2000), 250–51. See also Kathleen P. McClain, "Seeing Beyond the Traditional Image of Susanna and the Elders" (M.A. thesis, The University of Alabama at Birmingham, 2000), 47.

103. See Bal, "Between Focalization and Voyeurism," 167–68.

104. McClain, "Seeing Beyond the Traditional Image of Susanna and the Elders," 58 n. 94, agrees with Bal's assessment, even though she does not cite Bal. She notes that if Rembrandt's original vision for the Berlin *Susanna* was to have one Elder groping Susanna, then this would move Susanna away from the Venus tradition, which emphasizes concealment, not sexual contact.

105. Bal, "Between Focalization and Voyeurism," 167.

> The ridiculous overdressing of the men, with their pompous mantles and hats, the staff and seat for the one, the chain referring to his honorable function for the other. These elements hamper the viewer's gaze in that they activate the narrative of abuse of power with which most viewers will not automatically wish to identify. The position the viewer is invited to share, that of the Elder at the right of the painting, is thereby just too uncomfortable to allow the viewer to take up his objectifying, abstract, and delectating gaze very easily.[106]

Thus, Bal's reading of Rembrandt's Berlin *Susanna* claims that the eroticism and voyeurism present in other works depicting this theme is undermined by the particulars of the painting. Put another way, both Sluijter and Bal agree that Rembrandt altered the traditional representation(s) of Susanna in pictorial art during the Renaissance; they simply differ on the results of that alteration.

In sum, Rembrandt's two Susannas represent sites of competing claims as to their function(s) and effect(s) on viewers. Sluijter argues that Rembrandt's 1636 (Fig. 7) piece furthers the eroticizing tendencies of earlier Susannas by focusing on her individual figure and psychological state. Bal, on the other hand, claims that the Berlin *Susanna* resists these tendencies, even though it may appear to embrace them. In my opinion, both of the works resist the traditional iconographic meaning(s) found in traditional renderings due to the figure of Susanna. As Bonjione notes in her work, the Medici Venus in the *Venus pudica* pose "does not invite voyeurism and appears quite uncomfortable with the fact that anyone is observing her naked body."[107] However, unlike the classical Medici Venus and other renderings of Susanna, Rembrandt paints Susanna looking directly at the viewer, and this gaze, I would argue, contains no trace of erotic appeal or sexual suggestion.[108] If there is any acquiescence to the eroticizing tradition of other Susannas, I agree with Bal and Spolsky that it is of the sadistic variant, i.e., one would have to enjoy terror, confusion, and the potential of domination in order to find this Susanna sexually appealing. Thus, Rembrandt, like Gentileschi, resists the standard interpretations of Susanna as a sexual object and instead presents the viewer with a young woman shocked and horrified to find that she is being watched, one who appeals to the viewer both to turn away and to help her. In this regard, Rembrandt's Susannas build on mimetic and eroticizing tendencies, but they do so in order to critique them.

6.3. *Conclusion*

From the foregoing examination, it should be obvious that the story of Susanna had an interesting journey through the Renaissance. Due to the sheer number of artistic, musical, and literary interpretations, generalizations are difficult to make, but I would like to make a few observations on the foci of different genric traversals of the story.

106. Bal, "Between Focalization and Voyeurism," 168.

107. Bonjione, "Shifting Images: Susanna through the Ages," 114.

108. In Tintoretto's Louvre *Susanna and the Elders* (Fig. 2), Susanna's gaze out of the frame is not pleading or fearful. Due to the excessive presence of *vanitas* elements, as well as the fact that she is unaware of the presence of the Elders, her gaze cannot be taken as a cry for help.

In terms of music and literature, the focus with regard to Susanna is twofold. On the one hand, Susanna's faith in God over against the faithlessness of the Elders is used as an allegorical sign to serve the mimetic interests of various religious groups. For example, Birck and Rebhun use Susanna to emphasize Protestant values and mores, especially the importance of family. In Guéroult and Lupi's 1548 "Susanne un jour," the stress is on personal piety and the validity of the Huguenot movement in the face of the Catholic Church. On the other hand, Susanna's chastity and its opposite, the lust of the Elders, served to reinforce cultural prescriptions for feminine behavior, which also served religious ideologies. This tendency is also seen in Birck's play.[109]

In my opinion, the reason for the univocality of musical and dramatic renderings is linked to genric limitations. Put another way, lyrical songs were usually short during this period, and as such cannot paint a full picture of an incident like the story of Susanna. Additionally, dramatic works written for public performance had to take into account the transvestite nature of such performances, i.e., male players played all parts, regardless of the sex of a particular character. As such, little sexual intrigue and certainly no nudity was possible. Thus, Susanna's story was put to socio-religious uses, as opposed to the common artistic interpretation(s) of the narrative. In opposition to those works that highlight the mimetic and erotic level of the narrative, the works in this chapter either focus on the thematic level of the story or critique the more mimetic works. Put another way, the renderings in this chapter emphasize Susanna's faith and religiosity as opposed to the sexuality and voyeurism implicit in the apocryphal narrative. Altdorfer's painting, as well as Birck's play and Guéroult's poem, all highlight the religious nature of Susanna's story while using that religiosity to further their own religious agendas. Additionally, there are a number of paintings that depict Susanna as a nude that serve as counter-readings to the traditional, erotic renderings. I have dwelt at length on Gentileschi's contribution to this undercurrent, and Rembrandt's works also push in this direction. In addition, the Susannas of Ludovico Carracci; Frans Floris (1600; Vienna, Kunsthistorisches Museum); the School of Veronese (sixteenth century; Rome, Accademia Nazionale di San Luca); and Hendrick Goltzius (1607; Paris, Musée Municipal de Douai), also stand in this line of representation.[110] That is, by portraying Susanna as resisting or in fear of the advances of the Elders, these works serve to highlight not Susanna's voluptuous body, but rather the inappropriate and harmful behavior of the Elders, as well as Susanna's implicitly religious reasons for refusing their advances, which in turn reinforces the narrative's emphases on chastity and faith in God.

109. This inclination is also found in the work of Thomas Garter. See his *The Most Virtuous and Godly Susanna (1578)* (ed. B. I. Evans and W. W. Greg; Malone Society Reprints; Oxford: Oxford University Press, 1937).

110. For a recent assessment of Ludovico Carracci's Susanna paintings, see Bohn, "Rape and the Gendered Gaze," 259–86. I concur with Bohn's position that Ludovico Carracci's work resists the dominant interpretive *topos* of Susanna during the Renaissance, as exemplified by Tintoretto.

In sum, the interpretations of Susanna during the Renaissance display a remarkable variety, both of form and emphasis. We have seen the story utilized by Protestants and Catholics for religious, erotic, legal, and personal uses. Indeed, the almost universal themes and concerns in the apocryphal narrative make the story extremely malleable and almost invite diverse groups to take it up. This malleability, as well as the ability of different groups with divergent interests and agendas to see themselves in the story, accounts for the widespread dispersion of Susanna during the Renaissance. However, this dispersion is not the most important aspect of the Susanna theme during the Renaissance. In Chapter 5 as well as the present chapter, I have argued that renderings of Susanna have generally fallen into two categories: those that present a mimetic interpretation of the story, and those that focus on a thematic rendering. The former are harmful in that they seek to lure the viewer into a complicity with the Elders regarding their attempted rape of Susanna. In effect, these interpretations try to persuade their receivers that Susanna's beauty is responsible for the Elders' attempt to rape her, and that we have to share the Elders' view of Susanna. Assumptions of this sort reflect deep-seated beliefs regarding women that modern readers should resist. That is, by showing us ways in which interpreters have imaginatively defied the more mimetic, erotic tradition of Susanna interpretations, these works allow us to create our own ways of resisting the harmful emphasis on the erotic in the story of Susanna.

Part III

CONCLUSION(S) AND APPENDICES

Chapter 7

CONCLUSION(S)

We have traveled a great distance in the preceding six chapters. I have examined the story of Susanna and the situation(s) of women in the first century B.C.E., and then discussed how those situations were present during the Renaissance, as well as the way(s) in which Susanna's narrative was interpreted artistically, literarily, and musically. In this chapter, I will briefly review my findings and discussions in those chapters, and conclude this project with a consideration of the significance of my research, along with the importance of a story like Susanna to modern issues such as feminism and patriarchy.

In Chapter 2, I argue for a specific date for the story of Susanna, viz., the early first century B.C.E. To do so, I examined the socio-historical context(s) of that period, including the roles and issues embodied by women in the apocryphal narrative, including daughters, wives and women in public, women's religious devotion, and women as suspected adulteresses. After this examination, I discussed the reign of Salome Alexandra, and incorporated the work of Tal Ilan, who argues that Judith, Greek Esther, and Susanna were all used, if not composed, to serve as propaganda for her reign.[1] I concluded in that chapter that Susanna was composed during the first century B.C.E., and, due to many affinities with Judith and Greek Esther, was probably used in the manner Ilan claims.

Chapter 3 contains my extended reading of Susanna. Using James Phelan's narrative-rhetorical method of reading, as well as paying attention to issues of intertextual references and feminist insights, I read Susanna as primarily a thematic tale, as opposed to a mimetic story, i.e., a "realist" piece of writing. The thematic propositions put forth by the two main characters—Susanna and the Elders—can be stated simply: Susanna's actions and speech, along with the result of the story itself, posits the notion that her faith, her concept of the deity, is the correct one, over and against the character of the Elders, whose religiosity is sorely lacking and who are executed for actions stemming from this lack. Put another way, by composing the story of Susanna as we have it now, the author created a fictional world as well as certain themes or messages to be drawn from the goings-on in that world. My own reading of the story found the rhetoric of the story dominated by thematic concerns, i.e., the mimetic portrayal of the characters and their interactions takes a back seat to the message the story wants to posit through those characters and the plot.

1. See Ilan, "'And Who Knows,'" 127–53.

The second part of my project focuses on the Renaissance period and Susanna's existence therein. Chapter 4 analyzed women during this time period using the same four categories found in Chapter 2 in an attempt to determine if these societal attitudes were still present over fifteen hundred years later. My examination shows that, for the most part, the situation of women in the Renaissance is analogous to the expectations and behavior of women in the first century B.C.E. However, there seems to have been an intensification of interest in the issue of chastity and its implications for men and women that influenced the prescriptions for female behavior. Even so, women appear to have had more opportunities for public displays of religiosity, as well as educational prospects not present in the first century B.C.E.

In Chapter 5, I examined three painters whose work represents the best examples of an aesthetic interpretation of the mimetic level of the apocryphal story's rhetoric, with its emphasis on sexuality and voyeurism. I argued that these renderings are potentially harmful in that they present the Elders' lust for Susanna as both an outcome of her beauty as well as a "natural" feeling to be shared by the viewer. In Chapter 6, I discussed the work of five different interpreters who each resist or alter the dominant, mimetic rendering of Susanna. My choices are deliberately diverse, and include works of art, drama, and music. The last two groups of interpretations are especially important, since most surveys usually omit these discourses. In each case, I argued that the interpreter chooses to neglect the dominant interpretive tendency I discussed in Chapter 5 in favor of a more thematically oriented presentation of the subject. Put another way, these interpreters are more interested in Susanna's faith and religiosity than her nakedness.

Many scholars recognize the investment readers make when they encounter the story of Susanna and at the same time warn readers as to the deleterious effects of a naïve or surface reading. Amy-Jill Levine's following statement is representative:

> The text situates its readers as both accomplice and victim; the narrative renders us as voyeurs, looking on with the elders at the naked Susanna at her bath and at her trial. Like Susanna, we cannot leave the garden without shame. Our task is to read without having the interpretation of social setting bleed over into anti-Semitism, the critique of the title character succumb to sexism, or the analysis of the narrative descend into pornography.[2]

The assertion that the text forces readers into complicity with the Elders smacks of the renderings I discussed in Chapter 5. Thus, Levine's call for careful interpretation, as much as I support it, is based on a mimetic reading of the text, which in my opinion is not one supported by the rhetoric of the story. As I showed in Chapter 3, the mimetic level of the text is secondary to the thematic level and the assertions put forward therein. To be sure, we as readers must engage the mimetic level of the text, but the progression of the narrative clearly prioritizes the thematic level of the story's rhetoric, and, as such, to focus on the mimetic level, be it in feminist scholarship or artistic interpretation(s), is not only to miss the point

2. Levine, "Hemmed in on Every Side," 308.

of the story, it is to provide an incomplete interpretation of the story. This, in turn, can lead to a misplaced emphasis on the sexual and voyeuristic aspects of the story, which, as I showed in Chapter 5, can misrepresent the narrative as well as perpetuate harmful ideological messages about women and sex.

In Chapter 3, I raised the question of "guiltless gazing," i.e., the dangers of voyeuristic lust and, by extension, our role as readers and viewers. Put another way, when the reader or viewer is almost required to gaze at Susanna, sometimes along with the Elders but sometimes alone, what might be the result of such voyeurism? If we read the story of Susanna, then we know what the outcome is for the Elders. Knowing that outcome, if we, too, gaze on Susanna naively, could that gazing prove detrimental to us? That is, if we are aware that the Elders are punished for actions and lies stemming from their lustful voyeurism, and we also acknowledge that we must comprehend that lust for the story itself to function, how far do we have to take that comprehension? How persuaded do we have to be by the story to accept the fictional world of the narrator? Does the acceptance of that persuasion place us in a compliant position to that of the Elders?

All of these questions are important to the feminist analysis of biblical texts, as they address the connection(s) between interpretation and ethics in androcentric texts and societies. However, in the case of Susanna, these issues are asking the wrong questions. That is, by focusing on issues of sex and sexual aggression in the text, these questions miscomprehend the rhetorical force of the story and provide fodder for those wishing to emphasize the sexual and voyeuristic aspects of the narrative. Similarly, by claiming that the narrative somehow forces readers to adopt the position of the Elders without holding out the possibility of readers resisting that position, these issues take a dim view of the process of interpretation, meaning-making, and the power of the reader.

A different approach to the mimetic level of the text is in order. That is, if one acknowledges that the sexual and erotic emphases in the apocryphal narrative are meant to imply a larger thematic point, then one can more adequately address the mimetic level of rhetoric in the story without getting bogged down in the nakedness of Susanna and the sexual aggressiveness of the Elders. This approach, then, seek to question the way(s) in which the story makes its point vis-à-vis Susanna and the Elders' assumptions and actions. Put another way, Why is it that a story seeking to inculcate a particular view of religiosity in the first century B.C.E. would have portrayed Susanna the way it does?

The story itself links visual lust with a loss of proper religiosity. That is, the main reason the Elders are looking with lust at Susanna is because they have "turned their eyes away from Heaven and were not remembering the duty of doing justice." Since the Elders have forfeited their religious identity, they are able to ignore the social and religious boundaries against sexual violence. Their gazing at and subsequent actions against Susanna betray an assumption of Susanna as an object who can be utilized for their own sexual desires.

Part and parcel of this answer is that the attitudes and expectations regarding women present in and around the first century B.C.E. leads to the presentation of Susanna as an object to be gazed upon. Furthermore, it is entirely possible that the author of Susanna could have been influenced by sexually suggestive stories in the Hebrew Bible. Put another way, stories of rape (e.g. Dinah and the Levite's concubine) and sexual coercion, attempted or successful (e.g. Potiphar's wife, Bathsheba, and possibly Esther) might have conditioned the way(s) in which the author presents Susanna and the actions and assumptions of the Elders. Susanna certainly is a more complete character than some scholars assume, but we should remember that even though Susanna is a fictional subject, her subjectivity is provided by and seen through a male lens. Thus, her subjectivity as well as her character is a narcissistic one in an extra-textual sense, i.e., it is a reflection of the way(s) in which male authors, editors, and textual transmitters view women.

Even though modern forensic sexology is not often utilized in the field of Biblical Studies, it can in some cases provide a useful starting point for discussion. For example, in an interesting article F. M. Christensen mentions one common explanation for a possible link between pornography and sexual violence that he terms the "awakened desire" model. Put briefly, "since pornography arouses sexual feelings, in the absence of a willing partner, certain persons will be induced to use force in order to satisfy the aroused desires."[3] Christensen raises two main problems with this model, though neither of them applies directly to the Elders.[4] First, he notes that an argument could be made that pornographic materials satisfy, rather than arouse, sexual desires and as such can be seen as a substitution for sexual activity with another person, especially when used for masturbatory purposes. In the story of Susanna, though, the Elders' lust-filled gazing seems to have but one object: sexual union with Susanna, voluntary or otherwise. Second, Christensen notes that since almost all rapists are young men, their sexual libidos presumably need no pornographic crutch. Obviously, in our narrative, the two rapists are old men, and as such their sexual energy may have needed a jump-start, which is exactly what the image of Susanna bathing provided.

Even though this model seems to fit quite well with the situation in the story of Susanna, there is one overwhelming problem with it. If the sight of Susanna caused the sexual desire in the Elders that forced them to attempt to rape her, who is to blame for the sexual aggressiveness in the narrative? Shall we blame Susanna, whose beauty is specifically mentioned by the narrator? Shall we blame the Elders, who we are told are "wicked" before they ever speak? Christensen extrapolates this line of thought, and concludes with the following assessment:

> Suppose it is true, after all, that the existence of sexual materials [or in our case, attractive women] results in greater amounts of sexual arousal and sexual frustration in the population at large than would otherwise exist, and that this leads, among those willing to harm others to get what they want, to greater amounts of rape than would otherwise occur. Only those who see sexual desire as bad in the first place would assign moral blame to what gives rise to such desires, rather than merely blame the willingness to

3. F. M. Christensen, "The Alleged Link between Pornography and Violence," in *The Handbook of Forensic Sexology: Biomedical and Criminological Perspectives* (ed. James J. Krivacska and John Money; Amherst, NY: Prometheus Books, 1994), 422–48 (435).

4. See Christensen, "The Alleged Link between Pornography and Violence," 435.

> harm others and whatever produces it... What underlies the "awakened desire" argument, clearly, is conceiving "demon lust" as something that pollutes the soul rather than as a perfectly legitimate feeling.[5]

This "demon lust" is exactly what the narrator tells us that the Elders feel for Susanna in v. 8. In many of the standard artistic renderings of the story, one can see the assignment of blame to Susanna for causing such feelings of lust in the Elders through various means, e.g., the *vanitas* elements and the sundry gazes of Susanna, be they aimed at a mirror or the viewer.[6] However, according to Christensen's argument, the Elders are to blame for their willingness to injure Susanna to achieve their own goal, viz., sexual pleasure.

Aside from confirming my above reading of the Elders in Chapter 3, Christensen's argument raises another interesting point. As I note above, the idea that Susanna is somehow to blame for her own situation, or at least the suggestion that she may enjoy the advances of the Elders, is a *topos* we encountered in Chapter 5. If Christensen is correct in claiming that only someone who sees sexual desire or lust as negative could be able to condemn the cause of that desire, then we may be one step closer to explaining why so many portrayals of Susanna during the Renaissance depict an erotic nude instead of a courageous, frightened young woman. Because of the concern for chastity and the prevention of adultery during this time, as we saw in Chapter 4, artists may have seen fit to blame Susanna's beauty for enticing the Elders instead of their own religious, societal, and ideological values. In fact, the explanation becomes more suggestive when we recall that during the Second Temple period, when Susanna was composed, the act of looking at a woman was considered dangerous due to the importance of chastity. In some cases voyeurism or lustful gazing is equated with adultery. Thus, due to the negative view of sexual desire during both the first century B.C.E. and the Renaissance, the seeds were sown for later interpreters to view Susanna as the cause of the Elders' lust. In essence, because of the patriarchal need to control women's sexual activity, Susanna is somehow seen to be at fault for the Elders' activity, even though she is a model of wifely duties.

Given the difficulties with causally linking voyeurism and pornography to sexual violence or sexually aggressive behavior, as well as the emotionally charged debate surrounding this issue, one can sensibly ask how the audience encountering the story of Susanna and its aesthetic interpretations might be affected?[7] In

5. Christensen, "The Alleged Link between Pornography and Violence," 436–37.

6. As I noted in Chapters 5 and 6, there are several examples of Susanna gazing out of the frame at the viewer. However, of those examples I discussed, only the Louvre Tintoretto (Fig. 2) seems to be an eroticizing interpretation. In Chapter 6 I explained why I feel the two Rembrandt *Susannas* (Figs. 7 and 8) resist that sexualizing trend of interpretation.

7. For arguments against a causal connection between pornography and violence, see Lynne Segal, "Does Pornography Cause Violence? The Search for Evidence," in *Dirty Looks: Women, Pornography, Power* (ed. Pamela Church Gibson and Roma Gibson; London: British Film Institute, 1993), 5–21; Christensen, "The Alleged Link between Pornography and Violence," 422–48; and Deborah Cameron and Elizabeth Frazer, "On the Question of Pornography and Sexual Violence: Moving Beyond Cause and Effect," in *Feminism and Pornography* (ed. Drucilla Cornell; Oxford Readings in Feminism; Oxford: Oxford University Press, 2000), 240–53. Of course, there are femi-

other words, what is the harm, if any, in reading about and looking at all of these nude Susannas? Feminists, as well as modern criminologists, believe that voyeurism and the use of pornographic materials can be seen as symptoms of a larger attitude toward sex, and subsequently women. The harm in encountering nude Susannas lies in our own assumptions and predispositions about women and women's sexuality, which are informed by history, society, and perhaps most importantly, religion. Put differently, if we are unable critically or analytically to view or gaze upon Susanna, then we are in danger of allowing such patriarchal attitudes to propagate in our own society.

In Chapter 3, I discussed the narrative-rhetorical method of reading used by James Phelan. One of the assumptions of that method is that meaning is constructed through the interaction of text and reader. Phelan writes,

> The approach I am advocating shifts emphasis from author as controller to the recursive relationships among authorial agency, textual phenomena, and reader response, to the way in which our attention to each of these elements both influences and can be influenced by the other two.[8]

The importance of this point for our discussion is that if meaning is constructed, then there can be no stable constants in the process of encountering texts. In their work, Cameron and Frazer address this issue in the context of discussing the common comparison of consuming pornography with drug use. They write,

> A person does not have to interpret a line of cocaine in order to feel certain effects when it enters the bloodstream. S/he does have to interpret the picture of a dead and mutilated female body, along fairly narrow and conventional lines, in order to find it erotic. When someone looks or reads, they are constantly engaging, interacting with the text to produce meaning from it. The meaning is not magically, inherently "there" in the pictures or the words: the reader has to make it. The text does not independently have effects on readers or compel them to act in particular ways, as if they were passive and unreflecting objects. They are subjects, creators of meaning; the pornographic scenario must always be mediated by their imagination. (This, incidentally, is why pornography calls forth such a variety of responses; why not only individuals, but groups derive such different meanings from it.)[9]

That is, since meaning is flexible, we are able to negotiate within a range of possible interpretations, not simply one "correct" reading. As such, readers are not bound by "obvious" meanings in texts; alternative or counter-readings can be considered legitimate responses to textual stimuli.

nists who argue for a causal connection between pornography and sexual violence. One of the most influential works in this regard is Andrea Dworkin, *Pornography: Men Possessing Women* (New York: Perigee Books, 1981). A recent collection of essays and interviews also takes this stance. See Diana E. H. Russell, ed., *Making Violence Sexy: Feminist Views on Pornography* (Athene Series; New York: Teachers College Press, 1993). Even though these scholars have made persuasive arguments for the position that pornographic materials are harmful to women, I am not convinced that there is a causal relationship between sexually explicit texts and sexual violence.

8. Phelan, *Narrative as Rhetoric*, 19.
9. Cameron and Frazer, "On the Question," 251.

A related topic discussed by Phelan is the issue of resisting reading. Put briefly, when we encounter a text, we are asked to agree to certain propositions in order for our encounter of that text to be meaningful. However, this fact does not mean that we must heartily endorse every aspect of that text or every assumption that text makes. Phelan notes that readers can resist various presumptions of texts, even while adopting certain "givens" in a text for the sake of intelligible reading. He comments on what he terms partial resistance,

> Resistance is more likely to be satisfying and productive when it is partial, when we find ourselves in genuine disagreement with some parts of a work without entirely losing our respect for it. In these cases, we talk with the text and its author more as equals, acknowledging their power, but for that very reason, required to think hard about the nature and meaning of their limits. The dialogue established in these encounters can go on for a long time and can lead us to rethink some of our most fundamental commitments and beliefs.[10]

Thus, the process of partially disagreeing with a text can actually be more important that an outright dismissal. In the case of partial resistance, a textual consumer can find some value in a given text but at the same time fundamentally disagree with other presumptions found in the rhetoric of the piece.

With regards to Susanna and her Renaissance interpretations, this partial resistance is exactly what I would ask textual consumers to consider. That is, one of, if not *the*, overriding assumptions of the mimetic level of rhetoric in the apocryphal narrative as well as almost all of the interpretations during the Renaissance is the patriarchal view of women. In my opinion, there is little doubt that many aspects of the story and many interpretations are valuable, and perhaps even transformative for feminists. However, due to the underlying patriarchal view(s) of women in both the hyper- and hypotexts we have surveyed, feminists must take issue not only with the behavior of the Elders and the presentation of Susanna in aesthetic renderings, but even more importantly, with the assumptions that allow those discourses to function. In other words, we must not focus all our energy on ridding ourselves of the sneeze at the expense of the cold. Instead, we must approach the problem of patriarchal view(s) of women in a sustained fashion in an attempt to dismantle the conditions that allow them to fester.

As Gerda Lerner notes in her seminal work, *The Creation of Patriarchy*, one of the most important issues facing feminists today is "a radical restructuring of thought" that would allow patriarchal control over symbol systems to be dismantled.[11] Since meaning is constructed, and since we as readers can resist the rhetorical invitations issued to us by various texts, we are in a good position to challenge the hegemony patriarchy has established over various symbol systems. One of the most important contributions of feminist biblical scholarship has been to re-read biblical literature in an attempt to expose androcentric assumptions and scholarship, and therefore regain both symbolic and real influence in the arena of religious thought and practice. In the case of Susanna, once we as readers realize

10. Phelan, *Reading People, Reading Plots*, 188.
11. Gerda Lerner, *The Creation of Patriarchy* (New York: Oxford University Press, 1986), 220.

the harmful underlying assumptions and emphases found in the mimetic level of the narrative and, *mutatis mutandis*, subsequent aesthetic and scholarly interpretations, we can begin to resist those assumptions so that we can begin to develop ways to counter them in our own time.

Appendix 1

TRANSLATION OF SUSANNA (TH)[1]

(1) There was a man living in Babylon whose name was Joakim. (2) He took a wife whose name was Susanna, daughter of Hilkiah. She was exceedingly beautiful and fearful of the Lord. (3) Her parents were righteous and had taught their daughter according to the Law of Moses. (4) Joakim was extremely wealthy; he even had a garden bordering his house. The Jews would flock to him because he was the most honored of them all.

(5) Two Elders of the people were appointed as judges that year, concerning whom the Master had said: "Lawlessness came out of Babylon from Elders who judge,[2] who were supposed to guide people." (6) These Elders were spending much time in Joakim's house and all the people who were to be judged came to them there.

(7) When the people would run off at the middle of the day, Susanna would go into her husband's garden and walk around. (8) And every day, the two Elders would watch her entering and walking, for they were lusting for her.[3] (9) They had perverted their minds and turned their eyes away from Heaven[4] and were not remembering the duty of doing justice. (10) Both of them were deeply moved[5] by her, but neither disclosed his pain to the other, (11) for they were both ashamed to disclose their lust, their desire to be with her. (12) So, they watched eagerly each day to see her.

(13) One day they said to one another, "Let us go home, for it is time for a meal." So they went out and separated from one another. (14) But returning, they came upon each other; when each examined the other for the reason, they both confessed their desire [for Susanna].[6] As a result [of this confession], together they arranged a time when they would be able to find her alone.

(15) Later, when they were watching for a suitable day, Susanna entered as [she had done] before,[7] alone with two maids. She desired[8] to bathe in the garden

1. This translation is based on the Greek text of Th found in Ziegler, *Susanna, Daniel, Bel et Draco*.

2. The preposition ἐκ takes a double object here: πρεσβυτέρων and κριτῶν. I have chosen to use the latter object as a verbal adjective: "[those] who judge."

3. Literally, "They were in heat for her."

4. Literally, "they turned their eyes away to not look to Heaven,"

5. Or "were stupefied." More commonly, "were stabbed" or "wounded" by or over her.

6. The square brackets indicate that "for Susanna" is not in the text. This practice will be continued below.

7. Literally, "she entered as ever, yesterday and the day before."

because it was very hot. (16) There was no one there save the two Elders, hiding and watching her. (17) Then she said to the girls, "Bring me olive oil and ointment, and shut the doors of the garden so that I may bathe [in private]." (18) They did as she said: they shut up the doors of the garden and went out through the side doors to bring what had been commanded of them. They did not see the Elders because they were hiding themselves.

(19) As the girls were going out, the two Elders stood up and ran to Susanna. (20) They said, "Look, the doors of the garden have been closed and no one can see us. We are lusting for you; agree to be with us! (21) But if [you do] not, we will testify against you, that a young man was with you and because of this you sent the girls away from you." (22) Susanna sighed deeply and said, "It is narrow for me on all sides![9] For if I do this, it is death for me, but if I do not, I will not escape your hands. (23) It is chosen for me: I cannot do it; I will fall into your hands rather than sin before the Lord!"[10] (24) Then Susanna cried aloud with a great voice, and the Elders, opposite her, cried out [as well]. (25) One of them ran and opened the doors of the garden.

(26) When the people in the house heard the shouting in the garden, they rushed in through the side door to see what had happened to her. (27) After the Elders told their stories, the servants were intensely ashamed, for no such story had ever been told about Susanna.

(28) The next day, when the crowd came together to Joakim her husband, the two Elders came forth, full of unlawful intent against Susanna, to put her to death. Before the crowd they said, (29) "Send for Susanna, daughter of Hilkiah, Joakim's wife!" [The crowd] sent for her (30) and she came [with] her parents, her children, and all her relatives. (31) Susanna was exceedingly effeminate[11] and beautiful to the sight. (32) So that they might have their fill of her beauty, the evildoers ordered her to be uncovered, for she was covering herself.[12] (33) Those with her and all those seeing her were weeping.

(34) Standing in the middle of the people, the two Elders laid [their] hands on her head. (35) Weeping, she looked up to Heaven, for her heart trusted in the Lord. (36) Then the Elders said, "While we were walking about in the garden alone, [this] woman entered with two maids, shut up the doors of the garden, and dismissed the maids. (37) Then a young man, who was hiding, came to her and lay with her. (38) We, being in a corner of the garden, saw the lawlessness and ran to them. (39) Even though we saw them embrace,[13] we were not able to be in control because he was stronger than us. He opened the doors and rushed out. (40) We seized this woman and asked who the young man was, (41) but she did

8. Just as the Elders desired her.

9. Note a similar phrase in Josephus, *J.W.* 4.79.

10. Both "fall into" and "sin" are actually infinitives in Greek. I have chosen to render them as finite verbs.

11. Or "luxurious," "voluptuous."

12. This verse probably implies veiling.

13. Or "come together."

not wish to disclose [his identity] to us. These things we testify." The assembly believed them, as [they were] Elders of the people and judges; they condemned her to die.

(42) Susanna cried aloud with a great voice and said, "O God, the eternal, the one who knows hidden things, seeing all things before their beginning, (43) you know that they [the Elders] have borne false witness against me. Now, I am about to die even though I have done none of these [things] of which they wickedly accused me." (44) And the Lord heard her cry.

(45) And as she was being carried off to be killed, God awakened the holy spirit of a young man whose name was Daniel. (46) He cried aloud with a great voice, "I am clean[14] of this woman's blood!" (47) All the people turned to him and said, "What did you say?"[15] (48) Standing in the midst of them, he said, "Are you idiots, O Israelites? Would you condemn a daughter of Israel without closely examining or discovering the clear truth? (49) Return to the court! For these men have given false evidence against her." (50) So, all the people hastily returned. The [other] Elders said to [Daniel], "Come, sit down in our midst and report to us. For God has given you the right of an Elder." (51) Daniel replied, "Separate them far from one another and I will examine them."

(52) When they were separated one from the other, [Daniel] called one of them and said to him, "You old man of wicked days, your sins which you committed in the past have now returned: (53) making unjust judgments, condemning the innocent,[16] and acquitting[17] the guilty while the Lord said, 'An innocent one and a righteous one shall not be killed.' (54) Therefore, if you indeed saw this woman, tell me, under which tree did you see them having intercourse with each other?" He answered, "Under the mastic tree."[18] (55) Daniel replied, "Appropriately, you have lied and it will affect your own head![19] For already an angel of God has received the sentence from God and will split you in two!"[20]

(56) After [the first Elder was] removed, [Daniel] ordered the other to be brought.[21] He said to him, "Seed of Canaan and not of Judah! Beauty has deceived you and lust has twisted your heart! (57) You have done this[22] to the daughters of Israel and they, fearful, were having intercourse with you, but a daughter of Judah would not submit to your wickedness. (58) Now, therefore, tell me, under which tree did you catch them having intercourse with each other?" He answered, "Under the evergreen oak."[23] (59) Daniel responded, "Appropriately,

14. Or "innocent," "guiltless."
15. Literally, "What is this word which you have said?"
16. Literally, "the unpunished."
17. Or "releasing."
18. This word, σχῖνον, is the first part of a wordplay continued in v. 55.
19. This phrase is difficult to translate and to understand. Literally, it means: "Correct, you have lied in your own head."
20. The word for "he will split," σχίσει, finishes the wordplay in v. 54.
21. Literally, "He ordered to bring the other."
22. There seems to be no antecedent for "this."
23. This word, πρῖνον, is the first part of a wordplay continued in v. 59.

you have lied and it will affect your own head![24] For the angel of God is waiting with a sword to cut you in two,[25] so that you both will be destroyed!"

(60) [After this,] the whole assembly cried aloud with a great voice and praised God, who saves those hoping in him. (61) They rose up against the two Elders because out of their own mouths, Daniel convicted[26] them of bearing false witness. The assembly then did to them the same wicked thing [they were going to do] to their neighbor; (62) acting according to the law of Moses, they killed them. Thus, innocent blood was saved in that day.

(63) [Following this,] Hilkiah and his wife gave praise for their daughter together with her husband Joakim and all [their] relatives because [Susanna] was found innocent of a disgraceful deed.[27] (64) [Because of this,] Daniel was great among the people from that day and beyond.

24. See n. 19 above.
25. The word for "to cut," πρίσαι, finishes the wordplay in v. 58.
26. Literally, "associated."
27. Literally, "because a disgraceful deed was not found in her."

Appendix 2

SELECTED WORKS BASED ON SUSANNA DURING THE RENAISSANCE*

1. *Art*

Allori, Allesandro (1535–1607). *Susanna and the Elders*. Oil on Canvas. Lyon, Musée Magnin, sixteenth century.

Altdorfer, Albrecht (ca. 1480–1538). *Susanna in the Bath and the Stoning of the Elders*. Oil on Limewood. 74.8 × 61.2 cm. Munich, Alte Pinakothek, 1526.

Badalocchio, Sisto. *Susanna and the Elders*. Oil on Canvas. 63 × 43 cm. Sarasota, Fla., Ringling Museum of Art, 1610.

Bassano, Jacopo (ca. 1515–1592). *Susanna and the Elders*. Oil on canvas. 89 × 114.8 cm. Ottawa, the National Gallery of Canada, ca. 1556/66.

Carracci, Agostino. *Susanna and the Elders*. Engraving. Ca. 1595.

Carracci, Annibale (1560–1609). *Susanna and the Elders*. Etching and engraving. 346 × 305 mm. Washington, D.C., National Gallery of Art, 1590/1.

Carracci, Ludovico (1555–1619). *Susanna and the Elders*. Oil on Canvas. Modena, Banca popolare dell' Emilia, 1598.

—*Susanna and the Elders*. Oil on Canvas. 146.6 × 116.5 cm. London, National Gallery, 1616.

Cesari, Guiseppe (1568–1640). *Susanna in the Bath*. Oil on Copper, ca. 1610.

Domenichino (1581–1641). *Susanna and the Elders*. Oil on Canvas. 58.4 × 83.8 cm. Rome, Galleria Doria Pamphili, 1603.

Dyck, Anthony van (1599–1641). *Susanna and the Elders*. Oil on canvas. 194 × 144 cm. Munich, Alte Pinakothek, ca. 1625.

Floris, Frans (1516/19–1570). *Susanna and the Elders*. Oil on Wood. 150 × 210 cm. Florence, Galleria Palatina, Palazzo Pitti, ca. 1562/3.

Gentileschi, Artemisia (ca. 1593–1653). *Susanna and the Elders*. Oil on Canvas. 170 × 119 cm. Schonborn Collection, Pommerfelden, Germany, Schloss Weissenstein, 1610.

—*Susanna and the Elders*. Oil on Canvas. Moravská Galerie, Brno, Czech Republic, 1649.

Goltzius, Hendrick. *Susanna and the Elders*. Oil on Canvas. 67 × 94 cm. Paris, Musée Municipal de Douai, 1607.

Guercino (1591–1666). *Susanna and the Elders*. Oil on Canvas. 175 × 207 cm. Madrid, Museo del Prado, 1617.

—*Susanna and the Elders*. Chalk Drawing. 1649.

—*Susanna and the Elders*. Oil on Canvas. 133 × 181.2 cm. Parma, Galleria Nazionale, 1649/50.

* See also the extensive and comprehensive lists in Charles R. Lewis, "The Character of Susanna in the Arts of the Twentieth Century with a Survey of the Theme to the Present" (Ph.D. diss., Florida State University, 1993), 239–59; and Andrea Marie Willis, "The Theme of Susanna," 74–130.

Haarlem, Cornelius van (1562–1638). *Susanna and the Elders*. Oil on canvas. 98.5 × 87 cm. Ottawa, the National Gallery of Canada, ca. 1599.

König, Johann. *Susanna and the Elders*. Oil on Canvas. 23 × 33 cm. Nürnberg, German National Museum, ca. 1620.

Lastman, Pieter (1583–1633). *Susanna and the Elders*. Oil on Canvas. 42 × 58 cm. Berlin, Staatliche Museen, Stiftung Preussischer Kulturbesitz, Gemäldegalerie, 1614.

Pencz, George (1500–1550). *Susanna and the Elders*. Engraving. 46 × 74 mm, ca. 1532.

Reni, Guido (1575–1642). *Susanna and the Elders*. Oil on Canvas. 116 × 151 cm. Florence, Galleria degli Uffizi, 1622/23.

Rijn, Rembrandt van (1606–1669). *Susanna and the Elders*. 47.2 × 38.6 cm. Mauritshuis, the Hague, ca. 1636.

—*Susanna and the Elders*. Oil on Canvas. 102 × 84 cm. Staatliche Museen zu Berlin—Preußischer Kulturbesitz, Gemäldegalerie, ca. 1647.

Rubens, Peter Paul. *Susanna and the Elders*. Oil on Canvas. 175 × 200 cm. Madrid, Real Academia de Bellas Artes de San Fernando, ca. 1606.

—*Susanna and the Elders*. Oil on Canvas. 94 × 67 cm. Rome, Galleria Borghese, ca. 1607.

Saenredam, Jan (ca. 1565–1607). *Susanna and the Elders* (after H. Goltzius). Engraving. Before 1598.

The School of Veronese. *Susanna and the Elders*. Oil on Canvas. 72 × 98 cm. Rome, Accademia Nazionale di San Luca, sixteenth century.

Schöpfer, Hans. *History of Susanna*. Oil on Canvas. 100.8 × 149.9 cm. Munich, Alte Pinakothek, 1537.

Stanzione, Massimo. *Susanna and the Elders*. Oil on Canvas. 153 × 204 cm. Frankfurt, Städelches Kunstinstitut, seventeenth century.

Tintoretto (1518–1594). *Susanna and the Elders*. Oil on Canvas. 167 × 238 cm. Paris, the Louvre, 1550–1555.

—*Susanna and the Elders*. Oil on Canvas. 146.6 × 193.6 cm. Vienna, Kunsthistorisches Museum, ca. 1555.

—*Susanna and the Elders*. From a Series of Six Old Testament Paintings. Oil on Canvas. 58 × 116 cm. Madrid, Museo del Prado, ca. 1555.

—*Susanna and the Elders*. Oil on Canvas. 150 × 103 cm. Washington, D.C., Gallery of National Art, ca. 1575.

—(attr.). *Susanna and the Elders*. Oil on Canvas. 76.2 × 93 cm. Pittsburgh, Pa., the Frick Art Museum, ca. 1589.

Vorsterman, Lucas (1624–1666). *Susanna and the Elders* (after Rubens). Etching and engraving. 38.5 × 27.7 cm. 1620.

Wtewael, Joachim (1566–1638). *Susanna and the Elders*. Oil on Canvas. 116 × 155 cm. Arras, France, Musée Municipal, ca. 1613.

2. *Music*

Byrd, William (1543–1623). "Susanna Fair." Originally published in *Psalmes, Sonets, and Songs*, 1588. In *Consort and Keyboard Music, Songs and Anthems*. Rose Consort of Viols with Red Byrd. Tessa Bonner, Soprano. Naxos 8.550604, 1994.

Lassus [Lasso], Orlando di (ca. 1532–1594). "Susanne un jour." Originally published in 1560. In *Chansons and Madrigals*. The Toronto Consort. Meredith Hall, Soprano; Paul Jenkins, Organ. Dorian Discovery DIS-80149, 1994, 1996

—"Missa Susanne un jour." Originally published in 1577. In *Masses for Five Voices; Infelix Ego*. Oxford Camerata, Jeremy Summerly, cond. Naxos 8.550842, 1993.

Le Jeune, Claude (1527–1600). "Susanne un jour (7 Voices, 5 Viols)." Originally published in *Mellange de Chansons tant des vieux Autheurs que des Modernes*, (Paris: Le Roy & Ballard: 1572). In *Meslanges: Chansons et Fantasies de viols*. Ensemble Clément Janequin and Ensemble Les Éléments. Harmonia Mundi 1901182, 1985, 1995.

Lupi Second, Didier. "Susanne un jour." Originally published in *Premier livre de chansons spirituelles nouvellement composées par Guillaume Gueroult, mises en musique par Didier Lupi Second* (Lyons: Beringen, 1548).

3. *Literature*

Anonymous. *The Wiener (Viennese) Susanna*. Fifteenth century.

Birck, Sixt. "Susanna." 1532 (Ger.); 1538 (Lat.).

Garter, Thomas. *The Most Virtuous and Godly Susanna*. 1578.

Rebhun, Paul. *Ein geistlich Spiel, von der Gotfürchtigen vnd keuschen Frawen Susannen, gantz lustig und fruchtbarlich zu lessen*. 1536; rev. 1544.

Sacco, Tibortio. *Tragedia nova, intitolata Sosanna, raccolta da Daniello Profeta*. 1537.

Appendix 3

TRANSLATION OF "SUSANNE UN JOUR" BY GUILLAUME GUÉROULT

Susanne un jour d'amour solicitée	Susanna, one day solicited of love
Par deux viellards convoitans sa beauté,	By two old men coveting her beauty,
Fut en son coeur triste et déconfortée	Was in her heart sad and discomforted
Voyant l'effort fait à sa chasteté.	Seeing the effort made on her chastity.
Elle leur dit: "Si par desloyauté	She said to them: "If by dishonesty
De ce cors mien vous avez jouissance,	You take my body with pleasure
C'est fait de moy; si je fay resistance,	That is the end of me; but if I resist
Vous me ferez mourir en deshonneur;	You will make me die in dishonor;
Mais j'aime mieux perir en innocence,	But I would prefer to die in innocence,
Que d'offenser par peché le Seigneur."	Than to offend the Lord by sinning."

BIBLIOGRAPHY

Abbé, Derek van. *Drama in Renaissance Germany and Switzerland*. Melbourne: Melbourne University Press, 1961.

Africanus, Julius. "A Letter to Origen from Africanus about the History of Susanna." Page 385 in vol. 4 of Roberts and James Donaldson, eds., *The Anti-Nicene Fathers*.

Aikema, Bernard. *Jacopo Bassano and His Public: Moralizing Pictures in an Age of Reform, ca. 1535–1600*. Translated by Andrew P. McCormick. Princeton, N.J.: Princeton University Press, 1996.

Alberti, Leon Battista. *Della Famiglia*. Pages 27–326 in *The Albertis of Florence: Leon Battista Alberti's* Della Famiglia. Translated by Guido A. Guarino. Bucknell Renaissance Texts in Translation. Lewisburg: Bucknell University Press, 1971.

Alter, Robert. *The Art of Biblical Narrative*. New York: Basic Books, 1981.

Anonymous. "The Wiener Susanna." Pages 231–45 in *Fastnachtspiele aus dem fünfzehnten Jahrhundert: Nachlese*. Edited by Adelbert von Keller. Stuttgart: Schriften des litterarischen Vereins, 1858.

Anzelewski, Fedja. "Albrecht Altdorfer and the Question of 'the Danube School'." Pages 10–47 in Guillaud and Guillaud, eds., *Altdorfer and Fantastic Realism in German Art*.

Archer, Léonie J. *Her Price is Beyond Rubies: The Jewish Woman in Graeco-Roman Palestine*. Journal for the Study of the Old Testament: Supplement Series 60. Sheffield: JSOT Press, 1990.

—"The Role of Jewish Women in the Religion, Ritual and Cult of Graeco-Roman Palestine." Pages 273–87 in *Images of Women in Antiquity*. Edited by Averil Cameron and Amélie Kuhrt. Detroit: Wayne State University Press, 1983.

Bach, Alice, ed. *Biblical Glamour and Hollywood Glitz*. Semeia 74. Atlanta: Scholars Press, 1996.

—"Calling the Shots: Directing Salomé's Dance of Death." Pages 210–62 in *Women, Seduction, and Betrayal in Biblical Narrative*. Cambridge: Cambridge University Press, 1997.

Bächtold, Jacob. *Scweizerische Schauspiele des 16. Jahrhunderts*. Vol. 2. Frauenfeld, n.p., 1891.

Bakhtin, Mikhail M. "Discourse in the Novel." Pages 259–422 in *The Dialogic Imagination: Four Essays*. Edited by Michael Holquist. Translated by Caryl Emerson and Michael Holquist. Austin: University of Texas Press, 1981.

Bal, Mieke. "Between Focalization and Voyeurism: The Representation of Vision." Pages 138–76 in *Reading "Rembrandt": Beyond the Word–Image Opposition*. Cambridge New Art History and Criticism. Cambridge: Cambridge University Press, 1991.

—"The Elders and Susanna." *Biblical Interpretation* 1 (1993): 1–19.

—*Lethal Love: Feminist Literary Readings of Biblical Love Stories*. Indiana Studies in Biblical Literature. Bloomington: Indiana University Press, 1987.

Ball, C. J. "The Additions to Daniel II: The History of Susanna." Pages 323–43 in vol. 2 of *The Holy Bible: Apocrypha*. Edited by Henry Wace. 2 Vols. London: John Murray, 1888.

Barbaro, Francesco. "On Wifely Duties" [1415]. Pages 179–228 in *The Earthly Republic: Italian Humanists on Government and Society*. Edited by Benjamin G. Kohl and Ronald G. Witt. Philadelphia: University of Pennsylvania Press, 1978.

Barclay, John M. G. *Jews in the Mediterranean Diaspora: From Alexander to Trajan (323 BCE–117 CE)*. Hellenistic Culture and Society 33. Berkeley: University of California Press, 1996.

Barilli, Renato. *Rhetoric*. Theory and History of Literature 63. Minneapolis: University of Minnesota Press, 1989.

Barthélemy, D. *Les devanciers d'Aquila*. Vetus Testamentum Supplements 10. Leiden: Brill, 1963.

Baskins, Christelle L. "La Festa di Susanna: Virtue on Trial in Renaissance Sacred Drama and Painted Wedding Chests." *Art History* 14.3 (1991): 329–44.

Baumgartner, Walter. "Susanna: Die Geschichte einer Legende." Pages 42–67 in *Zum Alten Testament und Seiner Umwelt*. Leiden: Brill, 1959.

Becker, Georg. *Guillaume Guéroult et ses Chansons Spirituelles*. Paris: Librarie Sandoz & Fischbacher, 1880.

Berger, John. *Ways of Seeing*. London: BBC/Penguin, 1972.

Bernari, Carlo, and Pierluigi de Vecchi. *L'Opera Completa del Tintoretto*. Milan: Rizzoli Editore, 1970.

The Bible and Culture Collective. *The Postmodern Bible*. New Haven: Yale University Press, 1995.

Bickerman, Elias J. "The Colophon of the Greek Book of Esther." *Journal of Biblical Literature* 63 (1944): 339–62.

—*The God of the Maccabees: Studies in the Meaning and Origin of the Maccabean Revolt*. Translated by H. R. Moehring. Studies in Judaism in Late Antiquity 32. Leiden: Brill, 1979.

Binder, Donald D. *Into the Temple Courts: The Place of the Synagogues in the Second Temple Period*. Society of Biblical Literature Dissertation Series 169. Atlanta: Society of Biblical Literature, 1999.

Birck, Sixt. "Die history von der fromen Gottsförchtigen frouwen Susanna [1532]." Pages 3–97 in vol. 2 of Bächtold, ed., *Scweizerische Schauspiele des 16. Jahrhunderts*.

—"Die history von der fromen Gottsförchtigen frouwen Susanna [1532]." Pages 1–53 in vol. 2 of Brauneck, ed., *Sämtliche Werke*.

—"Susanna, Comoedia tragica [1538]." Pages 167–272 in vol. 2 of Brauneck, ed., *Sämtliche Werke*.

—"Susanna, a Tragi-Comedy [1538]." Translated by C. C. Love. No pages. Online: http://www.chass.utoronto.ca/epc/rnlp/susanna.html.

Bischoff, Cordula. "Albrecht Altdorfer's *Susanna and the Elders*: Female Virtues, Male Politics." *Racar* 23, nos. 1–2 (1996): 22–35.

Bissell, R. Ward. *Artemisia Gentileschi and the Authority of Art: Critical Reading and Catalogue Raisonné*. University Park, Pa.: University of Pennsylvania, 1999.

Boccaccio, Giovanni. *Concerning Famous Women* [1361]. Translated by Guido A. Guarino. New Brunswick, N.J.: Rutgers University Press, 1963.

Bohn, Babette. "Rape and the Gendered Gaze: *Susanna and the Elders* in Early Modern Bologna." *Biblical Interpretation* 9 (2001): 259–86.

Bonjione, Gail A. "Shifting Images: Susanna through the Ages." Ph.D. diss., Florida State University, 1997.

Booth, Wayne C. *The Rhetoric of Fiction*. Chicago: University of Chicago Press, 1961.

Boulding, Elise. *The Underside of History: A View of Women through Time*. 2 vols. Rev. ed. Newbury Park, Calif.: Sage, 1992.

Brady, Thomas A. Jr. et al., eds. *Handbook of European History, 1400–1600: Late Middle Ages, Renaissance, and Reformation*. 2 vols. Grand Rapids: Eerdmans, 1994–96.

Brauneck, Manfred, ed. *Sämtliche Werke*. 2 vols. New York: de Gruyter, 1976.

Brenner, Athalya, ed. *A Feminist Companion to Esther, Judith, and Susanna*. The Feminist Companion to the Bible 7. Sheffield: Sheffield Academic Press, 1995.

Brock, S. P. "Versions, Ancient (Syriac)." Pages 794–99 in vol. 6 of Freedman et al. eds., *The Anchor Bible Dictionary*.

Brooke, George J. "Susanna and Paradise Regained." Pages 92–111 in *Women in the Biblical Tradition*. Edited by G. J. Brooke. Studies in Women and Religions 30. Lewiston, N.Y.: Edwin Mellen, 1992.

Brooten, Bernadette J. *Women Leaders in the Ancient Synagogue: Inscriptional Evidence and Background Issues*. Brown Judaic Studies 36. Atlanta: Scholars Press, 1982.

Brown, Cheri A. "The *Susanna* Drama and the German Reformation." Pages 129–53 in *Everyman and Company: Essays on the Theme and Structure of the European Moral Play*. Edited by Donald Gilman. New York: AMS Press, 1989.

Brown, Cheryl Anne. *No Longer Be Silent: First Century Jewish Portraits of Biblical Women*. Gender and the Biblical Tradition Series. Louisville, Ky.: Westminster/John Knox, 1992.

Brown, Howard M., and Louise K. Stein. "The Music of the Reformation and the Council of Trent." Pages 273–80 in *Music in the Renaissance*. 2d ed. Prentice Hall History of Music. Upper Saddle River, N.J.: Prentice–Hall, 1999.

Brueggemann, Walter. *Genesis*. Interpretation: A Bible Commentary for Teaching and Preaching. Atlanta: John Knox, 1982.

Brüll, Nehemiah. "Das apokryphische Susanna-Buch." *Jahrbuch für Jüdische Geschichte* 3 (1877): 1–69.

Burchard, C., trans. "Joseph and Aseneth." Pages 177–247 in vol. 2 of Charlesworth, ed., *The Old Testament Pseudepigrapha*.

Burrus, Virginia. *Chastity as Autonomy: Women in the Stories of Apocryphal Acts*. Lewiston, N.Y.: Edwin Mellen, 1987.

Cameron, Deborah and Elizabeth Frazer. "On the Question of Pornography and Sexual Violence: Moving Beyond Cause and Effect." Pages 240–53 in *Feminism and Pornography*. Edited by Drucilla Cornell. Oxford Readings in Feminism. Oxford: Oxford University Press, 2000.

Camp, Claudia V. "Understanding a Patriarchy: Women in Second Century Jerusalem through the Eyes of Ben Sira." Pages 1–39 in Levine, ed., *"Women Like This"*.

Carroll, Michael P. "Myth, Methodology, and Transformation in the Old Testament: The Stories of Esther, Judith, and Susanna." *Studies in Religion* 12 (1983): 301–12.

Casey, Paul F. *Paul Rebhun: A Biographical Study*. Stuttgart: Steiner, 1986.

—*The Susanna Theme in German Literature: Variations of the Biblical Drama*. Abhandlungen zur Kunst-, Musik-, und Literaturwissenschaft 214. Bonn: Bouvier Verlag Herbert Grundmann, 1976.

Castelli, Elizabeth A. "Virginity and Its Meaning for Women's Sexuality in Early Christianity." *Journal of Feminist Studies in Religion* 2 (1986): 61–88.

Charlesworth, James H., ed. *The Old Testament Pseudepigrapha*. 2 vols. New York: Doubleday, 1983–85.

Chesnutt, Randall D. "Joseph and Aseneth." Pages 969–71 in vol. 3 of Freedman et al. eds., *The Anchor Bible Dictionary*.

Christensen, F. M. "The Alleged Link between Pornography and Violence." Pages 422–48 in *The Handbook of Forensic Sexology: Biomedical and Criminological Perspectives*. Edited by James J. Krivacska and John Money. Amherst, N.Y.: Prometheus Books, 1994.

Clanton, Dan W. "(Re)Dating the Story of Susanna: A Proposal," *Journal for the Study of Judaism* 34, no. 2 (2003): 121–40.

Clark, Kenneth. *The Nude: A Study in Ideal Form*. Garden City, N.Y.: Doubleday, 1956.

Clark, S. L., and David Duewall. "Give and Take: Good, Evil, and Language in Rebhun's *Susanna*." *Euphorion* 75 (1981): 325–41.

Cloke, Gillian. *This Female Man of God: Women and Spiritual Power in the Patristic Age, AD 350–450*. London: Routledge, 1995.

Coggins, Richard J. *Sirach*. Guides to Apocrypha and Pseudepigrapha. Sheffield: Sheffield Academic Press, 1998.

Cohen, Shaye J. D. "Ioudaios: 'Judaean' and 'Jew' in Susanna, First Maccabees, and Second Maccabees." Pages 211–20 in *Geschichte–Tradition–Reflexion: Festschrift für Martin Hengel zum 70. Geburtstag*. Vol. 1, *Judentum*. Edited by Peter Schäfer. Tübingen: J. C. B. Mohr (Paul Siebeck): 1996.

—"Women in the Synagogues of Antiquity." *Conservative Judaism* 34, no. 2 (1980): 23–29.

Collins, John J. *Daniel*. Hermeneia. Minneapolis: Fortress, 1993.

—"Marriage, Divorce, and Family in Second Temple Judaism." Pages 104–62 in *Families in Ancient Israel*. Edited by Leo G. Perdue et al. The Family, Religion, and Culture. Louisville, Ky.: Westminster/John Knox, 1997.

Cooper, Kate. *The Virgin and the Bride: Idealized Womanhood in Late Antiquity*. Cambridge, Mass.: Harvard University Press, 1995.

Craven, Toni. " 'From where Will My Help Come?' Women and Prayer in the Apocryphal/Deuterocanonical Books." Pages 95–109 in *Worship and the Hebrew Bible: Essays in Honor of John T. Willis*. Edited by M. Patrick Graham et al. Journal for the Study of the Old Testament: Supplement Series 284; Sheffield: Sheffield Academic Press, 1999.

—"Judith 9: Strength and Deceit." Pages 59–64 in *Prayer from Alexander to Constantine: A Critical Anthology*. Edited by M. C. Kiley. London: Routledge, 1997.

Crawford, Sidnie White. "The Additions to Esther." Pages 970–72 in vol. 3 of *The New Interpreter's Bible*. Edited by Leander Keck et al. 12 vols. Nashville, Abingdon, 1994–.

—"Has *Esther* been Found at Qumran? *4Qproto-Esther* and the *Esther* Corpus." *Revue de Qumran* 17 (1996): 307–25.

Crenshaw, James L. "Theodicy." Pages 444–47 in vol. 6 of Freedman et al. eds., *The Anchor Bible Dictionary*.

Culler, Jonathan. *Structuralist Poetics: Structuralism, Linguistics, and the Study of Literature*. Ithaca, N.Y.: Cornell University Press, 1975.

Dackerman, Susan. "The Danger of Visual Seduction: Netherlandish Prints of Susanna and the Elders." Ph.D. diss., Bryn Mawr College, 1995.

Danby, Herbert. *The Mishnah*. Oxford: Oxford University Press, 1933.

Dancy, J. C. "The Book of Judith." Pages 67–131 in *The Shorter Books of the Apocrypha*. Edited by J. C. Dancy. Cambridge Bible Commentary. Cambridge: Cambridge University Press, 1972.

Davies, W. D., and Louis Finkelstein, eds. *The Cambridge History of Judaism*. Vol. 2, *The Hellenistic Age*. Cambridge: Cambridge University Press, 1989.

Delcor, Mathias. "Le Livre de Judith et l'époque grecque." *Klio* 49 (1967): 151–79.

DeSilva, David Arthur. *4 Maccabees*. Guides to Apocrypha and Pseudepigrapha. Sheffield: Sheffield Academic Press, 1998.

—"The Wisdom of Ben Sira: Honor, Shame, and the Maintenance of Minority Cultural Values." *Catholic Biblical Quarterly* 58 (1996): 433–55.

Dobbins, Frank. *Music in Renaissance Lyons*. Oxford Monographs on Music. Oxford: Clarendon, 1992.

Dorothy, Charles V. *The Books of Esther: Structure, Genre and Textual Integrity*. Journal for the Study of the Old Testament: Supplement Series 187. Sheffield: Sheffield Academic Press, 1997.

Dworkin, Andrea. *Pornography: Men Possessing Women*. New York: Perigee Books, 1981.

Eisenbaum, Pamela M. "Sirach." Pages 298–304 in Newsom and S. H. Ringe, eds., *Women's Bible Commentary*.

Elder, Linda Bennett. "Judith's *Sophia* and *Synesis*: Educated Jewish Women in the Late Second Temple Period." Pages 53–69 in *Biblical and Humane: A Festschrift for John F. Priest*. Edited by Linda Bennett Elder et al. Atlanta: Scholars Press, 1996.

Engel, Helmut. *Die Susanna Erzählung: Einleitung, Übersetzung und Kommentar zum Septuaginta-Text und zur Theodotion-Bearbeitung*. Orbis biblicus et orientalis 61. Freiburg: Universitätsverlag; Göttingen: Vandenhoeck & Ruprecht, 1985.

Enslin, Morton S. *The Book of Judith*. Edited by Solomon Zeitlin. Jewish Apocryphal Literature 7. Leiden: Brill, 1972.

Exum, J. Cheryl. "Bathsheba Plotted, Shot, and Painted." Pages 19–53 in *Plotted, Shot, and Painted: Cultural Representations of Biblical Women*. Journal for the Study of the Old Testament: Supplement Series 215. Gender, Culture, Theory 3. Sheffield: Sheffield Academic Press, 1996.

—*Fragmented Women: Feminist (Sub)Versions of Biblical Narratives*. Valley Forge, Pa.: Trinity, 1993.

—*Plotted, Shot, and Painted: Cultural Representations of Biblical Women*. Journal for the Study of the Old Testament: Supplement Series 215. Gender, Culture, Theory 3. Sheffield: Sheffield Academic Press, 1996.

Fabre, Marie-Louise. *Suzanne ou les avatars d'un motif biblique*. Sémantiques. Paris: L'Harmattan, 2000.

Fahy, Conor. "Three Early Renaissance Treatises on Women." *Italian Studies* 11 (1956): 30–55.

Fantham, Elaine et al. *Women in the Classical World: Image and Text*. New York: Oxford University Press, 1994.

Fetterley, Judith. *The Resisting Reader: A Feminist Approach to American Fiction*. Bloomington: Indiana University Press, 1978.

Fewell, Danna Nolan, and David M. Gunn. *Gender, Power, and Promise: The Subject of the Bible's First Story*. Nashville: Abingdon, 1993.

Finkelstein, Louis. "Pharisaic Leadership after the Great Synagogue (170 B.C.E.–135 C.E.)." Pages 245–77 in Davies and Finkelstein, eds., *The Cambridge History of Judaism*. Vol. 2, *The Hellenistic Age*.

—*The Pharisees: The Sociological Background of their Faith*. 2 vols. 3d rev. ed. Philadelphia: The Jewish Publication Society of America, 1962.

Fishbane, Michael A. "Accusations of Adultery: A Study of Law and Scribal Practice in Numbers 5:11–31." *Hebrew Union College Annual* 45 (1974): 25–45.

—*Judaism*. Religious Traditions of the World. San Francisco: HarperCollins, 1987.

Fitzmyer, Joseph A. *The Gospel According to Luke I–IX*. Anchor Bible 28. New York: Doubleday, 1970.

Forster, E. M. *Aspects of the Novel*. New York: Harcourt, Brace, & World, 1927.

Fox, Michael V. *Character and Ideology in the Book of Esther*. Studies on Personalities of the Old Testament Series. Columbia: University of South Carolina Press, 1991.

Freedman, David Noel et al., eds. *The Anchor Bible Dictionary*. 6 vols. New York: Doubleday, 1992.

Frymer-Kensky, Tikva. "The Strange Case of the Suspected Sotah (Numbers V 11–31)." *Vetus Testamentum* 34 (1984): 11–26.

Garrard, Mary D. "Artemisia and Susanna." Pages 146–71 in *Feminism and Art History: Questioning the Litany*. Edited by Norma Broude and Mary D. Garrard. New York: Harper & Row, 1982.
—*Artemisia Gentileschi around 1622: The Shaping and Reshaping of an Artistic Identity*. Discovery. Berkeley: University of California Press, 2001.
—*Artemisia Gentileschi: The Image of the Female Hero in Italian Baroque Art*. Princeton, N.J.: Princeton University Press, 1989.
Garter, Thomas. *The Most Virtuous and Godly Susanna (1578)*. Edited by B. I. Evans and W. W. Greg. Malone Society Reprints. Oxford: Oxford University Press, 1937.
Gitay, Yehoshua. *Prophecy and Persuasion*. Forum Theologicae Linguisticae 14. Bonn: Linguistica Biblica, 1981.
Glancy, Jennifer A. "The Accused: Susanna and Her Readers." Pages 288–302 in Brenner, ed., *A Feminist Companion to Esther, Judith, and Susanna*.
—"The Mistress–Slave Dialectic: Paradoxes of Slavery in Three LXX Narratives." *Journal for the Study of the Old Testament* 72 (1996): 71–87.
Goldberg, Gisela. "Albrecht Altdorfer: The Battle of Alexander the Great against the Great Persian King Darius III at Issus in 333 B.C. (The Battle of Alexander)." Pages 245–68 in Guillaud and Guillaud, eds., *Altdorfer and Fantastic Realism in German Art*.
Goldstein, Jonathan A. "The Hasmonean Revolt and the Hasmonean Dynasty." Pages 292–351 in Davies and Finkelstein, eds., *The Cambridge History of Judaism*. Vol. 2, *The Hellenistic Age*.
González, Justo L. *The Story of Christianity*. Vol. 2, *The Reformation to the Present Day*. San Francisco: HarperSanFrancisco, 1985.
Grabbe, Lester L. *Judaism from Cyrus to Hadrian*. 2 vols. Minneapolis: Fortress, 1992.
—*Wisdom of Solomon*. Guides to Apocrypha and Pseudepigrapha. Sheffield: Sheffield Academic Press, 1997.
Greenspoon, Leonard J. "Theodotion, Theodotion's Version." Pages 447–48 in vol. 6 of Freedman et al. eds., *The Anchor Bible Dictionary*.
Gross, Rita M. *Feminism and Religion: An Introduction*. Boston: Beacon, 1996.
Grossman, Susan. "Women and the Jerusalem Temple." Pages 15–37 in Grossman and Haut, eds., *Daughters of the King*.
Grossman, Susan, and Rivka Haut, eds. *Daughters of the King: Women and the Synagogue*. Edited by. Philadelphia: Jewish Publication Society of America, 1992.
Gruen, Erich S. *Heritage and Hellenism: The Reinvention of Jewish Tradition*. Hellenistic Culture and Society 30. Berkeley: University of California Press, 1998.
Guillaud, Jacqueline, and Maurice Guillaud. *Altdorfer and Fantastic Realism in German Art*. Paris: Guillaud Editions New York: Rizzoli International, 1985.
Gundry, Robert H. *Matthew: A Commentary on His Handbook for a Mixed Church under Persecution*. 2d ed. Grand Rapids: Eerdmans, 1994.
Haberman, Bonna Devora. "The Suspected Adulteress: A Study of Textual Embodiment." *Prooftexts* 20 (2000): 12–42.
Haenchen, Ernst. *The Acts of the Apostles: A Commentary*. Translated by Bernard Noble et al. Philadelphia: Westminster, 1971.
Hale, John. *The Civilization of Europe in the Renaissance*. New York: Simon & Schuster, 1993.
Halpern-Amaru, Betsy. "The Journey of Susanna among the Church Fathers." Pages 21–34 in Spolsky, ed., *The Judgment of Susanna*.
Handel, George Frideric. *Susanna* [1748]. Philharmonia Baroque Orchestra. Conducted by Nicholas McGegan. Harmonia Mundi 907030.32. 1990.

Happé, Peter. "Two *Susannas*: Dutch and English Plays Compared." *Dutch Crossing* 20 (1996): 108–27.
Harrán, Don. "Stories from the Hebrew Bible in the Music of the Renaissance." *Musica Disciplina* 37 (1983): 235–88.
Harrington, Daniel J., S. J. *Invitation to the Apocrypha*. Grand Rapids: Eerdmans, 1999.
Harris, Ann Sutherland. "Artemisia Gentileschi." In *The Grove Dictionary of Art Online*. No pages. 1998. Online: http://www.groveart.com/index.html.
—"Artemisia Gentileschi: The Literate Illiterate or Learning from Example." Pages 105–20 in *Docere Delectare Movere: Affetti, Devozione e Retorico nel Linguaggio Artistico del Primo Barocco Romano*. Rome: Instituto Olandese a Roma, 1998.
Hayes, John H. *An Introduction to Old Testament Study*. Nashville: Abingdon, 1979.
Hayes, John H., and Sara R. Mandell. *The Jewish People in Classical Antiquity: From Alexander to Bar Kochba*. Louisville, Ky.: Westminster/John Knox, 1998.
Heltzer, Michael. "The Story of Susanna and the Self-Government of the Jewish Community in Achaemenid Babylonia." *Annali dell'Instituto Orientale di Napoli* 41 (1981): 35–39.
Hengel, Martin. *Judaism and Hellenism: Studies in their Encounter in Palestine during the Early Hellenistic Period*. Translated by J. Bowden. 2 vols. Philadelphia: Fortress, 1974.
—in collaboration with Christoph Markschies. *The "Hellenization" of Judaea in the First Century after Christ*. Translated by J. Bowden. London: SCM Press. Philadelphia: Trinity, 1989.
Henten, J. W. van. "The Story of Susanna as a Pre-Rabbinic Midrash to Dan 1:1–2." Pages 1–14 in *Variety of Forms: Dutch Studies in Midrash*. Edited by A. Kuyt et al. Publications of the Juda Palache Institute 5. Amsterdam: University of Amsterdam Press, 1990.
Herrick, Marvin T. "Susanna and the Elders in Sixteenth-Century Drama." Pages 125–35 in *Studies in Honor of T. W. Baldwin*. Edited by Don Cameron Allen. Urbana: University of Illinois Press, 1958.
Herrmann, Michaela. *Vom Schauen als Metapher des Begehrens: Die venezianischen Darstellungen der "Susanna im Bade" im Cinquecento*. Dissertationes 4. Marburg: Hitzeroth, 1990.
Hershey, George L. "Female and Male Art: *Postille* to Garrard's *Artemisia Gentileschi*." Pages 323–35 in *Parthenope's Splendor: Art of the Golden Age in Naples*. Edited by Jeanne Chenault Porter and Susan Scott Munshower. University Park, Pa.: University of Pennsylvania Press, 1993.
Hippolytus. "Fragments from Commentaries: On Susanna." Translated by S. D. F. Salmond. Pages 191–94 in vol. 5 of Roberts and Donaldson, eds., *The Anti-Nicene Fathers*.
Honegger, Marc, and Frank Dobbins. "Lupi Second [Lupi], Didier." In *The New Grove Dictionary of Music and Musicians*. 2d ed. No pages. 2001. Online: http://www.grovemusic.com.
Hopkins, Denise Dombrowski. "Judith." Pages 279–85 in Newsom and S. H. Ringe, eds., *Women's Bible Commentary*.
Horsley, Richard A., with John S. Hanson. *Bandits, Prophets, and Messiahs: Popular Movements at the Time of Jesus*. Harrisburg, Pa.: Trinity, 1999.
Horst, P. W. van der, trans. "Pseudo-Phocylides." Pages 565–82 in vol. 2 of Charlesworth, ed., *The Old Testament Pseudepigrapha*.
Hovey, Walter Read. *Treasures of the Frick Art Museum*. Pittsburgh, Pa.: The Frick Art Museum, 1975.
Hufton, Olwen. *The Prospect Before Her: A History of Women in Western Europe*. Vol. 1, *1500–1800*. New York: Knopf, 1996.
Hull, Suzanne W. *Chaste, Silent, and Obedient: English Books for Women, 1475–1640*. San Marino, Calif.: The Huntington Library, 1982.
Humfrey, Peter. *Painting in Renaissance Venice*. New Haven: Yale University Press, 1995.

Humphrey, Edith M. *Joseph and Aseneth*. Guides to Apocrypha and Pseudepigrapha. Sheffield: Sheffield Academic Press, 2000.

Ilan, Tal. "'And Who Knows Whether You have not Come to Dominion for a Time Like This?' (Esther 4:14): Esther, *Judith* and *Susanna* as Propaganda for Shelamzion's Queenship." Pages 127–53 in *Integrating Women*.

—"'Beruriah has Spoken Well' (*tKelim Bava Metzia* 1:6): The Historical Beruriah and Her Transformation in the Rabbinic Corpora." Pages 175–94 in *Integrating Women*.

—*Integrating Women into Second Temple History*. Texts and Studies in Ancient Judaism 76. Tübingen: Mohr Siebeck, 1999.

—*Jewish Women in Greco-Roman Palestine: An Inquiry into Image and Status*. Tübingen: J. C. B. Mohr, 1995. Repr., Peabody, Mass.: Hendrickson, 1996.

—"Queen Salamzion Alexandra and Judas Aristobulus I's Widow: Did Jannaeus Alexander Contract a Levirate Marriage?" *Journal for the Study of Judaism in the Persian, Hellenistic, and Roman Periods* 24 (1993): 181–90.

—" 'Things Unbecoming a Woman' (*Ant* 13.431): Josephus and Nicolaus on Women." Pages 85–125 in *Integrating Women*.

Jacob, Benno. "Das Buch Esther bei den LXX." *Zeitschrift für die alttestamentliche Wissenschaft* 10 (1890): 241–98.

Jagersma, H. *A History of Israel from Alexander the Great to Bar Kochba*. Translated by J. Bowden. Philadelphia: Fortress, 1985.

Jeremias, Joachim. *Jerusalem in the Time of Jesus: An Investigation into Economic and Social Conditions during the New Testament Period*. Translated by F. H. and C. H. Cave. Philadelphia: Fortress, 1969.

Johnson, Paul. *The Renaissance: A Short History*. Modern Library Chronicles. New York: Random House, 2000.

Kay, David M. "Susanna." Pages 638–51 in vol. 1 of *The Apocrypha and Pseudepigrapha of the Old Testament*. Edited by R. H. Charles. 2 vols. Oxford: Clarendon, 1913.

Kee, Howard Clark, trans. "Testaments of the Twelve Patriarchs." Pages 775–828 in vol. 1 of Charlesworth, ed., *The Old Testament Pseudepigrapha*.

Kelly, Kathleen Coyne. *Performing Virginity and Testing Chastity in the Middle Ages*. Routledge Research in Medieval Studies. London: Routledge, 2000.

Kennedy, George. *New Testament Interpretation Through Rhetorical Criticism*. Chapel Hill: University of North Carolina Press, 1984.

King, Margaret L. "Goddess and Captive: Antonio Loschi's Epistolary Tribute to Maddalena Scrovegni (1389)." *Medievalia et humanistica* 9 (1980): 103–27

—*Women of the Renaissance*. Women in Culture and Society. Chicago: University of Chicago Press, 1991.

Klausner, J. "Queen Salome Alexandra." Pages 242–54 in *The World History of the Jewish People: The Hellenistic Age*. Edited by Abraham Schalit. New Brunswick: Rutgers University Press, 1972.

Kloppenborg, John S., and Stephen G. Wilson, eds. *Voluntary Associations in the Graeco-Roman World*. London: Routledge, 1996.

Koenen, Klaus. "Von der todesmutigen Susanna zum begabten Daniel: Zur Überlieferungsgeschichte der Susanna-Erzählung." *Theologische Zeitschrift* 54 (1998): 1–13.

Kossmann, Ruth. *Die Esthernovelle: vom Erzählten zur Erzählung; Studien zur Traditions- und Redaktiongeschichte des Estherbuches*. Vetus Testamentum Supplements 79. Leiden: Brill, 2000.

Kottsieper, Ingo. "Zusätze zu Ester." Pages 111–207 in *Das Buch Baruch, Der Brief des Jeremia, Zusätze zu Ester und Daniel*. Edited by Odil Hannes Steck, Reinhard G. Kratz, and Ingo Kottsieper. Das Alte Testament Deutsch Apokryphen 5. Göttingen: Vandenhoeck & Ruprecht, 1998.

Kraemer, Ross Shepard. "Jewish Mothers and Daughters in the Greco-Roman World." Pages 89–112 in *The Jewish Family in Antiquity*. Edited by Shaye J. D. Cohen. Brown Judaic Studies 289. Atlanta: Scholars Press, 1993.

Kreitzer, Larry J. *The New Testament in Fiction and Film*. The Biblical Seminar 17. Sheffield: JSOT Press, 1993.

—*The Old Testament in Fiction and Film: On Reversing the Hermeneutical Flow*. The Biblical Seminar 24. Sheffield: Sheffield Academic Press, 1994.

LaCocque, André. *The Feminine Unconventional: Four Subversive Figures in Israel's Tradition*. Overtures to Biblical Theology. Minneapolis: Fortress, 1990.

Leach, Mark C. "Rubens and the Theme of Susanna and the Elders." M.A. thesis, University of Delaware, 1974.

Leclercq, Henry. "Suzanne." Cols. 1742–1752 in vol. 15, pt. 2 in *Dictionarre d'Archaéologie Chrétienne et de Liturgie*. Edited by F. Cabrol and H. Leclercq. 15 vols. Paris: Librarie Letouzey et Ané, 1953.

Lerner, Gerda. *The Creation of Patriarchy*. New York: Oxford University Press, 1986.

Levenson, Jon D. *Esther*. Old Testament Library. Philadelphia: Westminster, 1997.

Levin, Carole. "Advice on Women's Behavior in Three Tudor Homilies." *International Journal of Women's Studies* 6 (1983): 176–85.

Levine, Amy-Jill. "Hemmed in on Every Side: Jews and Women in the Book of Susanna." Pages 303–23 in Brenner, ed., *A Feminist Companion to Esther, Judith, and Susanna*.

—"Sacrifice and Salvation: Otherness and Domestication in the Book of Judith." Pages 208–33 in Brenner, ed., *A Feminist Companion to Esther, Judith, and Susanna*.

—ed. *"Women Like This" New Perspectives on Jewish Women in the Greco-Roman World*. Society of Biblical Literature Early Judaism and Its Literature 1. Atlanta: Scholars Press, 1991.

Levine, Lee I. *The Ancient Synagogue: The First Thousand Years*. New Haven: Yale University Press, 2000.

Levy, Kenneth Jay. "'Susanne un jour': The History of a 16th-Century Chanson." *Annales Musicologiques* 1 (1953): 375–408.

Lewis, Charles R. "The Character of Susanna in the Arts of the Twentieth Century with a Survey of the Theme to the Present." Ph.D. diss., Florida State University, 1993.

Löcher, Kurt. "Hans Schöpfers *Geschichte der Susanna* in der Alte Pinakothek in München." *Pantheon* 28 (1970): 279–83.

Luther, Martin. "Confession Concerning Christ's Supper [1528]." Pages 151–372 in *Luther's Works*. Vol. 37, *Word and Sacrament III*. Edited and translated by Robert H. Fischer. Philadelphia: Fortress, 1961.

—"Prefaces to the Apocrypha." Pages 335–54 in *Luther's Works*. Vol. 35, *Word and Sacrament I*. Edited and translated by E. Theodore Bachmann. Philadelphia: Fortress, 1960.

MacDonald, Dennis Ronald. *The Legend and the Apostle: The Battle for Paul in Story and Canon*. Philadelphia: Westminster, 1983.

Mack, Burton. *Rhetoric and the New Testament*. Guides to Biblical Scholarship. Minneapolis: Fortress, 1990.

MacKenzie, R. A. F. "The Meaning of the Susanna Story." *Canadian Journal of Theology* 3 (1957): 211–18.

Malina, Bruce J., and Jerome H. Neyrey. *Portraits of Paul: An Archaeology of Ancient Personality*. Louisville, Ky.: Westminster/John Knox, 1996.

Manchester, William. *A World Lit Only by Fire: The Medieval Mind and the Renaissance, Portrait of an Age*. Boston: Little, Brown & Company, 1992.

Mantel, Hugo. *Studies in the History of the Sanhedrin*. Cambridge, Mass.: Harvard University Press, 1961.

Mason, Steve. *Flavius Josephus on the Pharisees: A Composition-Critical Study*. Studia post-biblica 39. Leiden: Brill, 1991.

Mattila, Sharon Lea. "Where Women Sat in Ancient Synagogues: The Archaeological Evidence in Context." Pages 266–86 in Kloppenborg and Wilson, eds., *Voluntary Associations in the Graeco-Roman World*.

Matzel, Klaus, and Jörg Riecke. "Das Pfandregister der Regensburger Juden vom Jahre 1519." *Zeitschrift für Bayerische Landesgeschichte* 51 (1988): 767–806.

Mayes, A. D. H. *Deuteronomy*. New Century Bible Commentary. Grand Rapids: Eerdmans, 1981.

McCarter, P. Kyle Jr. *II Samuel*. Anchor Bible 9. New York: Doubleday, 1984.

McClain, Kathleen P. "Seeing Beyond the Traditional Image of Susanna and the Elders." M.A. thesis, The University of Alabama at Birmingham, 2000.

McKinlay, Judith. "Potiphar's Wife in Conversation." *Feminist Theology* 10 (1995): 69–80.

McLay, Tim. *The OG and Th Versions of Daniel*. Society of Biblical Literature Septuagint and Cognate Studies 43. Atlanta: Scholars Press, 1996.

Mendels, Michal Dayagi. "Susanna, Book of." Pages 246–47 in vol. 6 of Freedman et al. eds., *The Anchor Bible Dictionary*.

Miles, Margaret R. *Carnal Knowing: Female Nakedness and Religious Meaning in the Christian West*. Boston: Beacon, 1989.

Milik, J. T. "Daniel et Susanne à Qumrân." Pages 337–59 in *De la Tôrah au Messie: Etudes d'exegèse et d'herméneutique Bibliques Offertes à Henri Cazelles*. Edited by Maurice Carrez et al. Paris: Desclée, 1981.

—"Les Modèles Araméens du Livre d'Esther dans la Grotte 4 de Qumrân." *Revue de Qumran* 15 (1992): 321–99.

Miller, Clement A. "Rebhuhn [Rephuhn], Paul." In *The New Grove Dictionary of Music and Musicians*, 2d ed. No pages. 2001. Online: http://www.grovemusic.com.

Milne, Pamela J. "What Shall We Do with Judith?: A Feminist Reassessment of a Biblical 'Heroine.'" *Semeia* 62 (1993): 37–55.

Moore, Carey A. *Daniel, Esther and Jeremiah: The Additions*. Anchor Bible 44. Garden City, N.Y.: Doubleday, 1977.

—"Esther, Additions to." Pages 626–33 in vol. 2 of Freedman et al. eds., *The Anchor Bible Dictionary*.

—*Judith*. Anchor Bible 40. Garden City, N.Y.: Doubleday, 1985.

—"Judith, Book of." Pages 1117–25 in vol. 3 of Freedman et al. eds., *The Anchor Bible Dictionary*.

—"On the Origin of the LXX Additions to the Book of Esther." *Journal of Biblical Literature* 72 (1973): 382–93.

Muilenburg, James. "Form Criticism and Beyond," *Journal of Biblical Literature* 88 (1969): 1–18.

Mullett, Michael A. "The Catholic Reformation and the Arts." Pages 196–214 in *The Catholic Reformation*. London: Routledge, 1999.

Murray, Linda. *The Late Renaissance and Mannerism*. Praeger World of Art Series. New York: Praeger, 1967.

Nead, Lynda. *The Female Nude: Art, Obscenity and Sexuality*. London: Routledge, 1992.

Neusner, Jacob. *From Politics to Piety: The Emergence of Pharisaic Judaism*. 2d ed. New York: Ktav, 1979.

—*A History of the Mishnaic Law of Damages, Part Three: Baba Batra, Sanhedrin, Makkot*. Studies in Judaism in Late Antiquity 35. Leiden: Brill, 1984.

—*Introduction to Rabbinic Literature*. Anchor Bible Reference Library. New York: Doubleday, 1994.

—*Mekhilta According to Rabbi Ishmael: An Analytical Translation*. 2 vols. Brown Judaic Studies 148, 154. Atlanta: Scholars Press, 1988.

—*The Rabbinic Traditions about the Pharisees before 70*. 3 vols. Leiden: Brill, 1971.

Newsom, C. A., and S. H. Ringe, eds. *Women's Bible Commentary*. Expanded ed. with Apocrypha. Louisville, Ky.: Westminster/John Knox, 1998.

Nichols, Tomas. "Jacopo Tintoretto." In *The Grove Dictionary of Art Online*. No pages. 1998. Online: http://www.groveart.com/index.html.

Nickelsburg, George W. E. "4Q551: A *Vorlage* to Susanna or a Text Related to Judges 19?" *Journal of Jewish Studies* 48 (1997): 349–51.

Noth, Martin. *The Deuteronomistic History*. 2d ed. Translated by Jane Doull et al. Journal for the Study of the Old Testament: Supplement Series 15. Sheffield: JSOT Press, 1991.

Odorisio, Ginevra Conti. *Donne e società nel Seicento: Lucrezia Marinelli e Arcangela Tarabotti*. Edited by. Biblioteca di cultura 167. Rome: Bulzoni, 1979.

Origen. "A Letter from Origen to Africanus." Pages 386–92 in vol. 4 of Roberts and Donaldson, eds., *The Anti-Nicene Fathers*.

Pearce, Sarah J. K. "Echoes of Eden in the Old Greek of Susanna." *Feminist Theology* 11 (1996): 11–31.

Perelman, Chaim, and Lucie Olbrechts-Tyteca. *The New Rhetoric: A Treatise on Argumentation*. Notre Dame: University of Notre Dame Press, 1969.

Perelman, Chaim. *The Realm of Rhetoric*. Notre Dame: University of Notre Dame Press, 1982.

Pervo, Richard I. "Aseneth and Her Sisters: Women in Jewish Narrative and in the Greek Novels." Pages 145–60 in Levine, ed., *"Women Like This"*.

Peters, Melvin K. H. "Septuagint." Pages 1093–1104 in vol. 5 of Freedman et al. eds., *The Anchor Bible Dictionary*.

Pfeiffer, Robert H. *History of New Testament Times with an Introduction to the Apocrypha*. New York: Harper & Brothers, 1949.

Phelan, James. *Narrative as Rhetoric: Technique, Audiences, Ethics, Ideology*. Columbus: Ohio State University Press, 1996.

—*Reading People, Reading Plots: Character, Progression, and the Interpretation of Narrative*. Chicago: University of Chicago Press, 1989.

Pignatti, T., "Life and Work." Pages 9–56 in Francesco Valcanover and Terisio Pignatti. *Tintoretto*. The Library of Great Painters Series. Translated by Robert Erich Wolf. New York: Abrams, 1985.

Pilger, Robert. "Die Dramatisierungen der Susanna im 16. Jahrhundert." *Zeitschrift für deutsche Philologie* 11 (1879–80): 129–217.

Pollock, Griselda. "The Female Hero and the Making of a Feminist Canon: Artemisia Gentileschi's Representations of Susanna and Judith." Pages 97–127 in *Differencing the Canon: Feminist Desire and the Writing of Art's Histories*. London: Routledge, 1999.

Pomeroy, Sarah B. *Goddesses, Whores, Wives, and Slaves: Women in Classical Antiquity*. New York: Schocken, 1975.

Pretre, Jean-Claude. *Suzanne: les procès du modèle*. Paris: Bibliothèque des arts, 1990.

Price, David. "'Schweyg liebe tochter': A Reevaluation of Paul Rebhun's *Susanna* (1536)." Pages 40–49 in *Studies in German and Scandinavian Literature after 1500: A Festschrift for George C. Schoolfield*. Edited by James A. Parente, Jr. and Richard Erich Schade. Columbia: Camden House, 1993.

Rabinowitz, Peter J. "Truth in Fiction: A Reexamination of Audiences." *Critical Inquiry* 4 (1976): 121–41.

Rad, Gerhard von. *Deuteronomy*. Translated by Dorothea Barton. Old Testament Library. Philadelphia: Westminster, 1966.

—*Genesis*. Old Testament Library. Philadelphia: Westminster, 1972.

Rearick, W. R. "Jacopo Bassano and Changing Religious Imagery in the Mid-Cinquecento." Pages 331–43 in *Essays Presented to Myron P. Gilmore*. Vol. 2, *History of Art, History of Music*. Edited by Sergio Bertelli and Gloria Ramakus. Villa I Tatti 2. Florence: La Nuova Italia Editrice, 1978.

Rebhun, Paul. *Ein geistlich Spiel, von der Gotfürchtigen vnd keuschen Frawen Susannen, auffs new gemehret vnd gebessert, gantz lustig und fruchtbarlich zu lessen* [1536]. Pages 329–444 in *Deutsche Spiele und Dramen des 15. und 16. Jahrhunderts*. Edited by Hellmut Thomke. Frankfurt am Main: Deutscher Klassiker, 1996.

—*Susanna: Eingeleitet und redigiert von Walter Zitzenbacher*. Graz: Stiasny-Verlag, 1961.

—"Susanna: A Miracle Play about the God-Fearing and Chaste Lady Susanna, for Entertaining and Profitable Reading [1544]." Pages 27–97 in *German Theater before 1750*. Edited by Gerald Gillespie. The German Library 8. New York: Continuum, 1992.

Richardson, Peter, and Valerie Heuchan. "Jewish Voluntary Associations in Egypt and the Roles of Women." Pages 226–51 in Kloppenborg and Wilson, eds., *Voluntary Associations in the Graeco-Roman World*.

Ridolfi, Carlo. *The Life of Tintoretto* [1642]. Translated by Catherine and Robert Enggass. University Park: The Pennsylvania State University Press, 1984.

Robbins, Vernon K. *Exploring the Texture of Texts: A Guide to Socio-Rhetorical Interpretation*. Valley Forge, Pa.: Trinity, 1996.

—*The Tapestry of Early Christian Discourse: Rhetoric, Society and Ideology*. London: Routledge, 1996.

Roberts, Alexander, and James Donaldson, eds. *The Anti-Nicene Fathers*. 10 vols. New York: Scribner, 1885–87. Repr., Peabody, Mass.: Hendrickson, 1994.

Rosand, David. *Painting in Sixteenth-Century Venice: Titian, Veronese, Tintoretto*. Rev. ed. Cambridge: Cambridge University Press, 1997.

Rubin, Gayle. "The Traffic in Women: Notes on the 'Political Economy' of Sex." Pages 157–210 in *Toward an Anthropology of Women*. Edited by Rayna R. Reiter. New York: Monthly Review Press, 1975.

Ruether, Rosemary Radford. "Christianity." Pages 207–34 in *Women in World Religions*. Edited by Arvind Sharma. Albany: State University of New York Press, 1987.

Russell, D. S. *The Jews from Alexander to Herod*. New Clarendon Bible. Oxford: Oxford University Press, 1967.

Russell, Diana E. H., ed. *Making Violence Sexy: Feminist Views on Pornography*. Athene. New York: Teachers College Press, 1993.

Safrai, Hannah. "Women and the Ancient Synagogue." Pages 39–49 in Grossman and Haut, eds., *Daughters of the King*.

Safrai, S. "Education and the Study of the Torah." Pages 945–70 in vol. 2 of Safrai and Stern, eds., *The Jewish People in the First Century*.

—"Home and Family." Pages 728–92 in vol. 2 of Safrai and Stern, eds., *The Jewish People in the First Century*.

—"The Temple." Pages 865–907 in vol. 2 of Safrai and Stern, eds., *The Jewish People in the First Century*.

Safrai, S., and M. Stern, *The Jewish People in the First Century*. 2 vols. Compendia rerum iudaicarum ad novum testamentum 1. Philadelphia: Fortress, 1976.

Sakenfeld, Katherine Doob. "Numbers." Pages 49–56 in Newsom and S. H. Ringe, eds., *Women's Bible Commentary*.

Saldarini, Anthony J. "Sanhedrin." Pages 975–80 in vol. 5 of Freedman et al. eds., *The Anchor Bible Dictionary*.

Samuel, Alan Edouard. *Ptolemaic Chronology*. Münchener Beiträge zur Papyrusforschung und antiken Rechtsgeschichte 43. Munich: Beck, 1962.

Sanders, E. P. *Judaism: Practice and Belief, 63 BCE–66 CE*. London: SCM Press; Philadelphia: Trinity, 1992.

Schmitt, A. *Stammt der sogenannte "Θ"-Text bei Daniel wirklich von Theodotian?* Nachrichten [von] der Akademie der Wissenschaft in Göttingen 1. Göttingen: Vandenhoeck & Ruprecht, 1966.

Schneemelcher, Wilhelm. "The Acts of Peter." Pages 271–321 in vol. 2 of *New Testament Apocrypha*. 2 vols. Edited by Wilhelm Schneemelcher. Translated by R. McL. Wilson. Rev. ed. Louisville, Ky.: Westminster/John Knox, 1991–92.

Schroeder, H. J. *Canons and Decrees of the Council of Trent*. St. Louis, Miss.: Herder, 1941.

Schürer, Emil. *A History of the Jewish People in the Age of Jesus Christ*. 3 vols. New rev. English ed. by G. Vermes et al. Edinburgh: T&T Clark, 1973–86.

Segal, Alan F. *Rebecca's Children: Judaism and Christianity in the Roman World*. Cambridge, Mass.: Harvard University Press, 1986.

Segal, Lynne. "Does Pornography Cause Violence? The Search for Evidence." Pages 5–21 in *Dirty Looks: Women, Pornography, Power*. Edited by Pamela Church Gibson and Roma Gibson; London: British Film Institute, 1993.

Sered, Susan, and Samuel Cooper. "Sexuality and Social Control: Anthropological Reflections of the Book of Susanna." Pages 43–56 in Spolsky, ed., *The Judgment of Susanna*.

Shepherd, Simon, ed. *The Women's Sharp Revenge: Five Women's Pamphlets from the Renaissance*. New York: St. Martin's Press, 1985.

Sievers, Joseph. "The Role of Women in the Hasmonean Dynasty." Pages 132–46 in *Josephus, the Bible, and History*. Edited by Louis H. Feldman and Gohei Hata. Detroit: Wayne State University Press, 1989.

Sims, Mark Anthony. "The Basel Dramas of Sixt Birck." M.A. thesis, Vanderbilt University, 1991.

Skehan, Patrick W., and Alexander A. Di Lella. *The Wisdom of Ben Sira*. Anchor Bible 39. Garden City, N.Y.: Doubleday, 1987.

Sluijter, Eric J. "Rembrandt's Early Paintings of the Female Nude: *Andromeda* and *Susanna*." Pages 31–54 in *Rembrandt and His Pupils*. Edited by Görel Cavalli-Björkman. Uddevalla, Sweden: Risbergs Tryckeri, 1993.

—"Venus, Visus en Pictura." *Nederlands Kunsthistorisch Jaarboek* 42–43 (1991–92): 337–96.

Smith, Kathryn A. "Inventing Marital Chastity: The Iconography of Susanna and the Elders in Early Christian Art." *Oxford Art Journal* 16, no. 1 (1993) 3–24.

Smith, Patrick. *Susannah and the Elders*. San Francisco: Pancake, 1992.

Sobel, Dava. *Galileo's Daughter: A Historical Memoir of Science, Faith, and Love*. New York: Walker, 1999.

Sölle, Dorothée et al., *Great Women of the Bible in Art and Literature* (Grand Rapids: Eerdmans, 1993).

Spear, Richard E. *The "Divine" Guido: Religion, Sex, Money and Art in the World of Guido Reni*. New Haven: Yale University Press, 1997.

—"Reni, Guido." In *The Grove Dictionary of Art Online*. No pages. 1998. Online: http://www.groveart.com/index.html.

Spolsky, Ellen, ed. *The Judgment of Susanna: Authority and Witness*. Society of Biblical Literature Early Judaism and Its Literature 11. Atlanta: Scholars Press, 1996.

—"Law or the Garden: The Betrayal of Susanna in Pastoral Painting." Pages 101–18 in Spolsky, ed., *The Judgment of Susanna*.

Stern, Menahem, ed. *Greek and Latin Authors on Jews and Judaism*. 3 vols. Jerusalem: The Israel Academy of Sciences and Humanities, 1974–84.

Steussy, Marti J. *Gardens in Babylon: Narrative and Faith in the Greek Legends of Daniel*. Society of Biblical Literature Dissertation Series 141. Atlanta: Scholars Press, 1993.

Stocker, Margarita. *Judith, Sexual Warrior: Women and Power in Western Culture*. New Haven: Yale University Press, 1998.

Stradella, Allessandro. *La Susanna: Oratorio in due parti di Giovanni Battista Giardini a cinque voci, due violini e basso continuo* [1681]. Complesso Vocale Strumentale Camerata Ligure. Conducted by Esteban Velardi. Bongiovanni GB 2121/22–2, 1991.

Straus, Raphael. *Regensburg and Augsburg*. Translated by Felix N. Gerson. Jewish Communities Series. Philadelphia: Jewish Publication Society of America, 1939.

Stump, Eleonore. "Susanna and the Elders: Wisdom and Folly." Pages 85–100 in Spolsky, ed., *The Judgment of Susanna*.

Swete, Henry Barclay. *An Introduction to the Old Testament in Greek*. Revised by Richard Rusden Ottley. Cambridge: Cambridge University Press, 1914. Repr., Peabody, Mass.: Hendrickson, 1989.

Talbot, Charles. "Altdorfer." In *The Grove Dictionary of Art Online*. No pages. 1998. Online: http://www.groveart.com/index.html.

Tarabotti, Arcangela. *Inferno monacale*. Pages 231–38 in Odorisio, ed., *Donne e società nel Seicento*.

—*La semplicità ingannata: Tirannia paterna* and *Inferno monacale*. Pages 199–214 in Odorisio, ed., *Donne e società nel Seicento*.

Taylor, J. "The Women's Sharpe Revenge." Pages 159–93 in Shepherd, ed., *The Women's Sharp Revenge*.

Thomas, Keith. "The Double Standard." *Journal of the History of Ideas* 20 (1959): 195–216.

Tkacz, Catherine Brown. "Susanna as a Type of Christ." *Studies in Iconography* 20 (1999): 101–53.

The Toronto Consort. *Orlando di Lasso: Chansons and Madrigals*. Dorian Discovery DIS-80149 1994, 1996.

Tov, Emanuel. *Textual Criticism of the Hebrew Bible*. Minneapolis: Fortress; Assen: Van Gorcum, 1992.

Trenchard, Warren C. *Ben Sira's View of Women: A Literary Analysis*. Brown Judaic Studies 38. Chico, Calif.: Scholars Press, 1982.

Trible, Phyllis. *God and the Rhetoric of Sexuality*. Overtures to Biblical Theology. Philadelphia: Fortress, 1978.

—*Rhetorical Criticism: Context, Method, and the Book of Jonah*. Guides to Biblical Scholarship. Minneapolis: Fortress, 1994.

Turner, Nicholas. "Guercino [Barbieri, Giovanni Francesco]." In *The Grove Dictionary of Art Online*. No pages. 1998. Online: http://www.groveart.com/index.html.

Vives, Juan Luis. *The Education of a Christian Woman: A Sixteenth-Century Manual*. Edited and translated by Charles Fantazzi. The Other Voice in Early Modern Europe. Chicago: University of Chicago Press, 2000.

Warner, Marina. *Alone of All Her Sex: The Myth and the Cult of the Virgin Mary*. New York: Knopf, 1976.

Weaver, Elissa. "Spiritual Fun: A Study of Sixteenth-Century Tuscan Convent Theater." Pages 173–206 in *Women in the Middle Ages and the Renaissance: Literary and Historical Perspectives*. Edited by Mary Beth Rose. Syracuse: Syracuse University Press, 1986.

Wessley, Stephen E. "The Thirteenth-Century Guglielmites: Salvation through Women." Pages 289–303 in *Medieval Women: Dedicated and Presented to Professor Rosalind M. T. Hill on the Occasion of Her Seventieth Birthday*. Edited by Derek Baker. Oxford: Blackwell, 1978.

Wetering, Ernst van de. *Rembrandt: The Painter at Work*. Berkeley: University of California Press, 2000.

Wiesner-Hanks, Merry E. *Christianity and Sexuality in the Early Modern World: Regulating Desire, Reforming Practice*. Christianity and Society in the Modern World. London: Routledge, 2000.

Willis, Andrea Marie. "The Theme of Susanna and the Elders from the Late Fourteenth through the Early Sixteenth Century: A Study of History, Iconography and Societal Interpretations." M.A. thesis, University of South Carolina, 1998.

Wills, Lawrence M. *The Jewish Novel in the Ancient World*. Myth and Poetics Series. Ithaca, N.Y.: Cornell University Press, 1995.

Winston, David. *The Wisdom of Solomon*. Anchor Bible 43. Garden City, N.Y.: Doubleday, 1979.

Wood, Christopher S. *Albrecht Altdorfer and the Origins of Landscape*. Chicago: University of Chicago Press, 1993.

Zeitlin, Solomon. "Queen Salome and King Jannaeus Alexander: A Chapter in the History of the Second Jewish Commonwealth," *Jewish Quarterly Review* 51 (1961): 1–33.

—"There was No Court of Gentiles in the Temple Area." *Jewish Quarterly Review* 56 (1965): 88–89.

Ziegler, Joseph, ed. *Susanna, Daniel, Bel et Draco*. Pages 216–33 in *Septuaginta*. Vetus Testamentum Graecum auctoritate Academiae Scientiarum Gottingensis editum 16, no. 2. 2d ed. Göttingen: Vandenhoeck & Ruprecht, 1999.

Zimmermann, Frank. "The Story of Susanna and its Original Language." *Jewish Quarterly Review* 48 (1957–58): 236–41.

Indexes

Index of References

Index of Authors